Singing Ideas

DANCE AND PERFORMANCE STUDIES

General Editors:
Helena Wulff, *Stockholm University* and **Jonathan Skinner**, *University of Roehampton*

Advisory Board:
Alexandra Carter, Marion Kant, Tim Scholl

In all cultures, and across time, people have danced. For performers and spectators, the expressive nature of dance opens up spaces where social and political circumstances are creatively negotiated. Grounded in ethnography, this series explores dance, music and bodily movement in cultural contexts at the juncture of history, ritual and performance in an interconnected world.

Volume 1
Dancing at the Crossroads: Memory and Mobility in Ireland
Helena Wulff

Volume 2
Embodied Communities: Dance Traditions and Change in Java
Felicia Hughes-Freeland

Volume 3
Turning the Tune: Traditional Music, Tourism and Social Change in an Irish Village
Adam Kaul

Volume 4
Dancing Cultures: Globalization, Tourism and Identity in the Anthropology of Dance
Edited by Hélène Neveu Kringelbach and Jonathan Skinner

Volume 5
Dance Circles: Movement, Morality and Self-Fashioning in Urban Senegal
Hélène Neveu Kringelbach

Volume 6
Learning Senegalese Sabar: Dancers and Embodiment in New York and Dakar
Eleni Bizas

Volume 7
In Search of Legitimacy: How Outsiders Become Part of the Afro-Brazilian Capoeira Tradition
Lauren Miller Griffith

Volume 8
Choreographies of Landscape: Signs of Performance in Yosemite National Park
Sally Ann Ness

Volume 9
Languid Bodies, Grounded Stances: The Curving Pathway of Neoclassical Odissi Dance
Nandini Sikand

Volume 10
Collaborative Intimacies in Music and Dance: Anthropologies of Sound and Movement
Edited by Evangelos Chrysagis and Panas Karampampas

Volume 11
Staging Citizenship: Roma, Performance and Belonging in EU Romania
Ioana Szeman

Volume 12
Singing Ideas: Performance, Politics and Oral Poetry
Tríona Ní Shíocháin

Singing Ideas

Performance, Politics and Oral Poetry

Tríona Ní Shíocháin

First published in 2018 by
Berghahn Books
www.berghahnbooks.com

© 2018, 2021 Tríona Ní Shíocháin
First paperback edition published in 2021

All rights reserved. Except for the quotation of short passages
for the purposes of criticism and review, no part of this book
may be reproduced in any form or by any means, electronic or
mechanical, including photocopying, recording, or any information
storage and retrieval system now known or to be invented,
without written permission of the publisher.

Library of Congress Cataloging-in-Publication Data

A C.I.P. cataloging record is available from the Library of Congress

British Library Cataloguing in Publication Data

A catalogue record for this book is available from the British Library

ISBN 978-1-78533-767-3 hardback
ISBN 978-1-80073-182-0 paperback
ISBN 978-1-78533-768-0 ebook

Do Ghormfhlaith agus Amhlaoibh;
agus do mhná Mhúscraí.

For Gormfhlaith and Amhlaoibh;
and for the women of Muskerry.

Contents

List of Figures	ix
Acknowledgements	x

Chapter 1
Singing Ideas: An Alternative History of Thought — 1
  (Un)doing History: The Authority of Literacy and the
    Performativity of Thought — 5
  Oral Trouble and Women's Voices: Searching for Intellectual
    Traditions Beyond the Written Word — 9
  Singing Politics and Power in Society: Some Comparative Examples — 12
  Seizing Agency: Women of Song — 15
  Beyond the Limits of Textuality: Performing the Past and
    Performing Thought — 17

Chapter 2
'Where Everything Trembles in the Balance': Song as a Liminal Ludic Space — 23
  The Theory of Liminality — 24
  Performing Liminality: Poetry as a Symbolic Marker for Liminality
    in the Irish Tradition — 26
  A Journey to the Sacred and Back: The Liminality of the
    Aisling (Vision) — 29
  Song and Oral Poetic Performance as Ritual — 31
  Separating from the Profane: Ekstasis and Song — 34
  Moments of Potentiality: The Antistructure of Melody and Verse
    in the Irish Tradition — 36
  The Ritual Powers of (Song)Poetry: Satire, Insult and Fearlessness — 41
  The Potentiality of the Play-Sphere: The Challenging Discourse
    of Song — 43
  The Singer of Ideas as 'Seer of Communitas': The Liminality of
    Song and the Generation of Ideas — 51

Chapter 3
Singing Parrhesia: Máire Bhuí Ní Laeire, Song Performance and
Politics in Nineteenth-Century Ireland 56
    Máire Bhuí Ní Laeire: Nineteenth-Century Song Poet 59
    Irish-Language Song-Making: Poetry as Performance and the
        Aesthetics of Orality 65
    Multiformity and Oral Formulaic Techniques 69
    Local Agrarian Agitation and the Creation of the Poetic Radical 78
    Crisis and Charisma: The Song Poet as Prophet and Truth-Teller 86
    Identity and the Aesthetics of Orality: New Ideas and the Narrative
        of Belonging 104
    Framing the Revolution: Performing Antistructure and the Vision
        of the Revolution through Song 110
    From Generation to Generation to Regeneration: The Legacy
        of Ideas through Song 113

Conclusion. Singing Ideas in Society: Experience, Song and
'Passing Through' 125

Appendix of Songs and Lore 131

Bibliography 191

Index 201

Figures

Figure 2.1 Áine Uí Chuíll (2011) — 37
Figure 2.2 Cáit Ní Mhuimhneacháin (1941) — 37
Figure 2.3 Seán de hÓra (1973) — 38
Figure A.1 'S ar Maidin Moch is Mi 'r mo Leabain Bhuig [And Early One Morning While on My Soft Bed] — 139
Figure A.2 Maidin Mhuch ar Leabaig Bhuig [Early One Morning on a Soft Bed] — 142
Figure A.3 A Bhúrcaig Bhuí ón gCéim [Oh Yellow Burke from Céim] — 146
Figure A.4 Maidin Álainn Ghréine [One Lovely Sunny Morning] — 156
Figure A.5 Maidin Álainn Gréine [One Lovely Sunny Morning] — 159
Figure A.6 Maidin Álainn Gréine [One Lovely Sunny Morning] — 162
Figure A.7 Seo Leó, ' Thoil [Seo Leó, My Darling] — 167
Figure A.8 Cath Chéim an Fhia [The Battle of Keimaneigh] — 173
Figure A.9 A Mháir' Ní Laeire [Oh Mary O'Leary] by Máire Bhuí Ní Laeire and Donncha Bán Ó Luínse — 184

Acknowledgements

I gratefully acknowledge the following for kindly granting permission to publish songs and lore of Máire Bhuí herein: Seán Ó Súilleabháin, Chairperson of the Ballingeary Historical Society; Special Collections, UCC Library, University College, Cork; Dr Criostóir Mac Cárthaigh, the National Folklore Archive, University College, Dublin; Mary Mitchell-Ingoldsby, Director of the Traditional Music Archive, UCC; Raidió Teilifís Éireann; Mícheál Ó Conghaile, Director of Cló Iar-Chonnacht; Máire Ní Cheocháin; Áine Uí Chuíll; the Ó Cuív family, who kindly gave me permission to publish material from the private manuscript collection of the late Professor Brian Ó Cuív.

Chapter 1

Singing Ideas
An Alternative History of Thought

Singing is a cultural form both of great antiquity and of persistent contemporary relevance across many different cultures in the world today. Song, and its meanings, are by no means universal, and the diversity of singing traditions apparent even within Western European culture alone is striking – from Schubert's lieder honed by conservatoire training, to community choral performance, to punk, to metal, to highly produced popular genres, to oral traditional song; from the worker singing up a ladder, to a parent singing to a child, to an operatic diva in an elegant dress, to the young anarchist giving it all she is worth in a contemporary 'drunken tavern', to the background singing we cannot escape when shopping in the supermarket. This book focuses on the importance of one such facet of the rich tapestry of song and its cultural practices in Western Europe, that being the Irish-language singing tradition, but in doing so hopes to make a claim for the importance of song performance more generally in our understanding of the development of ideas in society – that claim being that a song is more than 'just a song'; rather it is a hotbed of thought and identity formation.

The dynamics of thought formation and singing will here be explored through a theoreticization of song and an analysis of the work of the nineteenth-century song poet Máire Bhuí Ní Laeire[1] (Yellow Mary O'Leary, 1774–c.1848), whose song composition responded directly to the lived experience of colonization under British rule in Ireland. The Ireland of the late eighteenth century into which Máire Bhuí was born was in the throes of the precarity and conflict that emerged from the British colonial project: the penal laws prohibited the participation of Irish Catholics in public office and prevented social mobility; economic policies favoured the minority elite of (mainly Protestant) landowners, whose wealth and status depended largely on the exploitation of the economically disadvantaged;

it was also a period marked by famine, both in the 1820s when Máire Bhuí was in her prime as a poet, and at the end of her life she witnessed the devastation of the Great Irish Famine (closer contextual analysis of the historic period will be offered in Chapter 3). During her lifetime, Máire Bhuí engaged her contemporary political world by singing ideas integral to the development of the anticolonial movement in Ireland.

In almost every respect Máire Bhuí Ní Laeire is markedly different from the great literate thinkers of her age: not only was she a farmer's wife, a mother to nine children and an Irish-speaking colonial subject, but she practised the richly echoic aesthetic values of the oral tradition, a poetic style that had at its centre the re-creative impulse of oral formulaic composition (Lord 1960, 1996; Buchan 1972; Foley 1981, 1991, 2002; McCarthy 1990; Nagy 1996; Ramey 2012). In many ways, the compositional craft she practised could not be more different to the 'measured' approach of the literate male European thinker: Máire Bhuí was less a rationalist and more a 'truth-teller', or parrhesiast, and a master of compelling song performance. Foucault analyses parrhesia as a concept that emerged in ancient Greece and that came to designate various forms of truth-telling in public regarding urgent political issues, usually with personal risk to the speaker (2011). Foucault argues that this form of truth-telling is influential in the subsequent history of modern politics, and provides a mode of critiquing power (Boland 2014). Máire Bhuí sung antiestablishment ideas, castigating the nobles and the wealthy, lamenting the abuse of the poor, and, most importantly, she sung ideas that delegitimized colonial power and legitimized the popular impulse for self-determination and sustained violent revolt. Her songs embody the fearless speech of parrhesia, encapsulating a strong sense of being compelled to speak the truth, or, more specifically, of being compelled to sing against the Empire. This is coupled with a distinctly prophetic voice strongly suggestive of her role as a charismatic prophetic figure (Weber 1978) in the millenarian movement of the 1820s in Ireland. Singing an anticolonial 'image of the world' in the Weberian sense of 'a stand in the face of the world', as redemptory of a senseless colonial reality, was central to her oral work of thought. This combination of the parrhesiastic fearlessness of her song and the charismatic authority she generated due to her exceptional abilities at verse-making gave an almost ecstatic intensity to her political thought.

Her art, unlike Kant or Paine, is neither marked by a performative preoccupation with the 'rational' nor a schism with tradition, but with a conscious yet re-creative continuity with an imagined past. And unlike the literate thinker, her works of thought lived and breathed in the very moment of song performance itself. That Máire Bhuí's songs were at once forms of music and forms of thought, to be re-created by subsequent singers and generations of singers, also sets her apart from her male, literate English-speaking contemporaries. However, it is in this very difference that the efficacy of the ideas she espoused lies: for to *sing* ideas is to create an ecstatic ludic space, a fleeting antistructure in which ideas and identity can be re-formed and new political realities articulated. Song performs and reimagines reality in a way that goes to the root of identity and belonging itself, in a way that a literate text perhaps cannot rival. Song is akin to what Arnold van Gennep describes as 'the great rhythms of the universe', a social form central to human existence that punctuates and renews everyday life (1960: 194). Song is an experience, a 'passing through'; song is a social and artistic process with the capacity to regenerate. Therefore song is more than just a 'text', orality is much more than just a precursor to words on a page, and its true potency lies in the moment of performance itself, in the very experience of song and singing in body and emotion. Song was a realm of possibility. It was this power of song that Máire Bhuí harnessed in her engagement with contemporary politics during her own lifetime.

Rather than look upon songs as documents reflecting history, therefore, they can equally be understood as social processes that have shaped history, as real-life moments in time that may have determined personal persuasions, political developments or the very way in which we interpret the world. Though the fall of the Bastille, for example, is well documented, we understand that it actually *happened,* that it was *an event.* We understand that any document depicting the Bastille does not fully represent the dynamics of the historical event or its significance and that the event existed beyond the text. And so it is for a song that has survived – it is more than a document, it is something that happened, it was a performance at which moment the song was thoroughly embroiled in the social and political machinations of contemporary society.

To understand the significance of singing for thought formation in society, therefore, it is crucial we go beyond the often narrow trappings of text and re-imagine the song as a living liminal moment of sheer potentiality, where structures have melted and new forms are yet to emerge. This moment of potentiality was of significance not just for the song-composer, such as Máire Bhuí, who wrought contemporary political meaning out of the traditional play-sphere of song, but also the listener and singer, who courted new ways of thinking and feeling through song. This is the moment where everything trembles in the balance (Turner 1982: 44), where both ideas and identity can be renewed. The intense communitas of singing is of particular significance here, for it is one thing for an idea to emerge at any given time in history, but it is another thing entirely for an idea to have a lasting impact and to become a central idea by which people interpret the world. Rather than viewing the oral tradition as a restrictive code that, as Ong once claimed, prevents human consciousness from achieving 'its fuller potentials' (1982: 14–15), it is argued here that oral poetry was a superb medium for both political thought and political engagement. The traditionality of Máire Bhuí's medium of thought, the song, would be integral to the impact of her ideas thereafter, for song is a richly performative social process that has the capacity to form the very ideas we live by and through which one's 'image of the world' can ecstatically be re-created (Weber 1978).

Máire Bhuí is one of a number of figures in Irish revolutionary history who have been neglected due to an overreliance on the part of historians on printed material in English from the period, which, as Morley has argued, is more reflective of 'the experiences of middle-class political activists in Dublin and Belfast' (2017: 242). Though Máire Bhuí is much less visible than O'Connell or Wolfe Tone,[2] I believe that her work is of immense significance in our attempts to understand the history of anticolonial thought in Ireland. Her radical verse falls outside the category of modernizing Jacobinism, such as was once described by Whelan in reference to the United Irish movement: 'The United Irishmen's necks were set in concrete, staring relentlessly forward' (1996: 61). However, her songs speak of a burgeoning political consciousness among the agrarian classes; her songs perform colonial experience and colonial subjection; she melds the identity of the collective to a developing anticolonial impulse in a seamless manner – her songs are at once deeply rooted in the past, yet speak of pressing contemporary experience. Her songs epitomize the symbiosis between ideas and identity, between thinking and feeling, and exemplify the ability of song to create the world anew. Máire Bhuí, therefore, was a *singer of ideas* of no small import who moulded a radical millenarian vision at a time when official Catholic parliamentary politics was distancing itself from the radicalism of the 1790s in Ireland.

The possibility of a tradition of thought that does not perform 'detachment' but rather performs parrhesia and ekstasis, as we see in the case of song, is worth considering. Indeed, when we think of ecstasy and thought as sisters, rather than pairing cold rationality alone with serious thought, a different picture of the world emerges. Song ritualizes the 'passing through' of experience, articulating and re-presenting the 'formative power of experience' (Szakolczai 2004, 2008) through verse and music. Song performs new meanings borne of this transitory and transformative nature of experience, and these 'experiential meanings' are in turn imbued with the intensity and liminal ekstasis of song performance, and thus melded to the collective narrative and 'reborn' as essential ideas to live by. The path of thought and political consciousness, therefore, lies not in 'cold' reasoning alone, but in the heated experience of 'truth' also, and in the transformative nature of experience.

In the chapters that follow I argue that song is best understood as a liminal experience that is foundational in the lives of humans, providing an expressive play-sphere through which thought and identity are formed and renewed, ultimately arguing that song engenders socio-processual thought of huge importance to the development of political ideas. Máire Bhuí Ní Laeire of nineteenth-century Ireland is taken as an exemplary singer of ideas who engaged with contemporary thought through the medium of traditional song. From the revolutionary period of 1796 to the turbulent 1820s in Ireland, Máire Bhuí sung ideas of great immediacy to the colonial subject, or perhaps one could go so far to say that she sung ideas that performed and ritually enacted colonial subjection and resistance. Máire Bhuí was responding to an extended period of crisis, uncertainty and danger for the community. It is my contention that song was an effective response that oversaw the experience of crisis and transition in the lives of ordinary people. Following Turner, I argue that performance is inherently renewing, similar to rites of transition that it so resembles, and that song created ideas that would reinvigorate collective identity, and renew the meaning of shared existence under colonial rule. As Eisenstadt states, 'All societies construct a social and cultural order designed in part to overcome the uncertainties and anxieties implied in existential givens' (1995: 310). Indeed, Eisenstadt understood the order transforming elements of culture as socially constructed and symbolically enacted. Song is one such performative symbolic enactment of antistructure in society. As Eisenstadt argues, however, the order-maintaining and order-transforming dimensions of culture are two sides of the same coin (1995: 323), or as Thomassen would say, antistructure is inherently structure-forming, and liminality moves towards reaggregation (2009: 20). The songs of Máire Bhuí can likewise be understood as illustrating the symbiosis of order-maintaining and order-transforming drives in culture: on the one hand the songs construct a strong we-image (Elias 1994) and collective narrative of unbroken continuity while also perpetuating an 'age old' tradition of song composition with supernatural overtones, while on the other the songs perform a contemporary radical drive towards anarchy, revolt and renewal. The 'new' radicalism of Máire Bhuí would ultimately become a legitimized web of ideas that would be central to subsequent political movements, and the status quo of the anticolonial movement that would gain traction in the early twentieth century. The singer of ideas, therefore, tells a different story of the ideas that shaped human society and culture to that of official history, and demonstrates the socio-processual ideas of singing experience and the performative dynamic of thought formation. Such an alternative history of ideas in which a woman of no letters engaged the colonial world is worth reliving and reimagining.

(Un)doing History: The Authority of Literacy and the Performativity of Thought

Thinking has long been considered a most 'serious' endeavour – that of the famous 'greybeards' of the university, for example, and certainly is associated with men (and, less often, women) of letters: scribes, philosophers, scientists, writers. Great works of thought are generally assumed to be written, and those who engage with the ideas that shape our very society are assumed to be readers. Writing and reading have long been central to the performative construction of seriousness and to the symbolic performance of rationality and objectivity in Western society. Reading and writing are central tenets of the story the modern Western world tells itself about itself: one of transcendent objective reason and critique.

The performance of objectivity underscores much of academic practice in modernity: the scholar is seen to occupy a neutral yet authoritative position from which he/she can cast a cold critical gaze over the object of study, and academic and popular literature on the merits of 'critical thinking' is now abundant (Boland 2013, 2014; Felski 2015). However, the philosophical and intellectual traditions of academia could also be said to be, in Weberian terms, webs of belief not just practised by elites and academics but constructed by them also. Thought itself and philosophizing and writing constitute *performative* cultural practices. These intellectual practices are as embroiled in social construction and symbolism as any other social custom, contrary to the very appearance of neutrality, detachment and transcendence that are core tenets of the performance of thinking in literate culture; or as Judith Butler might put it, the performativity of Western thought effectively conceals its genesis (1988: 522). The performance of thought in Western literate society is a compelling one: it is 'a performative accomplishment which the mundane social audience, including the actors themselves, come to believe and perform in the mode of belief' (Butler 1988: 520). Where literate intellectual culture perpetuates a compelling yet well-concealed performance of authority, truth and power, the oral tradition can be seen on the other hand as a 'disqualified knowledge' in the Foucauldian sense, excluded from the 'hierarchy of knowledges and sciences' (1980: 82).

Though literate culture is supremely dominant in modernity, this was not the case for most of history, and yet how we imagine the past is influenced primarily by written artefacts that can only communicate a fraction of the historical society of the time. The culture of literacy is so dominant that our preoccupation with literate sources is scarcely questioned, or acknowledged, and indeed the practice of literacy itself has become, according to O'Brien O'Keefe, 'virtually transparent' to us in modern times, with literate assumptions maintaining a sense of invisibility and remaining well hidden from ourselves (1990: ix). In attempting to understand the recent history of humanity in Europe, despite the prevalence of both oral cultures and illiteracy throughout Europe up until the twentieth century, scholars construct history for the most part drawing on whatever written evidence survives. History itself is the story that is told by the literate minority of the past, as represented by the literate elite in contemporary society. The contribution of thinkers from oral traditions scarcely hits the radar of Western academia.

This 'silence' on oral traditions points to an exclusion, or even a sacrificial mechanism being at play, that was supremely effective historically (Girard 1979): orality was the scapegoat that would ensure the status and prominence of literate culture, the sacrifice that would enable the social consensus and cohesion that would ensure the social dominance of literature and of literati. Literacy and intellectual practices embody the 'power of a discourse', performing the authority and power of knowledge convincingly (Foucault 1980: 83–84). Historically, the practitioners of the written word frequently had to deal with the competing communicative sphere of orality, and to perform an authority to literacy above that of orality would be key to ensure that written culture gain and maintain such a high status. Indeed such a burgeoning tension between oral and literate forms in ancient times can perhaps be read in Plato's famous attack on the poets, as a power play or a vying for legitimacy, as argued by Thomas and Kent Webb: 'Plato's attack on Homer and poetry shows the conflict between the practices of literacy and orality. Until the end of the fifth century, oral, traditional modes of thought served as the foundation of Greek life and culture' (1994: 3). Thus in ancient Greece, the transition from orality to literacy seems to have involved a contestation of power and status in society, rather than something that 'just happened'. This ideological battle between literacy and orality can perhaps be most acutely felt in more recent colonial times (Draper 2004). The conferring of superiority on written poetry as opposed to oral poetry, as discussed by Joseph Muleka (2014), was a power play that ensured that literate writers would hold greater authority and status in society, and this can be seen in the way in which some Western commentators portrayed the indigenous oral traditions of Africa as inferior. Muleka discusses how the poetic culture of Africa was relegated to 'non-poetry' in the eyes of Hegel and Long because it was an oral tradition, arguing that poetry was a mark of an 'advanced' civilization, aesthetic and serious, derivative of 'highly developed languages' (2014: 151). Oral poetic works, on the other hand, were dismissed as 'mere chants', the musicality of oral poetry viewed by Hegel as something of little relevance, bordering on unnecessary (Muleka 2014: 158). This Western colonial discourse of disenchanted cold rationality was to prove powerful politically.

Muleka rightly argues that such discourses were part of the 'politics of "superiorizing" and "peripherizing"' that is found so often in the interaction between the West and Africa (2014: 151). Muleka's arguments are highly relevant also to the recent work of Argyrou on the gift relation, and the manner in which the Western world has broken the cycle of gift-giving, by going forth into the world to bestow its gifts of thought, art and 'civilization' on other peoples and cultures, but not quite willing to accept the gift of thought, art, wisdom and beauty that other cultures have to give (2013). According to Argyrou, the West has broken the gift relation, which anthropologically is based not merely on bestowing gifts, but on receiving them with grace as part of a reciprocal cycle of human bonds and mutual respect (Mauss 1966). The ill-conceived notion of the West having everything that is worth giving (e.g. literacy, capitalism, industrialization, modernity itself) is a dysfunction of society and human interaction. Indeed, Argyrou asserts that the gift of 'rationality' is hollow, empty and merely negative (2013). Of course, this broken gift relation can also be seen in interactions between official or elite European cultures such as we have in the case of the modern day intelligentsia, and the oral cultures of contemporary and historical Europe. With the culture of literacy in Europe being so closely aligned to male culture historically, this is also a power play on gendered lines, as well as one between the powerful and the ordinary people. Therefore the 'peripherizing' dynamic so well described by Muleka between Europe and Africa can also be seen within Europe itself, between the powerful and the weak, between the modern and the traditional, between the literate male composer and the illiterate female composer. Literacy, therefore, is no neutral tool or practice, but is power-laden. Oral tradition thus poses a problem for the literate world, in that it disrupts the dominant discourse of truth and knowledge that is perpetuated by Western society, thus allowing us 'to rediscover the ruptural effects of conflict and struggle that the order imposed by functionalist or systemising thought is designed to mask' (Foucault 1980: 81). Even in the act of reimagining oral tradition as a central tenet of the development of ideas historically, the powerful discourse of objective literate Western reason is shaken.

This special status of literacy in the story that the West tells itself about itself is evident in the 'civilizing' dynamic put forth by both colonial powers and political elites in European countries, who attempted to impose order on the unwashed masses (Elias 1994, Van Krieken 2011). Literacy was central to societal control, power and order on many levels (Bartlett 2007). On the one hand denying access to literacy (as in the case of women or the poor in Western society) was a way in which patriarchal and hierarchical structures could be strengthened and maintained. On the other hand, popular literacy would later become part of the project of 'improvement' of both women and the lower classes, of civilizing the 'ignorant' or uneducated. The spread of literacy and education was ultimately to become the major social engineering project of the Western world. The belief in the diffusion of literacy as 'enlightening' illiterates was perhaps most acutely felt in the colonial project, as described by Hersch (2011). The heavy ideology of Western literacy and culture as civilizing and enlightening would be to the detriment of rich and sophisticated oral traditions of colonized peoples, whose status, through Western eyes, was considered lowly or primitive. As Voegelin said of the 'enlightening' and 'civilizing' impulse of modern man: 'The light of reason should fall into every corner of the human mind, and if it falls on a substance that is solid enough not to be dissolved by its rays, the obstacle should be destroyed because it is a scandal to enlightened man' (1975: 24).

The history of ideas has thus been informed by a masculine colonial construction of literacy as objective, advanced and transcendent. Neither orality nor literacy is considered here as a neutral form, therefore, but part of a wider negotiation and contestation of power in society in which academia is also embroiled. However, I also argue that the advent of literacy often did not inevitably signal the marginalization of oral forms, as in the case of the songs of Máire Bhuí, for example, and it would therefore be a mistake to assume that a society with an established literate culture does not also foster oral forms of huge social and political import, as can been seen in modern South Africa and Somalia. Through a comparative analysis of a selection of female and political song traditions that demonstrate the central role of song in political engagement, in social expression and in negotiating power in society, it will be argued that indeed it is a grave omission from our conceptualization of the development of thought in society to discount orality as a formative force for idea-making and for political agitation. These living and historical traditions of orality, which tell of the re-creativity and contemporaneity of oral tradition and of the vital relevance of song to power negotiations in society, will help us imagine an alternative history of ideas that had at its core the performative force of song.

Oral Trouble and Women's Voices: Searching for Intellectual Traditions Beyond the Written Word

To engage with what survives of the oral traditions of historical Irish-speaking women creates a 'gender trouble' (Butler 1990) all of its own: in the patriarchal realm of textuality the probability of influence as gleaned from oral fragments may not be enough to satisfy the standards of academic textual rigour; furthermore, the performance-centred aesthetics of orality elude easy classification by scholars more used to dealing with texts and documents. Máire Bhuí is a symbol of generations of women who engaged creatively with the world around them through their mastery of the oral tradition, but of whom we barely have a trace in our modern accounts of the history of thought. Though discourses and ideas emanating from oral cultures may have been pivotal in the development of thought and in various political movements or social transitions, this may completely elude the modern scholar, who must focus on textual 'evidence'.

Because of these 'lost traditions' of orality, the construction of history itself is reduced to a facade in which the values, ideas and activities of the minority literate culture can often be taken by modern scholars as authoritatively representative of the societies of the past, or as Morley recently commented regarding the failure of historians to engage with vernacular culture in the study of Irish politics and society, 'collective abdication of responsibility consigned the bulk of the Irish people to the role of non-speaking extras in the historiography' (2017: 2).

The songs that will be theorized in this book are compositions of Máire Bhuí, of which there are no urtexts: the songs are inherently prone to multiformity through re-creative transmission from singer to singer, and from generation to generation. The songs in this volume are therefore multivocal, attributed to Máire Bhuí, but also inextricable from the oral creative processes of the wider community and of generations of singers. This, however, is fitting to the political vision of Máire Bhuí, which was one that legitimized the authority of the people while evoking a beautifully re-creative tradition that had been developed by generations before her. Therefore though the songs cannot be said to be the definitive voice of Máire Bhuí in the literate sense, they could not be more true to the oral poetic tradition she herself practised. In this sense, when analysing the songs of Máire Bhuí, one is dealing with symbolic and conceptual thought that is multilayered and that cannot be neatly attributed to a single 'author'. As Lord said, 'the words "author" and "original" have either no meaning at all in oral tradition or a meaning quite different from the one usually assigned to them' (1960: 101). Furthermore, the very manner in which we imagine the poet is based on representations of her in the narrative tradition of the indigenous Irish-speaking communities of Cork. Máire Bhuí, though she was a historical figure, in our representation of her here she will always be tinged with the mythical, unextractable from the creative processes of orality and the imagination of the community. However, as Ó Giolláin argues, following Eliade, it is often in the mythical that a deeper 'truth' lies, and the meaning inherent in such creative forms is of particular significance to our reading of society (2005: 29). In engaging with the songs of Máire Bhuí, one is engaging with the tradition of many rather than that of the single author. As an interpretative work, this book is therefore drawing on the many interpretations of Máire Bhuí and her political concepts by practitioners of the oral tradition.

When contesting the engagement of women, such as Máire Bhuí, in the generation of political ideas in society, orality makes 'trouble' for the literate establishment. Not only do oral traditions often fall foul of the usual categorizations of literacy, particularly in their multivocal nature, as previously mentioned, but oral traditions also pose a challenge to the received discourse on the history of thought. In this sense, orality is a key feminist issue for academics, because it can be so conveniently stifled as 'unsubstantiated' scholarship, but also because it poses a genuine challenge to our reconstruction of history and to the very stories modern Western society tells itself about itself. Orality tells another story. Orality has the capacity to upset the status quo in that it challenges the very manner in which we imagine the history of our own society (Glassie 2012), and as Beiner has argued, 'The unique value of folk histories is that they do not conform to historical standards and therefore pose a radical challenge to historiography' (2007: 320). Oral traditions represent what Foucault calls *le savoir des gens*, hidden histories suppressed by official culture but that existed nonetheless (1980). In looking towards traditions of singing ideas we are exploring those 'hidden processes' of thought formation. Beyond the realm of male-dominated rhetoric and the official realm of literate political culture, therefore, there existed other voices.

In response to Spivak's question of 'Can the subaltern speak?', McLane argued that: 'If we have worried about whether the subaltern might speak, we may also consider the ways in which the subaltern (or more properly, the tenant farmer, the dairymaid, the genteel housewife, the aristocratic lady) *sang*' (2011: 11). Indeed, as will be argued later on, song provided a special medium by which the subaltern were allowed a voice that often was recognized even by the powerful in society. Often when the subaltern was not allowed to *speak* dissent, they were allowed to *sing* dissent. Song often functioned as a mediator of power in society. Also, in asking can the subaltern speak, it is important to acknowledge that, in this case, when the subaltern speaks it is multivocal, richly layered and does not conform to the single-author standard of modern literature. Furthermore, when the subaltern sings it is not just a text: it is a performance, a social process enmeshed in the workings of society, an elusive moment in time. In our exploration of these subaltern voices, therefore, it is vital that we embrace the multiformity, multivocality and complex echoic texture of oral forms. It is for this reason that the songs of Máire Bhuí here cannot be considered simply as single-author works, but this does not detract from their importance for thought formation in society. As Vansina argued in his work on oral tradition as history, oral traditions reflect both the past and the present all at once:

> Yes, oral traditions are documents of *the present*, because they are told in the present. Yet they also embody a message from *the past*, so they are expressions of the past at the same time. They are representations of the past in the present. (1985: xii)

Song that embodies the past is therefore also inherently contemporary and tied to the 'now' of the singing tradition. Neither does a song with a named author function as a literary text in the normal way, for it is intertwined with the creative processes of many individuals. If we are to consider the oral tradition that Máire Bhuí practised as being part of a subaltern culture, then this is how the subaltern speaks rather than in the clear-cut linear fashion that would be more familiar and convenient for modern academics. Though the issue of how modern academia can distort, suppress, co-opt or subjugate the subaltern voice will always figure in studies that dare to engage with orality, to abandon any attempt to listen to the subaltern would be even more problematic. As Vansina noted when arguing for the validity of oral forms, such as prophecy, in our study of history:

> Such sources should be recognized and not summarily dismissed as physical impossibilities and hence useless embellishments of some later age. Their very survival in tradition means something in terms of historical consciousness and of contemporary mentalities and ideologies. (1985: 7)

Likewise, song (and prophetic song in the case of Máire Bhuí) signifies 'oral trouble' for academics but, just like Vansina's prophecy, also embodies both historical and contemporary thought and political developments. A song such as 'Cath Chéim an Fhia' ('The Battle of Keimaneigh'), therefore, not only can tell us of the political thinking of the 1820s in Ireland, but is also linked to the development of anticolonial thought as the song travels through generations of singers down to the postcolonial era. Therefore song can be considered not a simple literary document, but the product of a 'chain of transmission', in Vansina's terms, echoing not just the historical anticolonial movement, but the mentality of successive generations also. It is this interpretative symbolic richness of song that is its great asset, as outlined by Vansina: 'Such data testify then to opinions and values held, to mentalities, and that is their value, not as testimony of fact' (1985: 31). It is inevitable, therefore, due to the fluid elusive performative nature of song, that a study such as this will essentially be one that seeks to reimagine, rather than establish concrete fact. As illustrated by Atkinson in his exposition on the imaginary contexts of the traditional ballad: 'Only an "imaginary" work can be pinned down in the manner of a text, and such a form is always necessarily subject to conjecture' (2014: 12). A written transcription of a song therefore has a rather tenuous relationship to the same song as it lives in performance: a song in its totality is not merely words set to a tune, but a moment of performance in time that eludes textual categorization. A study of song and thought formation is likewise subject to the 'necessary conjecture' to which Atkinson alludes. What can be considered the 'oral trouble' of song, however, can also be seen as its strength; fulsome rather than one-dimensional, multivocal rather than clear-cut, and, most importantly, deeply embedded in the thought and creative processes of many people. The song, therefore, is not the work of Máire Bhuí alone, but is the interpretative production of tradition bearers. Orality embodies, therefore, not just the ideas of the author, but the engagement of the singer and the community, giving us a sense of a *living* history of thought.

Therefore, following the work of Glassie, I argue that the song tradition offers an alternative history of thought to that of official history that is of immense value, a history of thought that was shaped 'beyond the centres of world power' (2012: 210). Glassie terms such histories of 'the vernacular intellectuals who endure obscurely in the ambit of neglect' as critical and alternative, articulating discourses that counterbalance the narrative of the establishment: 'It is critical, being the creation of subject, colonised historians – eloquent subalterns – and not historians who support and are supported by, dominant capitalistic and imperialistic powers' (2012: 210). This is the alternative tradition of thought to which Máire Bhuí belonged – one in which pertinent ideas were *sung* and *experienced* through singing.

Singing Politics and Power in Society: Some Comparative Examples

A number of traditions from modern times attest to the re-creative contemporary dynamic of oral culture and the pressing relevance of orality for power contestation and political engagement in society, helping us to reimagine the impact of singing ideas historically. Oral tradition is far from stagnant or limiting; oral tradition, as Foley would put it, is enabling (1995: xiv). Oral poetry is, as alluded to by Huizinga many years ago, the play-sphere par excellence, eminently capable of producing new forms suited to changing situations (1970). In contemporary oral traditions, song or oral poetry is often at the heart of political processes and idea formation as we see in the contemporary re-creation and articulation of traditional forms such as satire in Xhosa folk songs, which form a commentary on sociocultural conditions and political affairs (Dyubhele 1994), or songs of challenge and satirical comment in South West Ghana (Agovi 1995), or traditional song that engaged with the anti-apartheid struggle in South Africa (Gilbert 2007: 426; Gunner 2009). Indeed Agovi (1995), drawing on the work of Gyekye (1975) on traditional proverbs in Akan society, illustrates how oral culture is a powerful vehicle for ideas and a medium of philosophy. Furthermore, even in semi-literate or literate societies we cannot assume that these oral forms take a secondary role in public discourse and in the formation of the ideas that guide the lives of people. The women of Allah-Amin in Somalia, for example, were literate, but they still engaged in oral composition and performance independent of any written tradition: it was the oral tradition rather than the written tradition that influenced contemporary politics and opinion in that instance (Jama 1994). This is also why in eighteenth-century France with its well-established literate tradition the police expended significant time in tracking 'seditious' songs that were considered by the police to be 'a sign of incipient rebellion' (Darnton 2010: 127), songs that were so pervasive that they were found to be 'raining down everywhere'. Gunner (2009) rightly refers to 'the unruly power of song' – for these songs not only could spread with great rapidity through oral culture, but indeed could take on a whole life of their own thereafter with possibly disastrous consequences for the ruling establishment (Darnton 2010: 68, 79).

The dynamic re-creativity and potentiality of oral tradition is demonstrated by the utilization of oral poetry by the Somali Women's Democratic Organization during the Somali Civil War, for example, whose poetic discourses on themes of equality, self-sufficiency and socialism demonstrated the sheer contemporary relevance and influence of oral tradition (Jama 1994: 186). The experience of song performance itself was central to the impact of the message the oral poems conveyed, as Jama describes in the case of the female group Allah-Amin in Somalia:

> The traditional work songs are well known for their lively rhythms, and the group's poems were accompanied by clapping and wailing. At the same time the content of their poems was powerful and adept at touching the emotions of the listeners. The themes were mainly sad, serious issues reflecting the very real war situation. (1994: 196)

The ideas articulated by these Somali women poet-composers were both rooted in the tradition and of immediate contemporary relevance to listeners: they re-created work songs, religious songs and even curse-poetry and adapted them to new situations (Jama 1994: 197). Much like the tone of Máire Bhuí's compositions during the colonial period in Ireland, the songs of Allah-Amin should not be seen as 'mere entertainment', but as a call to arms (Jama 1994: 197). Thus song can be seen to occupy an important political space in Somali society, one in which ideas can be voiced and authority contested. This power of song goes beyond macro political issues; however, John William Johnson has illustrated how Somali work songs of 'low' prestige are entwined with power negotiations in society, and describes singing as 'an act of communication and even defiance between individuals and groups which are marginal in the power structure of Somalia and those who hold power in that country' (1995: 111). Johnson describes contexts in which song is a means of speaking out and engaging for individuals who, due to their low status, may otherwise be restricted in opposing the powerful in ordinary speech, concluding that that song 'catches the powerful off guard' (1995: 121). Song, therefore, can be seen to negotiate power, to intervene, to protest. This special status and perceived power of sung communication in Somalia is perhaps best illustrated by Johnson's anecdote of the radio announcer who was arrested for playing an oral poem over the airwaves to the public that was also audible to parliamentarians and who was subsequently charged with influencing parliamentary voting (1995: 115–17). This illustrates the dangerous potential of song: it was the understanding of the power of song as a vehicle of political influence that surely spurred the authorities to initiate the arrest.

Though it may echo strongly of the past, the oral tradition is inherently contemporary, a performative social process thoroughly entwined in the larger workings of society. This contemporaneity of orality was demonstrated in recent times by President Jacob Zuma in South Africa, when his political fortunes were adeptly redirected by his performance and re-creation of the song 'Umshini Wami' ('My Machine Gun'), which had a crucial role in mobilizing public support for Zuma. This was a song that echoed the anti-apartheid struggle, and its performance in 2005 enabled a marginalized group within the African National Congress to seize 'back agency and power to determine the flow of change in the new era' (Gunner 2009: 30). Crucially, this was not a 'new' song, and it was the echoic nature of Zuma's performance that ensured the extraordinary impact of the song in the dynamics of post-apartheid South African politics:

> Song was a means of capturing and giving expression to the aspirations, the anxieties and the vision of people in that particularly turbulent and painful moment in South Africa's history. That is the provenance of "Umshini Wami". It is a song from the belly of the struggle. (Gunner 2009: 38)

The power of collective memory and the power of echoes of collective experience result in the reconfiguration of the contemporary political scene. As Gunner describes, the oral tradition was a dynamic and engaging force, utterly entwined in new political ideas and motivations:

> Africa teems with the temporal and spatial journeying of various kinds of song, poetic speech and narrative. They travel, they metamorphose, they die, sometimes they are reborn and they give birth. They are the midwives to new ideas and social visions. They summon up collective memory with amazing speed. They can provide platforms for debate and for an evolving discourse on a range of topics. (Gunner 2009: 34)

In the case of 'Umshini Wami', song was at the centre of an evolving political powershift, and this attests to the extraordinary power of song in moulding the ideas that inform political action. Indeed, song was such a central tenet of Zuma's public persona and communicative abilities that one critic demanded 'more on policy from Zuma and less singing' in a national newspaper (Gunner 2009: 31). Likewise, the experience of song performance itself was to play a key role in swaying public support, as demonstrated by the euphoric reception of Zuma at the Congress of South African Trade Unions (COSATU), in which singing erupted, as described by Gunner (2009: 32). Song here is not peripheral, but central, operating at the very heart of politics. Zuma's song was of course building on a well-established tradition of social protest and anti-apartheid and anticolonial thought through song (Gunner 2009: 37). Much like the song craft of Máire Bhuí in nineteenth-century colonial Ireland, the oral tradition in South Africa was central to social protest and the creation of anticolonial political consciousness. In arguing, like Huizinga, that poetry is a foundational play-sphere in the lives of humans, we acknowledge that orality does much more than *preserve*, rather it *renews* and *re-creates* and can be an extraordinary force in challenging the status quo, political positions or, indeed, social norms.

Seizing Agency: Women of Song

In many oral cultures song is an important vehicle articulating that which would not be acceptable in ordinary speech. We see this, for example, in Somalia, whereby song was a means by which women could speak out, where otherwise it would be unacceptable for them to talk back to men (Johnson 1995: 112); in traditional Swazi society in the folk songs of women, who do not achieve full freedom of speech but are free to express their views and wishes through song (Dlamini 1994); and also in Dyula society, in which women exert influence through their mastery of an exclusively female genre of *kúrubi* songs, which pose a threat to the male status quo because of the potential for 'socially damaging speech' when performed at the end of Ramadan (Derive 1995: 126). Derive thus argues that song is an important expression of 'counter-powers' in society, particularly for the subjugated, and that it is tradition itself that enables this particular mode of social contestation: 'a genre authenticated by tradition is sometimes the only legitimate means of exerting compensatory or counter-powers' (1995: 129). Song is a lifeline that is essential to the lives of people. Song is therefore a regulatory force, a 'counter-power', used by the vulnerable to protect their interests and make their case. The kúrubi songs are clearly embroiled in the larger workings of the society to which they belong – these songs are 'alive' and integral to the negotiation of power for women.

> Through this genre, which is exclusively theirs, the women can effectively exert pressure. A husband or a son-in-law fears such public criticism – even though the rules of the genre require that the criticism remains allusive rather than direct – and their behaviour towards women may be mitigated by the fear of such an eventuality and such public criticism. (Derive 1995: 126)

The kúrubi songs are performed publicly before the entire community, men and all, but there are many other oral poetic practices that are performed exclusively or predominantly for women, such as the popular praises of Zulu women (*izibongo*) (Gunner 1995). These genres of female oral poetry are performed at a distance from men, leading to an increased subversion in the poetic discourses themselves. These poetic praise forms, as practised by women, challenge the norms of patriarchy and create a special demarcated space in which the dominant patriarchal discourses of society can safely be challenged or undercut (Gunner 1995: 192). Zulu women actively subvert and re-create the praise form to their own ends, and the pressing relevance and contemporaneity of oral poetry is clear: the oral tradition flows through and navigates women's social experiences, enabling their voice; enabling the expression of their own thoughts and experiences under patriarchy. It is clear that the oral tradition of song and poetic performance, rather than being passive, lent itself to active engagement and subversion.

The case of the female izibongo compositions in recent times, as described by Gunner, resonates strongly with both the tradition of the Irish-language lament or *caoineadh* (keen) and the Scottish Gaelic waulking songs. In both cases these were performance contexts that were either predominantly female (in the case of the caoineadh) or exclusively female (in the case of waulking songs). These oral traditions developed by women over countless generations drew heavily on received formulas and themes, but, as we generally find in orality, the art of the composer was in the re-creation and effective working of the traditional material as Lord has argued (1960). Though the traditional lament, which incorporated a significant element of praise poetry, was performed at the wake and was integral to the rite of passage that saw the deceased move on to the next world and enabled the community to come to terms with the passing of a loved one, the traditional Irish lament was also a vehicle through which these female poet-composers voiced grievances specific to the role and status of women in society (Bourke 1988). Bourke compares the tradition of keening and waulking in the protest against subjection, injustice, indignity and abuse common to both forms. Both these traditions were highly ritualistic, creating a time outside of ordinary time in which women could speak out (Bourke 1988: 13). Indeed, much like women in oral cultures of modern times, as discussed above, the medium of oral poetry was central to the emotional, social and intellectual life of Irish- and Gaelic-speaking women, who were for the most part excluded from scribal practices and the transmission of Irish manuscripts. Indeed, even with the advent of literacy among women in Scotland, song remained a core medium of expression, their mastery of which was widely recognized (Perry 2008). In modern times as we cast our eye over times past, it does a serious disservice to these women of song if we conceptualize the history of ideas in terms of canonical written texts alone. Though we can never return to the period during which the oral tradition in Ireland was truly thriving and therefore cannot equal contemporary studies of living traditions entirely, examples of oral traditions from recent times and the role women play in them would suggest that song as a medium warrants serious consideration. When compared with the female poet-composers of Somalia and their influence on political affairs through performance of oral verse, we have good reason to suppose, based on historic and folklore accounts, that Máire Bhuí Ní Laeire of nineteenth-century Ireland could have had a similar influence in a culture that at the time was steeped in song and oral verse.

Beyond the Limits of Textuality: Performing the Past and Performing Thought

In the cases discussed above, what is striking is that oral poetry was effective beyond the words uttered. The ideas that were to abound in oral verse – be it the injustice of male domination in the personal lives of women, or protest at subjection or the development of socialist ideals through song – were all amplified through the singing experience. It was the performance of poetry in its totality and its consequent experiential meaning that would change ideas, affiliations and actions. Zuma's song and performance whipped up emotions and euphoria that would change the direction of public life, while the women of Allah-Amin through their engaging performance with clapping and wailing would touch the minds of listeners, much like the Scottish women of the waulking songs, who would pound out a rhythm that would create a cathartic experience of female expression. Song is noisy; it demands attention and can intervene in the lives of people. Thus in Dyula society the power of the public performance of the female poetic form of kúrubi protected women's interests, and the public ritual of the Irish lament performed by a highly emotional keening woman of wild appearance, with howls and clapping of hands, would go beyond words alone in making meaning out of the passing of life for the community. Song was larger than a 'text', therefore, and was a social process integral to human society in which power was negotiated, experience was ritualized and contemporary ideas were formed and articulated. These traditions themselves illustrate beyond argument, I believe, the sheer relevance and vitality of oral creativity and practices for thought and politics in society well into modern times.

What of our search for oral intellectual traditions of the past, however, as we look for traditions and practices that are either long extinguished or the knowledge of which has been muted? Since the groundbreaking work of Parry and Lord, Western scholars have begun to consider that much of the literary manuscript material that has survived to present times is likely in many cases to be reflective of a predominantly oral rather than literate society (O'Brien O'Keefe 1990; Nagy 1996; Acker 1998). This is due to the formulaic character of many works that were transmitted in manuscript form and also the multiformity that is considered so typical of oral transmission, which often pervades different versions of poetic compositions that were transmitted by manuscript. It is these aesthetic differences, connected to the moment of performance itself by Parry and Lord in their writings, which inspired many medieval and classical scholars to reimagine the lifeworld of canonical masters such as Homer as an oral culture. Thus canonical literature began to be reimagined as oral. Scholars such as Gregory Nagy have strongly argued for Homer as an oral composer, as well as highlighting the ritualistic performance context of lyric forms from classical times, such as sympotic songs and the important role of song in the ancient world (1996, 2004). If this is the case, then the ancient world so revered by modern Europeans (to the point of even being mentioned in the constitution of the European Union), which we imagine as one of great sophistication and advancement, had in fact at its core a thriving oral culture. However, the oral formulaic theory, though employed by many scholars (myself included), is far from uncontested. As is inevitable, the past has escaped us: nothing can be unequivocally proven and we can never return to the world of Homer; we have neither sound recordings nor extensive ethnographic material to guide us.

It is possible, however, in our reliance on written documents, to take our belief in the authority of the written word a little too far: historical documents and pieces of parchment, for all their inherent value, only tell us so much, nor can the same written artefacts be taken as neutral objective representations of historical reality. One gaping omission from such written documents, as already mentioned, is the female voice: the history of the West is for the most part a history of men. However, if we look towards the oral tradition, which was practised widely by women, though little of it was recorded, we see who our foremothers were and what they were doing. Máire Bhuí, for example, though mentioned in two manuscript sources from the mid-nineteenth century, was not part of a scribal circle, yet she arguably had more influence politically than any contemporary literate Irish-language poet during her lifetime and beyond. Máire Bhuí was a master of orality not of the written word. However, the oral tradition she practised could rival the literate tradition as a vehicle of thought and political agitation. Therefore, even though the likes of Máire Bhuí do not automatically figure in our conceptualization of the development of political thought and activism in Ireland alongside Wolfe Tone and O'Connell, that is not to say that during her lifetime she was hindered by illiteracy. Much like Muleka's reading of the peripherizing of oral poetry by Western colonial discourse, the oral poetic practices of women were brushed to the side within patriarchal scholarly discourse within the West. Rather than recognizing the immense richness of these traditions, such as keening, waulking and other types of oral verse, as developed by women over generations, literacy came to be seen as enlightenment, as emancipation from a backward or unsophisticated oral tradition. Only with literacy would women be able to take their rightful place among men, or so we were led to believe.

However the songs of Máire Bhuí tell a different story, one of an illiterate woman who through mastery of song composition would become a central ideamaker in the politics of her own society. The oral tradition was no hindrance to Máire Bhuí; rather it was what enabled the formulation and articulation of a millenarian political vision that would grip the imagination of the community and indeed of subsequent generations of singers. No transcription of a song can do justice to the real-life experience of singing, which is emotive, ritualistic, challenging and identity-forming: to be a master of oral poetry was to be a master of oral performance, to be master of social space that was alive through song. In order to understand the influence of the political spheres of orality, therefore, the limits of textuality must be challenged.

Firstly, it is important to recognize that social processes that were central to political developments historically, if not recorded in writing, will have the appearance of never having happened at all. In this sense written reports are powerful not merely because of their ability to record, but in their ability to *erase* by omission. Secondly, one must look beyond textuality to the implications of performance itself, thus exploring how oral culture can truly play a pivotal role in thought formation and politics. Thirdly, the multivocality of orality, inherently re-creative, belonging at once to the individual artist and the community as a whole, poses problems to scholars in how it differs from fixed texts and testimonies; however, it is essential not to discount the validity of songs in historical and social analysis due to this multiformity integral to many oral forms, but embrace it. As Bourke famously argued in her seminal paper on the traditional Irish lament, 'Performing not Writing', if we hope to do justice to historical women of song and oral verse, we must take heed of the oral compositional craft and performance practices they mastered, rather than treating their oral works as being the same as literary compositions: 'Publishing women's oral poetry as though it were a literary production contributes to the undervaluing of women's creative output in the Irish tradition – even when the poetry is being celebrated as great art' (1991: 31). In embracing women's oral creativity and intellectual engagement, however, it is inevitable that we push the boundaries of textuality and historicity itself.

In arguing that we must imagine beyond the limits of textuality, I am also arguing for the persistent relevance of oral performance forms even after the spread of literacy. Even though Máire Bhuí could not read or write, popular literacy in English was widespread during her lifetime, and song coexisted with other media of political debate, such as popular print forms and traditional manuscript transmission (Ó Conchúir 1982; Ó Ciosáin 1997; Ní Úrdail 2000). However, I argue that song had not as yet been effectively marginalized by popular print in the nineteenth century, and that song must be recognized as a central vehicle for political ideas, agitation and consciousness-building, a point that has been effectively argued by Palmer McCulloch in relation to female poetry and song in eighteenth-century lowland Scotland (2003). Following Palmer McCulloch, I argue that the important sphere of song has been marginalized in our modern conceptualization of history to the detriment of our understanding of the historical processes that have informed political development. This imbalance, which has focused on the works of thought that belong to the predominantly male sphere of literacy at the expense of works of thought of orality, which involved the active participation of women, needs to be addressed. As McCulloch explains,

> "listening to the women" in poetry and song not only means bringing back into the eighteenth century world picture the place of song alongside Enlightenment philosophy, historical studies and the printed poetic forms of Ramsay, Ferguson and Burns. It also means bringing what Virginia Woolf called "women's values" into our understanding of this important historical period. (2003: 453)

Though orality was the creative and intellectual medium of the majority of Irish-speaking women in the nineteenth century, it also belonged to the majority of Irish-speaking men. What is significant about oral culture in nineteenth-century Ireland is, unlike literate culture, it did not exclude women to the same extent. I do not claim, by any means, that the Irish song tradition was a solely female tradition, nor do I suggest that the oral tradition was akin to a utopian egalitarian art form from a gender perspective. What I do suggest, however, is if we seek out the Irish-speaking women who contributed to the ideas that shaped the society of the past, we will not find them among literate circles, but in the oral culture in which they were given freer reign. Rather than viewing the literate tradition, for all its riches, as freeing women from the trappings of the oral tradition, the agency of these women composers and singers – who were enabled by a tradition that they themselves developed, maintained and practised alongside men over generations – merits recognition.

Women may not have had access to official political hierarchies, or may not figure in the male-dominated public discussions and debates that were recorded in print from the eighteenth and nineteenth centuries, but they sang and they composed. We see, therefore, despite restrictions placed upon women in their participation in public life, that oral culture enabled women's voices and thought processes. Furthermore, oral culture in the case of song also ensured that women, such as Máire Bhuí, had a public voice, despite their exclusion from official circles. It is highly significant that in the colonial period in Ireland – in which women were restricted in certain areas of political life – song prevailed as a medium of political thought and engagement for women, remembering that women as well as men sung the radical verses of Máire Bhuí and other poet-composers. Where women may have been excluded from male-dominated political organizations such as the United Irishmen, they were experiencing and singing radical concepts through song. This is not entirely dissimilar to the case of women in some traditional societies, who are allowed liberty in song, despite restrictions on their free speech and participation in ordinary life.

The song form is very different from the male-dominated rhetorical tradition of political treatises and pamphleteering. Song does not perform cold rational authority in the way that a philosophical tome does, and song does not impose order through the performance of impartial reasoning. However, song does perform an authority of its own, an older authority to that of all-male literate circles: song performs an ecstatic authority more akin to the transformative experience of ritual that we find in non-Western traditional cultures. The authority of song is one of both thinking and feeling, of ekstasis, of body, emotion and mind all together. Where text is cold, song is hot. Where modern textual culture performs detachment, song performs immediacy. Though inherently ephemeral, the moment of song creates a time outside of ordinary time that can reconfigure ideas and influence action. It is this very difference between the politics of official culture and the politics of song that might make us inclined to dismiss song as 'unserious'. However, there is a very great seriousness to play, as argued by both Huizinga and Turner, despite any appearance of triviality when compared with the spheres of political thought of official culture. An alternative tradition of thought is to be found, therefore, if we look beyond the philosophy of calculated reason and detachment, which has come to the fore in the West since the time of Hobbes and Descartes, and look instead to ecstatic forms of political thought, such as song, which is one of the oldest and most enduring play spheres of humanity.

Notes

1. The spelling that most accurately represents the dialect pronunciation of the poet's surname, Ní Laeire, is preferred here and reflects the editorial methodology as explained in

the appendix. Other spellings of the poet's surname include the standardized Ní Laoghaire or Ní Laoire.

2. Daniel O'Connell (1775–1847), known as the Liberator or the Emancipator, was the most prominent figure of the parliamentary movement to secure Catholic emancipation under British imperial rule in Ireland. Theobald Wolfe Tone (1763–1798) was the leader of the 1798 United Irish Rebellion, an Irish anticolonial uprising that was heavily influenced by the French and American revolutions (see Morley 2002, 2017).

Chapter 2

'Where Everything Trembles in the Balance'
Song as a Liminal Ludic Space

Singing creates a pivotal space in the social and political lives of people, as we have seen in the performance of traditional verse in a number of postcolonial societies (as mentioned in the previous chapter), in which singing often occupies a key role in the contestation of power in society. We have also seen that for some female oral cultures song has provided a most crucial medium of expression for women who have serious social restrictions placed upon them regarding free speech or access to official political networks. It is clear, therefore, that in both historical and anthropological terms song is much more than 'just a song', song is much more than a 'past-time': rather it is a 'great rhythm of humanity' at the very core of social, intellectual and political life (van Gennep 1960). Gunner rightly argues that song has an 'unruly power' to it, with immense capacity to challenge or upset social and political norms (2009). In this chapter, the dynamics of this power of song will be explored through a theoreticization of song as liminal, as a pivotal social process integral to thought and identity formation in society. It will be here argued that the medium of song has a meaning beyond words alone, functioning much like a rite of transition, and thus encapsulating the regenerative and subversive dynamics of liminality. Song symbolizes and actualizes an in-between liminal experience, a period of symbolic antistructure, in which society can be challenged and the social hierarchy temporarily suspended, in which the *unspeakable* can become *singable* and the unthinkable thinkable. Song is a quintessential play-sphere through which new ideas and motivations can be generated. This is both true of the individual oral composer who 'plays' with tradition, adapting old forms to new contexts, re-creating the meaning of the traditional anew, but also of the singer or listener/participant, whose way of thinking can be re-created by the very experience of song itself. Therefore, traditional song should not be seen as narrow, restrictive or unchanging: rather it should be understood as essentially playful and prone to the generation of new forms. Song can also be understood as a cathartic moment of reckoning that performs an intense sense of possibility, or even an almost sacred sense of subversion. Therefore, in seeking to understand the import of song in the generation of ideas historically, we must look beyond the text to the liminal symbolism of song poetry, and to the critical moment of song performance itself, the moment in which song comes alive. For it is in this 'sheer potentiality' of the liminal moment of song, wherein 'everything trembles in the balance' (Turner 1982: 43), that the power of singing ideas lies.

The Theory of Liminality

In his groundbreaking study *Les Rites de Passage* published in 1909, Arnold van Gennep classified rites of passage as consisting of three distinct stages: pre-liminal, during which time the neophytes are separated from ordinary life; the liminal phase, during which time the neophytes live in an in-between state outside of ordinary society; and the post-liminal stage, during such time as the neophytes are reaggregated into society and are conferred with a new social status (1960: 11). Van Gennep's study included the comparative analysis of the forms and characteristics of many non-Western rites of transition, and argued that a rite of passage involves the loss or suspension of social status, leading to a new status being conferred on the individual. Thus transition rites in numerous societies were seen as ritualizing the 'passing through' of an individual from one stage in life to the next; for example, from boyhood to manhood, in changes of status such as marriage and motherhood, or indeed in becoming a member of a secret society. The rite of passage, according to van Gennep, involved being 'reborn' into society, and to enable this a period of separation from ordinary society was enacted during which time social norms would melt away and the neophyte would become a 'non-person' who would eventually be re-created anew and ascribed a new role and meaning in society.

Since the translation of van Gennep's book to English in 1960, his work, which was marginalized by the academic establishment in France during his lifetime, has enjoyed a renaissance among anthropologists, folklorists, literary scholars and sociologists (Thomassen 2014: 21–70). The most important of these scholars was Victor Turner, who was inspired by van Gennep's schema of the three phases of the ritual process to delve deeper into the dynamics of social transition and change. In particular it was van Gennep's analysis of the liminal phase of the rites of passage that would prove so influential: a period of symbolic social 'death' that ultimately would end in social 'rebirth', during which time the suspension of normal social structures was performatively enacted and richly signified by such customs as removal to the wilderness, near-naked appearance, lowly status, reversal of hierarchies and licentious behaviour (van Gennep 1960: 65–115). Following the work of van Gennep, Turner used the term 'antistructure' to describe the special dynamics of liminality, that special social phase where norms and structures melt temporarily to enable a new status to be conferred upon the ritual subject. Turner describes liminality as an ambiguous state, an in-between state that is 'neither here nor there':

> Liminal entities are neither here nor there; they are betwixt and between the positions assigned and arrayed by law, custom, convention, and ceremonial. As such, their ambiguous and indeterminate attributes are expressed by a rich variety of symbols in the many societies that ritualize social and cultural transitions. Thus liminality is frequently likened to death, to being in the womb, to invisibility, to darkness, to bisexuality, to the wilderness, and to an eclipse of the sun or moon. (1969: 95)

Not only did Turner add significantly to our understanding of rites of transition through his study of the Ndembu people, but he also began to see the tripartite structure of ritual in other aspects of society and human expression. Specifically, he realized that liminality had a dynamic role in human life, and that the antistructure of liminality was akin to a 'storehouse of possibilities', a playful realm where lack of structure would enable new forms to come to the fore (1990: 12). Turner further elaborated on the experience of liminality for the ritual subject, in particular the sense of ecstatic communion felt by initiands during liminality, something that he termed communitas. This communitas would be seen by Turner as the seedbed of new forms and ideas, as a realm of possibility that contrasted with the structured limits of ordinary life (1969: 132). Communitas was also a compelling emotional experience borne of the companionship of loss of status during liminality, an experience that had a certain 'magic' to it, that would be key to the 'spirit' of the new forms and ideas emanating from liminal experience (1969: 139). Indeed, his interest in liminality as a realm of possibility would lead to his publication of *From Ritual to Theatre: The Human Seriousness of Play* in 1982 in which he applied the theory of liminality to various aspects of modern social life, including the arts and leisure activities, most particularly theatre. Here Turner terms the play-forms of modern consumerist society as 'limanoid', as post-liminal forms that do not enact rites of transition, but still have all the trappings of the liminality associated with transition rites, and act as kernels of creativity in society.

We see, therefore, following van Gennep and Turner, that liminality involves the suspension of the ordinary structures of society. It is an upside down in-between space that does not adhere to the usual rules and societal norms. As Turner describes:

> It is, quintessentially, a time and place lodged between all times and places defined and governed in any specific biocultural ecosystem ... by

the rules of law, politics and religion, and by economic necessity. Here the cognitive schemata that give sense and order to everyday life no longer apply, but are, as it were, suspended – in ritual symbolism perhaps even shown as destroyed or dissolved. (1982: 84)

Liminality, therefore, entails the dissolution of ordinary structures and the suspension of the norms that govern ordinary life. We also see that liminality is one hell of an experience – it turns the world temporarily on its head, it makes the subject a 'blank slate' (Turner 1969: 103). In it the subject feels the sheer possibility of existence, the 'thrill' of antistructure, as well as a deeply felt sense of communitas with fellow humans; ultimately liminality can create the ritual subject anew.

Liminality does not just 'happen', however, it has to be symbolically performed, as demonstrated by the rich cross-cultural data cited in the above studies. Following Turner and van Gennep, I argue that song itself symbolizes and performs the liminal. It is liminality as a creative realm of possibility, as an experience in which 'everything trembles in the balance', as Turner would say, that concerns us here in our study of song. Our conception of song should not be reduced to a text, therefore, but rather is a moment outside of ordinary time in which the structures of ordinary social life temporarily melt. It is this 'free-ing up' of liminal antistructure that means that song is more than just a reflection of important social processes happening 'elsewhere' in society; rather, song is a liminal extraordinary moment in which new ideas and new identities can be born. Therefore the characteristics of liminality as classified by van Gennep and Turner, and later by Thomassen, of structurelessness, of inverted norms and hierarchies, of play, of possibility and of potentiality is of immediate relevance to our understanding of the import of the practices of singing for humans. The significance of this is twofold: for liminality can indeed generate new ideas and models for living, but at the same time liminality is a process through which the subject is reborn. The ideas of antistructure, therefore, are here understood as being inextricably linked to the experience of rebirth that van Gennep and Turner associate with liminality. This means that the medium of song is of particular importance not only in relation to the development of political thought, but of political identity, affiliation and activism also, as will be discussed later. Firstly, however, we must look to how song poetry symbolically performs liminality.

Performing Liminality: Poetry as a Symbolic Marker for Liminality in the Irish Tradition

In following the theoretical framework of Arnold van Gennep, Pádraig Ó Riain argued for the prevalence of liminal characteristics in representations of the *gelta* or 'wild men' of the Irish tradition (2014 [1972]). The most famous of these liminal personae is Suibne Geilt or Wild Sweeney, who in more recent times was also the basis of *Sweeney Astray* by the English-language poet Séamus Heaney (1983). Ultimately arguing that the *geilt* persona of the Irish tradition symbolized loss of status, the transitional or liminal markers of these personae during 'the state of madness', according to Ó Riain, were identified as follows:

1. The madman takes to the wilderness: Suibne, Mac Dá Cherda, the 'Norse' *geilt*, Cú Chulainn, an unidentified *dásachtach*.
2. The madman perches on trees, or runs along them; Suibne, Mac Dá Cherda, the 'Norse' *geilt*.
3. The madman collects firewood: Mac Dá Cherda, Cuanna.
4. The madman is naked, hairy, covered with feathers or clothed in rags: Suibne (naked, hairy, in rags), the 'Norse' *geilt* (feathers).
5. The madman levitates and/or performs great leaps: Suibne (levitates, leaps), Cú Chulainn (leaps), Gal Gaoithe (levitates or leaps?), unidentified *gelta* (levitate), Bolcán, *rí na Fraince* (levitates), the *builedach Tailche Tairbe* (leaps).
6. The madman is very swift: Suibne, the 'Norse' geilt, Mac Dá Cherda, Conall Clocach.
7. The madman is restless and travels great distances: Suibne, Cú Chulainn Mac, Dá Cherda, Conall Clocach, an unidentified *dásachtach*?
8. The madman experiences hallucinations: Suibne?, Muirchertach mac Erca.
9. The madman observes a special diet: Suibne, Mac Dá Cherda, Conall Clocach.

(Ó Riain 2014 [1972]: 176–77)

The parallels drawn by Ó Riain between the Irish geilt and characteristics identified by van Gennep in his comparative study of rites of passage were highly convincing, most notably the near-naked appearance of the geilt and his adornment with feathers, the wilderness context, the observation of a special diet and indeed the performance of madness, which Ó Riain explicitly relates to similar representations in van Gennep's work (2014 [1972]: 200). Other scholars followed suit, observing other quintessentially liminal characters and contexts in the Irish tradition. The first of these was Angela Partridge (now Bourke), who argued for the in-between status and characteristics of the traditional Irish keening woman or lamenter, the ritual specialist of the Irish funeral or 'wake' (1980): the keening woman had a special 'wild' attire and unkempt appearance, bore naked breasts and let her hair down, never stopped moving and travelled great distances, was in some accounts able to perform great leaps, and was also known to have a sort of 'special liminal diet' in the drinking of blood. It was these striking similarities between the keening woman and the wild man that also led Bergholm more recently in her study of Suibne Geilt to classify the keening woman as a kind of 'bereaved novice' (corresponding to Ó Riain's earlier description of Suibne as a 'mad novice') whose behaviour was borne of the liminal experience of grief:

> The behaviour of the *bean chaointe* is by definition both ritualised and transitional; allowing for Ó Riain's generalised use of the term, the bean chaointe could perhaps be characterised as a 'bereaved novice', whose behaviour is not determined by her deranged mental state, but rather by the grief that marks her temporary isolation from the community for the duration of the transitional period. (2012: 157)

Though representations of the keening women and the wild men show remarkable resemblance, as outlined by Partridge and subsequently Bergholm, there is one other central characteristic or behaviour that links both of these liminal personae: the ability to speak in verse. Both are *compelled* to speak in verse during the transitional phase. I believe, therefore, that verse-making should also be added to other established liminal markers in the Irish tradition as an extension of Ó Riain's initial list. Joseph Nagy also alludes to this specific connection between the gift of poetry and loss of status in the case of Suibne Geilt:

> The moment that a person receives the inspiration to see and speak like a poet can also be the moment that he is robbed of his identity, his autonomy, and his freedom from the tyranny of words, both his and those of others. This is precisely the moment undergone by the figure of Suibne in the late Middle Irish text edited and translated here by J.G. O'Keefe. (1996: 2)

Suibne or 'Wild Sweeney', for example, lost his mind having been cursed on the battlefield during the battle of Mag Rath. From that moment onwards he lived in the wilderness outside of normal social structures; he frequented the branches of trees, he wore special attire, he observed a 'weird' diet and he also was bestowed the gift of poetry. Indeed, he spoke only in verse. When Sweeney is finally re-aggregated into normal human life, he loses the ability to speak in verse. Likewise, in folklore accounts of the keening woman, when she becomes grief-stricken she travels great distances (with her bare feet being cut by stones in some instances) also speaking in verse – which is reflective of the ex tempore poetic genre of the keen central to the death ceremony of the traditional Irish. Therefore, both in the case of the wild man and of the keening woman, poetry is connected unequivocally to the liminal phase – that of the outcast in the wilderness on one hand, and that of the overseer of the rite of passage from this world to the next on the other. This is further supported by the extensive work of Joseph Nagy on the hero Finn from the Irish tradition, who is described by Nagy as speaking in verse in liminal prophetic contexts (1985: 21–26), and who also argues that the Irish poet is imbued with special knowledge and often represented as crossing a metaphysical boundary between this world and the next, thus illustrating the in-between status of the Irish poet (1985: 36). The gift of prophecy, which can be considered a sister gift to poetry in the Irish tradition, had already been connected by Kenneth Jackson in a 1940 article on Suibne to the state of madness – to what was understood by later scholars as liminality (Jackson in Nagy 1996: 4). The work of Dáithí Ó hÓgáin on the poet in the Irish tradition (1982), which included folklore sources from the twentieth century, does not incorporate the theory of liminality into his analysis, yet he describes many similar traits to both the wild men and the keening women above to the traditional image of the Irish poet, who he describes as an intermediary (i.e. an in-between figure) between this world and the next (1982: 196–98, 266–80). Furthermore, many folklore accounts describe poets as speaking solely in verse, much like the liminal personae described above (Ó hÓgáin 1982: 5–6, 93–103). This liminality of the Irish poet as represented in Fenian literature is also illustrated by Nagy, who argues that the 'liminal zones of the world' are central to the shamanic qualities of the Irish poet:

> It is in the liminal zones of the world, areas traversed or actually inhabited by the poet, that he awaits and receives supernatural knowledge, or it is from these liminal zones that he sets out to penetrate the otherworld and acquire the knowledge that it offers to the fili. (1985: 37)

Poetry is therefore deeply connected to liminality in the Irish tradition, and I argue that it is an important symbol that performs and actualizes rites of passage, as in the case of the traditional lament; that signals loss of status, as in the case of wild Sweeney; but also symbolizes the sacred intermediary or 'in-between' status of the poet.

A Journey to the Sacred and Back: The Liminality of the Aisling (Vision)

The performative liminality of song and song-makers in the Irish tradition is also evident in the pervasive use of the wilderness theme in the traditional vision poem or aisling as the backdrop to the appearance of the *spéirbhean*, or sovereignty goddess figure, to the poet. Ó Riain identifies the wilderness theme as the central trope of the liminal phase: 'The wilderness would appear to have been the pivotal element of the theme, supplying the background for most of the motif-content of the second or transitional stage of the novitiate' (2014 [1972]: 201). Ó Riain also considers the wilderness to be 'an actual topographical area of transition' in the Irish tradition (2014 [1972]: 201). This is of course reflective of many examples from van Gennep's comparative study, such as the initiation rites of secret societies of the Congo, which involve seclusion in the forest (1960: 81), and the wilderness is also deemed as a central signifier of the liminal by Turner (1969: 95). The wilderness signifies being 'outside' of society, both thematically in the tales of the wild man, but also socially and topographically in the case of 'real-life' transition rites. The song poet who opens a vision poem with this time-honoured theme of seclusion is clearly setting out the markers of liminality, such as Máire Bhuí in the opening to her most famous composition 'Cath Chéim an Fhia' ('The Battle of Keimaneigh'):

> Cois abha Ghleanna 'n Chéama i nUíbh Laeire 'sea ' bhímse
> mar a dtéann a' fia insan oíche chun síor-cholla sóil,
> a' machnamh seal liom féinig a' déanamh mo smaointibh,
> ag éisteacht i gcoíllthibh le bínn-ghuth na n-eón;
> (Ní Shíocháin 2012: 212)

> [By the river of the glen of Keimaneigh in Iveleary that I frequent
> where the deer goes at night to sleep soundly,
> thinking to myself and making my ideas,
> listening in the forest to the sweet voice of the birds]

Here Máire Bhuí is using a traditional theme of orality whose meaning goes beyond the aesthetic to the sacred itself. Rather than being just a pondering upon the serenity and beauty of nature for poetic effect, the wilderness theme here represents separation from the profane world (van Gennep 1960) and signals that a near-sacred truth is to be unveiled by the poet in the lines that follow. This is commonly found among numerous composers of the aisling genre, such as Eoghan Rua Ó Súilleabháin, and even the trance-like state of liminality is represented by various renditions of the aisling theme, as can be seen in Aogán Ó Rathaille's famous line: 'Aisling ghéar do dhearcas féin ar leaba is me go lag-bhríoch' ('A sharp vision I saw while lying weak in my bed'); or a combination of both the theme of seclusion or separation from normal society and a trance-like vision-state such as the traditional 'Tráthnóinín déanach i gcéin cois leasa dhom/ Táimse im chodladh is ná dúistear me' ('One evening late while I was far away near a fairy fort/ I am sleeping and do not wake me'). The roots of the wilderness theme run deep in the Irish tradition, and symbolically belong to the 'limbo of statuslessness' of the in-between, both socially and imaginatively. The aisling theme as a whole also compares interestingly to descriptions of rites of passage of the 'magician' or shaman in the work of van Gennep. Drawing on the work of Marcel Mauss on the Ural-Altaic shaman, for example, van Gennep describes the passage of the shaman, who is understood as being possessed by spirits (which involves 'hallucinations, phobias, epilepsy, trances, catalepsy, etc.') then withdraws to the woods, to solitude, or to the tundra, during which time spiritual beings appear to him, and subsequently he is eventually reborn into society and travels from village to village (1960: 180). There are significant parallels between his classification of the shaman's rite of passage and the aisling or vision theme in the Irish poetic tradition, which can be summarized as follows:

1. The poet is alone in the wilderness, in solitude by the woods or a river, or alternatively lying in bed in solitude, etc.
2. Sometimes a sleep- or trance-like state is depicted.
3. An otherworldly female personification presents herself to the poet in the context of the wilderness or solitude and tells him a message of great import.
4. The poet returns to the world and relays this important message to the people.

Here the poet is separated from society in the liminal realm of the wilderness, experiences the higher truth communicated to him by an otherworldly woman, and then the poem usually closes with his return to the world of men, in which he tells of the message he heard while removed from normal society. In this sense, the aisling corresponds to van Gennep's classification of separation, transition and reaggregation. Similarly to the rite of passage of the shaman described by van Gennep, thematically the aisling depicts a 'passing through' of sorts or a journey to the sacred and back. In this sense, the aisling itself is therefore like a poetic rite of passage with strong shamanic undertones. In opening 'Cath Chéim an Fhia' with the wilderness theme, or in composing in the aisling form, Máire Bhuí was doing much more than depicting a pretty scene: she was symbolizing the sacred authority of the song poet as a liminal persona.

Song and Oral Poetic Performance as Ritual

Van Gennep classes numerous poetico-religious forms as rites in themselves; he classifies a curse or a spell as a direct rite, and vows and prayers as indirect rites (1969: 8). By this account the performance of the spell or curse in itself constitutes a rite of sorts. Given that in the Irish tradition a curse is often performed through poetry or song, and that Ó Madagáin has argued that the vocables of the traditional lullaby were a charm to protect the baby (1992a), it can be argued that the song form itself, if not a rite, certainly seems to have a ritual basis.

The liminal ritual character of oral poetic performances, such as the waulking songs, the Irish lament and even the modern day singing tradition has also been illustrated by scholars. Angela Bourke, for example, refers to the traditional Irish funeral or wake as a 'highly marked interaction among the living, a ceremony of transition' (1993: 160). Therefore the performance of the *caoineadh* was part of a larger context of the performance of an upside down in-between space, one which, due to the context of wake games and frivolity alongside poetry of grief, was both carnivalesque and ultimately renewing:

> During this sort of wake, the world was turned upside down, recalling the carnivalesque of medieval and renaissance Europe. The marginal time of the funeral and wake represents what Mikhail Bakhtin calls 'the people's laughter' of universal upheaval and renewal. (Bourke 1993: 163)

The keening woman herself was akin to an ecstatic figure, bordering on mad in her behaviour, what Bourke would call a kind of holy fool, or even a tragic actor who created a cathartic experience through her mastery not just of words but of the fullness of oral poetic performance, including wailing, clapping and of course the music of the caoineadh (Ó Madagáin 1978: 200; Nic an Airchinnigh and Ó Laoire 2015). As Bourke describes: 'Her willingness to experience disturbing emotions to the full provided a catharsis for everyone who witnessed her performance' (1993: 165). For Bourke, the keener was the very embodiment of the state of transition that was being experienced by the community (1993: 166). Much like we have seen with other forms of oral poetry or song, the liminality of performance also enabled the performer to engage in challenging discourses, in this case in the rhetoric of resistance as described by Bourke that was passed along in the tradition and that otherwise may not have been tolerated by society. The keening woman was both ecstatic and disruptive, and yet these traits seem to have been central to her power and influence, to the licence she had both to speak out and ritually guide the community through transition (1993: 175).

Similarly, in the lives of women in Scotland the waulking songs were integral to the highly ritualized activity of waulking the cloth, which was 'communal and religo-magical in nature' and even included offerings to the *loireag* or fairy-woman believed to be present during the waulking (Speer 1985: 25). Speer is explicit in her analysis of waulking as a ritual process, following the work of Turner (1985: 30). Not only are the women separated from ordinary society, removed to a specially designated waulking space, but the performance of the waulking songs, which includes the sustained rhythm of working the cloth, works up a marked intensity, much like the ecstasy-inducing rhythmic practices associated with many ritual traditions. This intensity verging on the ecstatic is also noted by Speer: 'According to several historical accounts, the singing often became so high-spirited that the performers seemed possessed or demonic' (1985: 26).

The ritualistic characteristics of song have also been commented on by scholars of Irish-language song as apart from the lament tradition already mentioned, most recently by Ó Laoire in his analysis of dance and song on Irish-speaking Tory Island in the late twentieth century (2002). Ó Laoire discusses the transformative bodily experience of the play of dance as a ritual set apart from ordinary time (2002: 143, 170–76), which sets the scene for singing later in the evening and is considered the high point of the evening for many. It was at this high point that the *teas mothúchánach* or emotional heat was to be felt (2002: 176). Following

Gadamer and Turner, Ó Laoire therefore argues for the seriousness of play and of the central liminal role of evenings of dance and song on Tory Island as symbolically actualizing a time outside of ordinary time in which antistructure enables danger and contest, as well as the heat of intense meaning and the social bonds of communitas. Therefore, we see that where dance is a symbol of play that demarcates the liminal, likewise song is found at the centre of the ritualistic liminal play-sphere well into modernity, and integral to the regenerative experiences that speckle human life.

This ritual-like character of song performance context is prevalent in traditional Irish culture beyond Tory Island, of course. Irish singing occasions perform a time outside of ordinary time in a space set apart from ordinary life, in which members of the community sing for each other, through which an intense sense of meaning and communitas is created. The following description by Sewell of the performance of ritual could easily be mistaken for a singing session in a house, or in the local public house in Ireland:

> In most religious rituals, the participants are collected into a place marked off as sacred and then participate in a series of activities that induce a certain emotional state – quiet awe, rapt attention, terror, intense pleasure, or frenzied enthusiasm, as the case may be. (1996: 870)

Traditional singing performance is eagerly anticipated by members of the community. It is a time set apart from ordinary working life in which participants listen intently, interact and participate, and experience the emotional heat referred to by Ó Laoire in his study of song on Tory Island. Again this is typical of ritual contexts, such as that described by Alexander:

> Nor are all attendees only observers. At various points in the ritual, those merely watching the ritual performance are called upon to participate sometimes as principals and at other times as members of an attentive chorus providing remonstrations of approval through such demonstrative acts as shouting, crying and applause. (2004: 536)

However, there is reason to believe that song is not just one part of liminal experience, but is a central custom that symbolizes the liminal itself. Song is a performative speech act with a power beyond ordinary speech, similar to Barber's description of the power of the text (which in her formulation can be either written or oral): 'texts are hot spots of language: concentrations of linguistic productivity, forms of language that have been marked out to command heightened attention – and sometimes to stimulate intense excitement, provoke admiration and desire, or be the mainstay of memory' (2007: 3). The moment the singer's mouth opens, the combination of oral verse and music symbolizes that a special space is being performed, that something is happening, that social custom must heed the extraordinary import of singing, be it playful, or serious or both.

Separating from the Profane: Ekstasis and Song

As indicated by Turner in his study of liminality in society, the experience of communitas is also linked to the experience of ekstasis through song. Song removes us from the profane – it is a journey through a sacred liminal time that leads us back to the profane again. The ecstatic nature of song is demonstrated by many song cultures, such as the Jelimusow female praise singers of Malian music (Durán 1995). Not only is the traditional jeliw interesting as an example of the high social standing of female singers in the oral tradition, some of whom were of such importance that they were advisors to the king, like Sira Mory Diabaté, a late female *ngaara* or 'great singer' (1995: 202), but also gives us insight into the liminal ecstatic characteristics of song. Here the ngaara, which is considered to be the highest level of praise singer, is considered to be possessed by a gift, as Durán describes:

> The musicians say that ngaaraya is neither taught nor inherited; it is believed to be a gift from God, a state almost of possession that overtakes the singer, often induced by the inspired playing of the accompanists. (1995: 202)

The singer has shamanic overtones, therefore, and reminds us of van Gennep's description of transition rites of the shaman to the sacred world and back again. The words of song are not of the everyday, but are understood as being more penetrating than ordinary speech as the proverb tells us: 'The art of the ngaara is a thing of great wonder … mere use of words and mastery of the word are not the same' (Durán 1995: 202). It is clear in the Malian tradition, therefore, that song has an ecstatic almost otherworldly quality to it, that it removes the singer and the listeners from the profane world. Much like Ó Laoire's analysis of the emotional heat of Irish traditional song, the ecstatic intensity of the singing of the *ngaaraya* is considered hot and even potentially dangerous:

> It is not uncommon for a woman singer in the midst of an improvisation, to ask the accompanists to 'cool down' their instruments, which might otherwise draw her into the deep art of ngaaraya (kana mbila ngaarayala). Ngaaraya is considered powerful – draining for the singer and dangerous for the listeners, not the least because they too may go out of control and commit exaggerated acts of generosity. (Durán 1995: 202)

The above is an amazing expression of Turnerian communitas – the ecstatic heat of the aesthetic moment of song including the danger of the liminal antistructure performed by the singer and her musicians. Also part of this ecstatic tradition of song is truth-telling and the fearless speech of the sacred liminality of song, as told by senior musician Jeli Baba Sissoko of Mali: "'If a *ngaara* talks, someone will be offended, because the *ngaara* speaks his/her mind and the truth. The *ngaara* is not afraid of anything …'" (Durán 1995: 204).

This ecstatic experience, which would be termed 'trancing' by Becker, is an integral part of the experience of song in many cultures, an experience that is beyond the literal, and even embodied (2004). Trancing is the altered state of consciousness brought about by music and song in a ritualistic context. The practice of 'trancing', which Becker classifies as a process rather than a state, is ubiquitous in numerous non-Western cultures, but also is present in secular Westernized culture in the form of 'deep-listening', which is a term used by Becker to describe the transcendental experience of listening to or experiencing music outside of religious contexts per se:

> Deep listening is a kind of secular trancing, divorced from religious practice but often carrying religious sentiments such as feelings of transcendence or a sense of communion with a power beyond oneself. (2004: 2)

The power of music and song performance to create time outside of time, and a time of ekstasis, literally 'outside of oneself', is well established and indeed is not limited to religiosity alone. Even in secular traditions, therefore, there is a strong sense of 'communion with a power beyond oneself' often involved in musical experience either as a player/singer or as a listener. We see in Becker's description of this transcendent experience of music the overtly liminal characteristics of communion with the sacred and an altered state of consciousness. Indeed, music, as described in Becker's study of trancing, can be seen literally to enact the tripartite structure of van Gennep's theory:

> Many firsthand accounts of experienced and skillful trancers testify to the catalytic role of music in the transition into trancing, in the sustaining of trancing, and in the transition back to normal consciousness (Rouget 1985: 72, Kapferer 1991: 264, Friedson 1996: 6). (2004: 3)

Here music is seen to perform and actualize liminality. Music separates the subject from the profane world, sustains the liminal experience of altered consciousness and sees the subject back to the ordinary world and normal consciousness again. Trancing involves a separation, transition and reaggregation that is musically enacted. The semiotics of musical creativity, therefore, can be said to mark a 'passing through' for the listener, and I believe that this is the case in the Irish-language singing tradition.

The liminal, ecstatic, traversiary status of music in the Irish tradition is apparent in folklore representations of otherworldliness in music. As demonstrated by uí Ógáin, there is a very definite connection between music or song and the otherworld in Irish folklore, with some songs and tunes being attributed to an otherworldly source, such as 'Raghad-sa 's mo Cheaití', or 'Port na bPúcaí' (1988: 194), songs that have passed over to us from another realm. In older manuscript sources, such as the stories of Finn and the Fianna, musicians, such as the famous Cas Corach, were often in-between figures who moved between the world of mortals and the otherworld (Dooley and Roe 2008: 101–2). Music and song were understood as being able to travel from the otherworld to this one, as mediating cultural forms between worlds. Even some exceptional singers from the twentieth century have sometimes been spoken of as having been touched by the other world or by the 'good people' or 'fairies', and of course there are numerous folklore sources that tell of prodigious musicians being kidnapped by the fairies due to the excellence of their music. What was otherworldly in music was a mark of aesthetic beauty of such a high calibre that it was almost touching the divine. Therefore, from narrative representations down to aesthetic and performance practices of the music itself, song can be said to symbolize a temporary separation from the profane world and an intense though fleeting sense of potentiality.

Moments of Potentiality: The Antistructure of Melody and Verse in the Irish Tradition

It is time to delve a little deeper into that moment of potentiality that song creates and how melody and verse symbolically embody a sense of (sometimes ecstatic) play and can be understood as performing antistructure, thus separating the singer/listener temporarily from the profane world. Indeed, when comparing different forms of poetry in society, the antistructure of play is perhaps most acutely felt in oral verse, which, unlike the textual traditions of modernity, is unfixed and whose form is changeable and ultimately in the hands of the oral performer at hand (Lord 1960, 1996; Buchan 1972; Ó Coileáin 1988; Nagy 1996; Foley 2002; Ní Shíocháin 2009, 2012, 2013b). The moment of oral performance is truly one of potentiality, in relation to both words and music: musical motifs may lead one way or another, depending on the performance, and likewise, poetic formulas can lead in numerous directions re-creating the words of song. James Cowdery describes the motific structure of traditional Irish song as being a system of 'potentialities', for example:

> certain melodic moves are seen to belong together not as a fixed chain of events, but more as a system of potentialities. These motives can recombine in various ways, expanding or contracting, to make new melodies which still conform to the traditional sound. (1984: 499)

Cowdery's conclusions were drawn from a comparative analysis of common motifs in different songs from the tradition. However, his concept of potentialities in Irish song melody is equally applicable to the recomposition of song airs in performance by singers, as I have discussed elsewhere (2009, 2012). When different airs to the same song are compared, such as we find in Máire Bhuí's compositions, we see that certain motifs recur, but, just as Cowdery described, can lead in different directions. The moment of performance is therefore inherently a moment of musical play. The Irish song tradition is one of creative transmission (Ní Shíocháin 2009). This can be demonstrated by a comparative analysis of different renditions of the song 'Maidean Álainn Ghréine' ('One Lovely Sunny Morning'), which is attributed to Máire Bhuí. When the singing of Cáit Ní Mhuimhneacháin and Áine Uí Chuíll are compared, for example, though we find common melodic ideas, those same melodic concepts do not necessarily lead to the same end or come from an identical starting point.

Figure 2.1 *Áine Uí Chuíll (2011)*

Figure 2.2 *Cáit Ní Mhuimhneacháin (1941)*

In the above examples, we see that the beginning of both songs differ, only to lead to a similar motif in bars 3 and 4 of both Áine Uí Chuíll's rendition and Cáit Ní Mhuimhneacháin's rendition. From bars 5 onwards in both versions we see again the development of a common motif, but significant differences in the articulation of the rhythm. The creativity of the singer in performance is central therefore to the 'structure' of the air, and motifs – rather than being fixed – can lead one way or another. Indeed, even within the same performance of a song, such as we find with Seán de hÓra's rendition of 'Maidin Álainn Ghréine', we find that the singer demonstrates this re-creative dynamic of the singing performance. To illustrate this re-creativity of song performance, I give the opening melody from two different verses from the same song performance:

Figure 2.3 Seán de hÓra (1973)

In the above examples from the singing of Seán de hÓra, we see how he changes the opening melody in the different renditions of the melody of the verse, as illustrated above. Indeed, the musical potentialities that Cowdery talks of can even be heard to be at play in the creative process of a single song performance: we see that motif 1 (M1) and motif 2 (M2) in A1 are interchangeable with the 'new' motifs of Mx and My in A2, but that they all resolve to motif 3 followed by motif 4 to complete the line. This type of re-creative process in singing, in which the air is varied and ornamented in performance, is typical of sean-nós singing. Indeed, in the singing of Peáití Thaidhg Pheig, for example, we find that the rendition of a song by the same singer changes from performance to performance, as demonstrated by the three different renditions of 'Cath Chéim an Fhia' ('The Battle of Keimaneigh') released by Acadamh Fódhla on compact disc in 2011. Thus the very 'structure' of the song air is therefore realized in the moment of performance itself; the fleeting moment of performance is where the form the air will take is realized, and then it is gone.

There is an argument to be made, of course, that this re-creative impulse is at the core of the aesthetic experience of both Irish traditional music and Irish traditional song. It is precisely in the re-creation of older forms that the true art of traditional music lies: it is the variation of common tunes that drives the ecstatic experience of traditional dance music, for example, that leads the listener to 'lose the head' (as was the mantra of young men involved in traditional music circles from Ballyduff Upper in West Waterford in the 80s and 90s), that creates the individual style that captivates the listener, or that drives the dancer into a state of euphoria. Likewise, the art of the singer is in his or her play on the melody. This musical play is intrinsic to the feeling of elation in singing experience; it is the musical play that makes the listener feel that they are going to lose control of themselves altogether. Therefore, the play of music not only can be said to demonstrate the re-creativity of tradition, but also symbolizes and creates the very experience of antistructure, whereby one is caught in a moment of sheer Turnerian potentiality, of unbridled possibility, where one cannot quite tell what the musician or singer will conjure up next but cannot wait to hear it. The listener is experiencing something beyond structure, an in-between moment of anticipation that produces a thrill, an excitation of play. Therefore, a musical tradition such as this, which has at its core the dynamic impulse of creativity, is in itself central to the performative enactment of the liminal in the lives of people. The potentialities of traditional melodies not only create the very structure of the music through performance, but are also part of an ecstasy-inducing tradition, as depicted by song collector A.M. Freeman when describing the experience of the creative twists and turns of traditional singing and its effect on the audience in Ballyvourney in 1914:

> His tricks and idiosyncrasies have claimed the whole of your attention in the first verse. You do not even know what the tune is like. You must

listen carefully this time. But he has begun again so slyly, that in your perplexity you did not notice it. How far has he got in this, his second move to outwit you? Heavens! His eyes are flashing again! He is going to sing his long note and flourish! He does so, this time receiving congratulations from the audience. Those sitting near enough to him lift one of his hands and shake it: those further off praise him and wish him length of life. But the emotional moment passes ... (1920: xxii)

Here the 'tricks' and 'flourishes' and artistry of the singer rouse the audience, creating a heightened experience of aesthetic pleasure. Indeed, this sometimes intense ecstatic experience of traditional Irish singing was further illustrated by Freeman when remarking on the song performances of illiterate singer Peg O'Donoghue in Co. Cork in 1914, from whom he collected numerous songs, saying, 'When singing a complete song she becomes ecstatic' (Freeman 1920: xix; Ó Madagáin 1985: 135).

The importance of creative transmission of music among traditional musicians and singers is well established; however, we can also see that the words themselves also have some of the antistructure of liminality. The variation of words and lines, what Lord terms multiformity (1996) or what Gregory Nagy terms *mouvance* (1996), abounds in the song tradition, though less pronounced from the late twentieth century onwards in some quarters. Therefore in the humorous chanson de la mal-mariée 'An Seanduine Dóite' ('The Old Burnt Man') in Irish we see that lines and half-lines not only are unfixed or interchangeable with others, much like Cowdery's concept of potentialities, but furthermore that some of the lines that change have no small comic effect, which would suggest conscious recomposition on the part of singers as is demonstrated, for example, in the following multiforms that close each verse in the song:

1. 'S b'oiriúnaí dhuit sagart ar maidin ná óigbhean
   [and a priest in the morning would be more suited to your needs than a young woman]
   (Ó Cróinín 1980: 333)

2. Is dá mbeinnse i mbéal dorais ná beirimse beo ort
   [and if I were to come to your door, may I not find you alive]
   (Nic Dhonncha 2003)

3. Ó luigh ar do leabhaidh is gur marbh a éireoidh tú
   [Oh lie down on your bed and may you be dead when you wake up!]
   (Ó Cathasaigh 2009: 106–7)

We see, therefore, that multiformity, as oral theorists would call it, or potentialities, as Cowdery would say, are not only part and parcel of oral transmission, but are also central to the creation of a realm of possibility through music and verse. There is therefore no urtext, in the modern sense, in the singing tradition, and both the words and music are intrinsically playful. As Nagy describes:

> The nightingale moves his song, which as we have seen is inherently both recurrent and recomposed, much as every new season of spring is a joyous event of inherent recurrence and recomposition, even re-creation. (1996: 36–37)

As described by Ó Madagáin and Ó Laoire, the combination of the melody and words is a deeply felt aesthetic experience for the traditional singer and his/her community. Part of the aesthetics of song are the poetic formulas, themes and musical motifs that perform traditionality, that create a performance that echoes of the practices of generations of singers and composers. However, also intrinsic to this traditionality is the re-creative impulse of orality and performance, and it is these aesthetic values of re-creativity that serve as central markers of liminal experience through song, as a time outside of ordinary time, of heightened feeling and meaning. For it is in the very moment of performance itself that the song itself is realized. When considering song as a play-sphere integral to social and intellectual life, therefore, the very structure of the song form can be understood as an expression of play and of antistructure, and of sheer potentiality.

The Ritual Powers of (Song)Poetry: Satire, Insult and Fearlessness

Liminality confers ritual powers on the novitiate, and similarly song can be seen to have a certain licentiousness to it, or subversive qualities that are 'immune' to the usual rules, social norms or hierarchies. Many song forms are strongly linked to liminal behaviours, such as the funeral lament, as already mentioned. Another salient example is satire. Satire through song often confers powers upon the weak or lowly, temporarily suspending the social hierarchy, posing a distinct danger to those in power, something that resonates strongly with the insult-throwing by the novitiate at elders during the liminal phase of rites of passage (Turner 1969: 101–2). Much like such insult-throwing and mud-flinging being 'allowed' during liminality, the performer of satire is likewise given licence to question authority without any fear of consequence, such as described by Bosman in 1704 on observing the Avudwene satirical songs being performed:

> a perfect liberty is allowed and scandal so highly exalted that they may [the artists] freely sing of all the faults, villainies and frauds of their superiors as well as inferiors, without punishment or so much as the least interruption ... (Bosman in Agovi 1995: 48)

This has led to satire having consistent political clout in many societies and cultures, such as those described by Ruth Finnegan in her studies on oral culture in Africa (1977), and which is described by Agovi in relation to Nzema Avudwene festival songs:

> What we have in *avudwene,* therefore, is not just a catalogue of gratuitous insults arising from the simple fact that the occasion demands and guarantees immunity. Rather there is a conscious attempt to raise insult into a swerving instrument of public policy. (1995: 60)

Here we see that satirical festival songs not only reflect the subversion of liminality, but also serve to regulate social structure and the exercise of power, which is the raison d'être of antistructure – that is, to renew ordinary life. The fear of satire is well established in the Irish poetic tradition, with no one being above insult, much like in the Avudwene tradition. Such was the status of both the poet and satire in Gaelic society that it was believed in the Irish tradition that poetic satire had the power to even kill or maim (Ó hÓgáin 1982: 335–48). The ritual powers of poetry in Irish are to be found from the earliest representations of the poet down to folklore representations into the modern era itself, as illustrated by Bergin's description of the Irish bardic poet in his seminal essay in 1912: 'At an earlier period he had been regarded as a dealer in magic, a weaver of spells and incantations, who could blast his enemies by the venom of his verse, and there are traces down to most recent times of a lingering belief, which was not, of course, confined to Ireland in the efficacy of a well-turned malediction' (1970: 4). Indeed, Knott tells us in Irish manuscript sources the terms *fili* (poet) and *druí* (druid) frequently appear as interchangeable terms (1960: 8), with the bardic poet, whose compositions were performed to music for the Gaelic court, engaging not only in satire but in poems of remonstrance, protest and repeals for redress of injustice (1960: 66, 70).

In addition to these special powers associated with song and poetic performance, many song composers occupied a distinctly liminal position in society. This is demonstrated by the outsider status of the Irish poet in the work of Dáithí Ó hÓgáin, one of the best examples of which is perhaps Pead Buí, who had a filthy appearance and used to wander the countryside by himself, but had an incredible gift of poetry and indeed had the ability to cure certain ailments with charms, and also had a charm to expel or attract rats (1982: 381–82). Likewise, the Irish poet is often represented as having an almost freakish talent – such as we see in the tales of the poet Tomás Rua Ó Súilleabháin, of whom it was said that his first words were in verse (Ó hÓgáin 1982: 80). The poet is therefore both part of the community and yet an outsider figure, certainly one who occupies a position different to that of ordinary mortals. In this way, the image of the Irish poet in folklore is not entirely dissimilar to that of the Ewe oral tradition, in which the oral poet is akin to an outcast of sorts, albeit a gifted outsider figure of huge significance to society:

> Song texts by major Ewe oral poets reveal the poets as loners, frequently celebrated and even envied but marginalised individuals, expressing their opinions from beyond the mainstream of their communities though eternally engaged with issues central to communal life. (Anyidoho 1995: 244)

This 'loner' image of the poet is also expressed in the Irish tradition through the use of the wilderness theme, which is indicative of liminality (Ó Riain 2014 [1972]) and often used by poets in their compositions, such as depicted by Máire Bhuí herself when describing her own compositional process: 'a' machnamh seal liom féinig a' déanamh mo smaointibh'/ 'thinking a while to myself, making my ideas' (Ní Shíocháin 2012: 212–15). Indeed, Anyidoho argues that expressions of loneliness, marginality and low social status of oral poets in the Ewe tradition are not necessarily a real reflection of the actual circumstances of the poet, but rather reflect the special role and social standing of the poet (1995: 244). This extraordinary status is what enables the composer's fearless poetic speech, who, due to maintaining a sufficiently ambiguous social position, has literally nothing to lose and nothing to fear (1995: 249). Thus the poet is often an 'untouchable' liminal figure, with licence to criticize, much like the intense questioning and subversion we associate with the transition phase of the ritual process. Therefore the oral poet is often a 'gifted' figure, who, like Pead Buí, may be of a lowly dishevelled appearance, and this 'outsider' status is highly suggestive of the powers conferred upon the weak as part of liminality, as described by Victor Turner.

The Potentiality of the Play-Sphere: The Challenging Discourse of Song

Song can spell trouble for those in authority. This is why the police pursued song with incredible effort and no small success in eighteenth-century France, and also why Dublin Castle similarly kept tabs on seditious songs among the people of Ireland during the colonial period (Murphy 1979; Darnton 2010; Moylan 2016). The overtly political power of song will be dealt with in more detail in the second half of this book, but for now let us take a look at the licence given to song to articulate ideas and to challenge norms in society that otherwise may not be tolerated in ordinary speech or in other social interactions. In many cultures, song gives a voice to those who otherwise would have no voice, as discussed earlier. Certainly, there is a boldness to song (in the Hiberno-English sense of the word) that is permitted by society. Song is almost a sacred place of subversion. This, of course, echoes strongly of both van Gennep and Turner's description of the novitiate, who criticize and challenge the leaders of their society while undergoing a rite of passage: though lowly, the novitiate paradoxically are given licence to insult, loot and pillage, which would not be tolerated of members of ordinary society. As described by van Gennep:

> During the entire novitiate, the usual economic and legal ties are modified, sometimes broken altogether. The novices are outside society, and society has no power over them, especially since they are actually sacred and holy, and therefore untouchable and dangerous, just as gods would be. (1960: 114)

It is this particular dynamic of the ritual process that means that the liminal and the 'inferior', as described by Turner, can be associated with 'ritual powers' (1969: 100–3). Song symbolically constitutes a similar sacred space, in which challenging discourses that may not be tolerated in ordinary speech can be aired 'safely'. In this sense, song has a dangerous streak to it and poses a challenge to society – but this right to challenge is protected by the understanding of song as sacred, as a symbolic 'separation from the profane world' in van Gennep's terms (1960: 96, 99). The role of many song poets reflect what Turner would call the powers of the weak with which the liminal persona is imbued, as epitomized by characters such as the court jester and 'other oddities' in society, and in representation of holy beggars, third sons, little tailors or such like from folk literature (1969:109–11). Turner comments of the court jester, for example:

> They were privileged to throw into the water any of the great nobles 'who had offended them and their sense of justice during the last year' ... These figures, representing the poor and the deformed, appear to symbolize the moral values of communitas as against the coercive power of supreme political rulers. (1969: 110)

Similarly, the song form empowers the subaltern in many cultures, and enables voices that challenge, question, mock or regulate the status quo in society. Song, at least in the metaphorical sense, reserves the right to fling great nobles into the water. If we take the case of the aforementioned Irish song 'An Seanduine Dóite' ['The Old Burnt Man'], for example, we see that the most outrageous statements are made in respect of the old man to whom the young woman (the heroic long-suffering protagonist) is married. Again we see that the multiformity of traditional song generated numerous hilarious formulations of the young woman's various plots to rid herself of the corpse-like old man, including such sub-themes as follows: that she was ill-advised to marry the old man; she would rejoice at the death of the old man; she would poison him to be rid of him; she would bring home a young man for herself and throw the old man out into the ditch; and that she wishes to bury the old man and walk out with the young men. Such variations upon these sub-themes can be found in different renditions of the song, for example:

Dá bhfaighinnse mo sheanduine báite i bpoll móna,
A chosa a bheith briste, is a chnámha a bheith leonta,
Thabharfainn abhaile é is do dhéanfainn é a thórramh,
Is do shiúlóinnse amach leis na buachaillí óga.
(Nic Dhonncha 2003)

[If I were to find my old man drowned in a boghole,
his legs broken and his bones sprained,
I would bring him home and wake him [i.e. perform his funeral rite]
and I'd walk out with the young boys!]

Dá bhfaighinnse mo sheanduine báite i bpoll móna,
thabharfainn abhaile é is do dhéanfainn é a thórramh,
bhainfinn an craiceann dó is dhéanfadh sé bróga,
is chaithfinn amach go dtí na buachaillí óga é.
(Ó Cathasaigh 2009: 106–7)

[If I were to find my old man drowned in a boghole,
I would take him home and wake him [i.e. perform his funeral rite],
I'd remove his skin out of which I'd make shoes,
which I'd throw out to the young boys!]

The gruesome and the bizarre all figure in the abuse directed at this symbol of patriarchal societal restriction and personal unhappiness. In a society where marriage matches were a central part of social organization up until the twentieth century, this kind of brazen talk was thoroughly enjoyed. All of these discourses are sung with no small sense of glee, of course, and it is a light-hearted song. There was no ill-consequence to singing such ideas. However, the humour is also tinged with a real sense of sadness and injustice. The play of song, therefore, may broach what is risky or serious in the guise of humour. We see seriousness appearing in some more sombre verses that we find in the song, such as the following verse from the singing of renowned Cork storyteller, Amhlaoibh Ó Luínse:

Triúr a bhí agamsa am cheangal le hiarlis:
Mo mháthair is m'athair 's an sagart chó dian leo.
Téid siad abhaile nuair a chaithid an féasta
'S is annamh a thagaid am theagasc ná am fhéachaint.
(Ó Cróinín 1980: 333)

[Three people were tying me to a changeling:
my mother, my father and the priest who was as severe as them both.
They go home after the feast [wedding feast] has been consumed
and they rarely come to advise me or to see me.]

The protagonist of the song, the young woman who was traded by her parents to the old man, powerless in her own personal fortunes, is imagined through song as castigating her marriage, her husband and the status quo with abandon. She has (and we all have) a great laugh at the expense of the old man. In the song of the tormented young wife, the hierarchy of real-life patriarchal society is thus inverted: in the song the woman fantasizes of the demise of the old man and her subsequent release from marital bonds. In reality, numerous young women had to bite their lip and put up with their marriage arrangement for better or worse. In song, however, the whole institution of arranged marriage was gleefully targeted, and patriarchy itself was not above insult. Thus such a satirical voice may have served to regulate and to modify social customs or power relations in society. Thus song truly performs antistructure, and allows for the opposite of the norms of society, and for a freeing up of strictures. This special quality of poesis is summed up by Huizinga:

> *Poesis* is, in fact, a play function. It proceeds within the play-ground of the mind, in a world of its own which the mind creates for it. There things have a very different physiognomy from the one they wear in 'ordinary life', and are bound by ties other than those of logic and causality. (Huizinga 1970: 119)

Song is a play-sphere that enables ideas and discourses that may be unimaginable or at least unutterable in real life because song is not bound by the structures of 'ordinary life' in the same way as ordinary speech. This play of song should not be seen as solely the realm of mockery and humour by any means, however; the play of song can be deadly serious and thus can allow for some of the darker sides of human existence to be articulated.

This can be seen in another genre that speaks of female experience in patriarchal society, that being the chanson de jeune fille, or the song of the abandoned woman. Seán Ó Tuama, in his study of Irish-language love songs, remarked that of all the love genres there was truthfulness and sincerity to the song of the abandoned woman that was often lacking from courtly love songs (1960: 77). To this day songs on this theme are revered by singers, and the most famous of which, 'Dónall Óg', is a regular feature at singing sessions and at the Oireachtas, the foremost sean-nós singing competition in Ireland. Indeed, as was suggested by Ó Tuama, the discourses of the women's experiences in the songs touch a nerve, and seem to resonate strongly with female experience even in modern Irish society. We see taboo issues being voiced through song, of sexual relations outside of marriage, of pregnancy out of wedlock and the devastating effects that this has on women in a society that shuns women who do not conform to the patriarchal model. Though one could interpret such discourses as a warning to young women to be guarded in their behaviour towards men, one could also interpret such songs as voicing the injustice endured by the women represented in the songs. Arguably, there is no example from the song genre of the abandoned woman more chilling than the following verse from Bess Cronin from West Cork, which tells of a young woman who has successfully hidden her pregnancy from her family and who conceals her baby in a cave:

> Is dóigh lem' mhuintir gur maighdean acu me,
> Nuair a bhím-se féinig am' chladhaire banarthlan;
> Bíonn mo laogh agam i bpluais na carraige
> Agus istoíche thriallaim leis an ngealaigh air.
> (Ó Cróinín 2000: 52)

> [My family believe I'm a virgin,
> when actually I'm a fool of a wet-nurse;
> I keep my lamb in the rocky cave
> and visit him when the moon is high.]

Some of the discourses in the song of the abandoned woman are very raw, almost fearless, like the above excerpt. It is of particular significance that during the eighteenth century, for example, when the consequences of conceiving a child out of wedlock in Ireland, as in the rest of Europe, was dire, that the human story of such women, be it real or imagined, was being sung. It seems that these discourses, which perform female experiences in a patriarchal society, were allowed to be sung long before the status quo would change. Indeed, this particular rendition by Bess Cronin is particularly striking in its parrhesiastic character, when the female voice launches a mighty attack upon the dishonourable and reckless actions of her male lover. Unlike other articulations of the same theme, which may focus more on the depressed state of the woman and her nonetheless unwavering love for the man, this song performs a curse upon the offending lover that matches the plight of the offended woman herself:

> A ógánaigh óig, bhís anuraidh am' mhealladh-sa,
> Agus tán tú i mbliana a d'iarraidh m'atharrach;
> Cuirim-se Dia go dian 'na sheasamh leat,
> A' leagadh do chlú agus a' dúchtaint t'aigne.

> A ógánaigh óig, más a d'iarraidh mná thu
> Go seolaidh Dia i gcuan í fháil tu;
> Úrlár lom fé mhórán gárlach –
> A n-athair dall agus iad gan mháthair.
> (Ó Cróinín 2000: 52)

[Oh young man, last year you were seducing me,
and this year you are pursuing someone else;
I put God standing sternly beside you,
knocking your reputation and darkening your mind.

Oh young man, if it's a woman you are looking for,
may God send you such:
a bare floor under many offspring,
their father blind and they without a mother.]

One must remember, of course, that a curse through poetry was serious business in the Irish tradition, and therefore the sentiment is further amplified by the medium of song. In a society where unmarried mothers found themselves as outcasts, almost as non-people, it is striking that song enabled such a voice. We see, therefore, that song enabled a commentary upon social ills and injustice in the contemporary life of singers, and articulated ideas that in essence questioned the validity of the social norms that governed practices of courtship and marriage. In 'Do Gheallais Domhsa' ('You Promised Me'), as sung by Bess Cronin, which in many ways can be interpreted as a multiform of 'Dónall Óg', the powerless female outcast castigates the male figure, whose status in society is secure and protected by gender norms. In society he is safe – but not in song.

Another example of the sacred truth-telling of song comes from the mouth of the oral poet Máire Ní Dhroma, locally known as 'Molly na Páirce', from Co. Waterford (Ó Gealbháin 2015). Máire Ní Dhroma composed one of the few famine songs that has survived, 'Na Prátaí Dubha' ('The Black Potatoes'). The song speaks from within the human crisis of the Great Irish Famine; it is incredibly poignant and sad, but also angry. Through her mastery of oral poetry through song, Máire Ní Dhroma castigates the powerful in society and even goes so far as to say that God did not create the great hunger that herself and her community were experiencing. Máire Ní Dhroma is a parrhesiast who is compelled to sing out about the social injustice of starvation that she witnessed and experienced:

Tá na bochta seo Éireann ag plé leis an ainnise,
Buairt is anacair is pianta báis,
Leanaí bochta ag béiceadh is a scréachadh gach maidin,
Ocras fada orthu is gan dada le fáil.

Ní hé Dia a cheap riamh an obair seo;
Daoine bochta a chur le fuacht is le fán,
Iad a chur sa phoorhouse go dubhach is glas orthu,
Lánúineacha pósta is iad scartha go bás.

(Tóibín 1978: 19–20)

[These poor people of Ireland are contending with wretchedness,
worry and distress and pains of death,
poor infants shout and scream each morning,
a long hunger upon them and with nothing to be had.

It was not God who created this,
nor who made the poor destitute,
nor who put them sorrowful in the poorhouse under lock and key,
where married couples are separated until death.]

Indeed, it was this challenge by Máire Ní Dhroma that the famine was not God's will that apparently led to the song being censored by the Catholic Church, who insisted that the famine was indeed the will of God (although there are conflicting accounts of this, and the song still managed to survive in the oral tradition into the twentieth century) (Tóibín 1978; Ó Gealbháin 2015). It is to the God that did not inflict famine upon the Irish poor that she pleads for help, imploring the Almighty to remedy the plight of the starving masses and literally to floor the infamous poorhouse, a symbol of the oppression of the poor, to the ground:

A Dhia na Glóire, fóir is freagair sinn;
Scaoil ár nglasa is réidh ár gcás;
Is an bheatha arís ó do chroí go gcasair orainn
Is an poorhouse go leagair anuas ar lár.

(Tóibín 1978: 53)

[Oh God of Glory, help us and answer us;
Release our bonds and remedy our plight;
and may the life from your heart chance upon us again
and may you knock the poorhouse to the ground.]

However, her pleas to God at times verge on chastisement, with the suggestion that God has deserted the poor, that God is nowhere to be found in the wretched hunger-stricken existence, as described in the song: 'Níl aon chuimhne againn oíche ná maidin ort' ('We have no memory of you day or night'). The premise, as described by Agovi in the Avudwene song tradition (1995), that no one, even the king, is beyond the challenge of song seems to be borne out by Máire Ní Dhroma's communication with God on high also. When speaking directly to God, Ní Dhroma is respectful yet bold, and the authority of the speech act of poetry is palpable even when addressing the Creator himself. This in itself is an incredible expression of the challenge that song can pose. Ultimately, however, the grievance of the godless unnatural situation for the Irish poor is relaid at the feet of the powerful among mortal men, and no reserve is expressed in her depiction of the nobles who sit idly by while people are dying of hunger:

Mo thrua móruaisle go bhfuil mórán coda acu,
Gan tabhairt sásaimh don obair seo do Rí na nGrás,
Ag feall ar bhochta Dé nach bhfuair riamh aon saibhreas
Ach ag síorobair dóibh ó aois go bás.

(Tóibín 1978: 120)

I pity the great nobles who have plenty,
without giving any satisfaction to the work of the King of Graces,
but treacherously mistreating God's own poor who never got any riches
but eternally work from birth to death.]

This fearless speech could almost be termed a 'critical voice' in modern terms, whereby Máire Ní Dhroma not only represents the horrendous experience of famine for the community through song, but also accuses those who she deems responsible. And song was the medium best fitted to do so. Song, through symbolizing liminality, also symbolizes the right to protest. Song symbolizes and actualizes the sacred power of the weak in challenging the powerful. This challenging and subversive dynamic of song is found in other cultures also, as previously discussed, in which women are sometimes prohibited from making their case in ordinary speech, but may do so in song, as we have seen in Somali oral poetry, the Dyula tradition and the Irish lament or caoineadh. In all cases, the discourses of song are practically beyond reproach and untouchable. Anthropologically, therefore, song is connected to the powers of the weak that we associate with liminality, as depicted by oral poet Komi Ekpe of the Ewe song tradition, who said of himself: 'Komi Ekpe has become the leper-animal,/ He fears no living man' (Anyidoho 1995: 250). Likewise, the keening woman in her wildness and unbridled behaviour is allowed to speak of such issues as social injustice and domestic violence in poetic performance. As Bourke has argued, for the keening woman, the very performance of unhinged poetic wildness is licence for saying what she wants, and speaking out is tolerated because of the performative meaning of the keen itself as out of the ordinary (1993: 175). Indeed the kind of 'performative madness' demonstrated by the keening woman, or the asocial wildness as depicted by the oral poet Komi Ekpe, belongs to the symbols of liminality that we associate with rites of passage, such as described by Arnold van Gennep in relation to the Arioi of Tahiti, for example: 'Whoever wanted to join presented himself, dressed and decorated in an unusual fashion, and behaved as if mentally deranged …' (1960: 83, cf. Ó Riain 2014 [1972]: 200). Practitioners of song and oral poetry, therefore, also perform important symbols of liminality, or antistructure. Much like rites of transition, the antistructure of song temporarily suspends the social hierarchy and enables those of lower or marginal status to have a voice, where they might not have one in ordinary life. What is striking in all these situations is that the powers that be respect the sacred space of song to challenge society itself. In this sense song can be said to be integral to the negotiation of power in society and indeed to the articulation of ideas that challenge social norms. This is where the importance of song lies: as an in-between space where ideas and society itself can be challenged, renewed and reinvigorated. Song, therefore, can be seen as a special sacred space, an upside-down time outside of ordinary time, in which what is troublesome, dangerous or taboo can be aired – and without any ill consequence for the singer.

The Singer of Ideas as 'Seer of Communitas': The Liminality of Song and the Generation of Ideas

Turner's concept of communitas refers to the deep human bonds of solidarity, shared experience and elation that occur among neophytes in rites of transition and, according to Turner, is integral to the experience of liminality. Communitas is also related to ecstatic elements of ritual experience, in particular what Turner classifies as existential communitas, communitas of 'the moment', what William Blake might term 'a winged moment as it flies' (Blake in Turner 1969: 132). Existential or spontaneous communitas is the opposite of structure, and communitas is 'of the now' (1969: 113). Communitas is borne of the in-between, of the 'what if', is both reaffirming and euphoric in essence, frequently associated with mystical power and it balances against the structured world: 'structure tends to be pragmatic and this-worldly; while communitas is often speculative and generates imagery and philosophical ideas' (1969: 133). Here Turner clearly posits communitas as creative in contrast to the more rigid structure of ordinary life. Ó Laoire already has ascribed the generation of communitas as integral to the experience of singing on Tory Island in the twentieth century, of this compelling feeling of communion, mutual understanding and realization among participants in singing occasions (2002). This euphoric or deeply felt sense of communitas is of course connected to the aesthetic experience of song, as already mentioned, of the beauty and meaning of the words, the marriage of music and rhyme, and the twists and turns on the part of the singer that create a crescendo of ecstasis. The sense of there being a higher truth to song also echoes of the 'charism or grace sent by the deities or ancestors' in rites of passage that is felt as part of existential communitas (Turner 1969: 137–38). Indeed there is an ecstasy to communitas that is formative in and of itself. Therefore, the singer of ideas, such as Máire Bhuí Ní Laeire, in this instance, not only has mastered a tradition of verse and music composition and performance that is beautiful, but a tradition of creating a meaning-laden liminal experience that can inspire existential communitas, re-create the meaning of the world and reconfigure identity itself. Máire Bhuí is akin to what Turner would term a 'seer of communitas' or a master of symbolic thought (1969: 142). Song is much more than just a 'text', rather it is a social process akin to the 'magic circles' described by van Gennep that shift as a person undergoes rites of passage through their lifetime.

Thus the 'magic circles' pivot, shifting as a person moves from one place in society to another. The categories and concepts which embody them operate in such a way that whoever passes through the various positions of a lifetime one day sees the sacred where he has seen the profane, or vice versa. Such changes of condition do not occur without disturbing the life of society and the individual, and it is the function of rites of passage to reduce their harmful effects. (1960: 13)

Song also has the capacity, much like a rite of passage, to cause a person to see the sacred where he has previously seen the profane, literally marking the passage from profane to sacred and back again. As has been argued by Szakolczai (2009), and Horvath, Wydra and Thomassen (2015) more recently, transition and liminality are key processes not just in overt ritual practices in society such as were discussed in depth by van Gennep, but also are central to the experiences of communities of people who live through periods of great change, both on a societal and a personal level. As van Gennep describes above, transition rites safely see the person or the community through change of status or situation, and are therefore a regulating rhythm in the life of the community. In the Irish tradition, as in many cultures, song also responds to transition and change, makes meaning out of crisis and restores the person and society to an equilibrium. This particular dynamic of Irish song in enabling people to cope with overwhelming emotion has been discussed at length by Ó Madagáin, who refers in his study to the old Irish saying 'An ceol a ligeann an racht' ('Music/song releases intense emotion'). In his study, Ó Madagáin refers to the story of a traditional song entitled 'An Chéad Mháirt d'Fhómhar' about a man who tragically lost his son in a boating accident, and who was completely overcome with grief until such time as he was able to sing about the tragedy. Having composed his song, having released the great emotion, he was able to come to terms with his grief and re-enter normal society again (1992b). Ó Laoire also refers to a similar case of a family on Tory Island whose brother died in America and whose body never returned home. An old love song 'A Phaidí a Ghrá' on the theme of a woman abandoned by her lover was repeatedly requested by this particular family at social gatherings. The song now became a metaphor for their own plight, and hearing this song sung seemed to be central to how they would cope with their tragic loss (2002: 212–20). In both cases, song can be seen to see the person through a great change or sudden tragedy in their lives. So much like how the transition rite creates a topsy-turvy inverted world of possibility from which the neophyte will be created anew and ascribed a new status in society, song also on the one hand creates an imaginative world of possibility, while at the same time acting as a regulating force that renews ordinary life. In the chapters that follow, I will discuss how song also had a role in seeing the community through periods of precarity, hunger and crisis, in overseeing and making meaning out of transition and change.

Turner's theoreticization of communitas not only expresses the extraordinary 'magic' of the liminal moment of song, but also the ways in which communitas can generate new ways of thinking that in turn can become incorporated into post-liminal structured existence. Existential or spontaneous communitas is 'a phase, a moment, not a permanent condition', just like a song. However, Turner argues that existential communitas can give rise to normative communitas, which he describes as existential communitas that is 'organized into a perduring social system', and also ideological communitas, which he describes as 'utopian models of societies based on existential communitas' (1969: 132). Therefore the ideas of the 'winged moment' of existential communitas can in turn be incorporated into the more this-worldly structure of ordinary life. Liminality, therefore, can be a turning point in social and political development, a moment of potentiality that can send society on a new course.

Examples of such ideological communitas might include the Jacobinism of the French Revolution, for example, or various utopian models such as communism or its estranged sibling liberal capitalism, that emerge from the communitas of great societal transitions or crises to become enduring principles by which people live their lives, and indeed rule their communities. The significance of liminal communitas is in its capacity to generate new ideas and new models for living while at the same time being a moment of communion with others and of communal realization that is almost touching the divine. The ideas of communitas have all the trappings of 'truth' about them. Thus communitas can be a most compelling force in the lives of humans and is as much about identity and the self as it is about abstract ideas. Indeed, it is precisely this marriage between ideas and identity that is of particular relevance to this current study. Turner also suggests that liminality, as it involves the destruction of status and of the social, is particularly prone to levelling of hierarchies and egalitarian ideas, such as 'universal justice, comradeship and brotherhood between all men, the equality before God, the law or the life force of men and women, young and old, and persons of all races and ethnic groups' (1969: 134). He suggests that Shakespeare's Gonzalo's commonwealth, for example, is an expression of pure liminality in which the inversion of social norms and levelling of class and hierarchy in a utopian world where all men live as equals is a precursor to Rousseau's political ideas centuries later. One could infer that the play-sphere of song, through performing liminality, is similarly prone to generating utopian egalitarian modes of thinking.

In the Irish tradition we see a picture emerging of song and song-composers that indicates the huge symbolic weight of song as a liminal marker in traditional Irish society. Not only can we connect the gift of poetry to the liminal phase, as we find in the case of Wild Sweeney and keening women, but we also see that contexts of song performance, such as those described in recent times by Lillis Ó Laoire on Tory Island, are highly ritualized, functioning as an important renewing transition or antistructure in social life. In addition, the song poets themselves are seen to perform liminality in folklore representations of them, which include a certain restlessness, borderline ecstatic behaviour and often times a distinctly wild or unkempt appearance, as well as the ability to speak in verse with the ease of ordinary speech. The poets are often akin to 'in-between' figures or extra-social commentators on society who utilize the symbols of liminality in their poetic discourses, as in the case of the aisling genre. Furthermore, the traditional poet embodies the dangerous power of the liminal in his/her mastery of satire, a threat from which no member of society, no matter how elevated their status, is immune.

We have seen how the play of song is inherently re-creative even on a structural level and that the unfixity and multiformity of oral verse and music can also be seen as an expression of play in itself that is integral to the experience of liminality through song, and indeed integral to the aesthetic pleasure or near-ecstatic rush of singing experience. What is traditional is also playful and the re-creation of formulas, themes and musical motifs in themselves signify a creative antistructure to social life. Traditional verse, though conservative on one level, particularly in relation to themes and overall narrative structure, is very far from set in stone, and cannot rightly be considered to be a limiting cultural practice or a primitive form from which we needed to be emancipated through modernity and literacy; rather song is a foundational cultural practice that *enables* the generation of new forms that are integral to thought formation in society. Through the performance and actualization of liminality, traditional song is a seedbed of challenging discourses and new ideas at the same time as conserving age-old themes and song forms. The manner in which one such song poet, Máire Bhuí Ní Laeire, did precisely this and actively engaged through song in the political scene of the millenarian Rockite movement in the 1820s in Ireland will be discussed in depth in the next chapter.

If one returns for a moment to the political writings of Wolfe Tone when compared with the ideas sung by Máire Bhuí Ní Laeire, the contrast between the medium of their ideas is not merely superficial in its consequence. When the liminal ecstatic experience of singing is compared with the reading experience of the printed word, the power of song not just to pose new ideas but to see a person 'through' life's experiences is striking. Song is more than 'just a song', it is more than 'just words'; song is a highly charged ritualistic space in human society that is potentially transformative. Crucially, it is in the totality of the experience of song – rather than song as some kind of textual artefact – that the significance of song for thought and society lies.

When a song is sung, much like a rite of transition, it removes the singer or listener from the profane world, performs liminality, and at the close of the performance brings the singer and audience back to the profane world again. As described by Becker (2004) and Rouget (1985), the emotional and cognitive experience of music and song is profound. The embodiment of song, which according to Becker is experienced 'with our skins, our pulse rates and with our body temperature', means that as a medium of thought there is a particular power to song that perhaps the printed text in nineteenth-century Ireland could not rival (2004: 6). If we are to depart, therefore, from the narrow conception of the history of ideas as belonging exclusively to a Western intellectual culture that performs cold detachment and rationality and look instead towards the ideas that are generated as part of an intellectual tradition that performs emotional heat, sacred truth and liminality, a fuller picture of the genealogy of thought in society emerges. We begin to see the oral tradition not as a primitive version of sophisticated literary works, but as a powerful play-sphere that was much more than a text – a social process in which thought formation and identity formation combined. And there we will find not just men of thought but women of thought also. It is my intention in the analysis that follows, therefore, to further develop the premise of oral theory that the performance practices of oral poetic traditions are key to our understanding of oral art forms. However, the performance paradigm of oral theorists will be extended beyond words to the meaning of performance itself as a regenerative formative practice in society.

Chapter 3

Singing Parrhesia
Máire Bhuí Ní Laeire, Song Performance and Politics in Nineteenth-Century Ireland

This chapter will explore the story of Máire Bhuí and her songs, the oral tradition she practised and the radical millenarian political vision she articulated through song. The formative power of song and singing will be illustrated through an analysis of the work of this prominent nineteenth-century song poet, who is considered here as an exemplar of singing ideas. Her work will not be considered as merely a product of the political climate of the time, however, but rather as a pivotal social process that was at the centre of thought formation and political activism in the contemporary world of the song poet. Though Máire Bhuí composed in a traditional idiom that drew heavily on received formulas and themes, we see that the re-creative dynamic of oral traditionality not only was utterly capable of engaging with the contemporary world, but of moulding and articulating ideas that arguably had a lasting impact on the development of anticolonial thought in Ireland. The prophetic overtones to her songs suggest that the traditional authority of the song poet, as a quasi-shamanic figure possessed of a higher truth, was at play, and that song therefore conferred an authority on the ideas sung by Máire Bhuí that the written word could scarcely rival. Máire Bhuí did not perform knowledge in the same way that a writer of the literate enlightenment tradition might; however, she was a master of symbolic thought who sung compelling ideas that were rooted in the lived experience of colonization and articulated through the rich poetic tapestry of the oral tradition. These were ideas that were experienced and relived through singing, that could pierce the consciousness of the subject and constitute fleeting pivotal moments in the history of anticolonial agitation. Song was a realm of what is described by Turner as the '"subjunctive mood" of sociocultural action' (1982: 84), encapsulating a sense of intense possibility. For a song poet, such as Máire Bhuí, experiencing the precarity and injustice of the colonial system, this 'subjunctivity' of song would give an added immediacy and intensity to the idea that an alternative future to that of the colonial order was even possible. Máire Bhuí's repertoire tells of a colonial epoch synonymous with famine, uncertainty, marginalization and dissolution of order. She was a 'seer of communitas' in the Turnerian sense, a master of the performative act of song, responding to an acute time of crisis in the community, who, in evoking the traditional charismatic authority of the song poet, would delegitimize colonial authority and create a vision of a new authority of 'the people'. Her visionary ideas within song would become integral to the ideology that would drive the rebellion during her own lifetime and beyond. Thus the songs of Máire Bhuí speak to the centrality of singing to anticolonial thought and consciousness and represent an alternative history of ideas to that told by official documents or written record.

British conquest in Ireland can be traced back to the settlement of the Old English or Anglo Normans in the twelfth century, however a more aggressive approach by the British authorities to 'civilizing' Ireland emerges in the sixteenth century (Montano 2011: 369), and arguably it was in the century that followed the defeat at the Battle of Kinsale (1601) that Ireland became a fully fledged colony of Britain (Howe 2000: 31). During the seventeenth century, and particularly following the devastation of the Cromwellian wars and plantations (1649–1658) and the defeat of Jacobite forces during the Williamite wars (1688–1691), the Gaelic order essentially collapses, with up to 80 per cent of Irish lands being transferred to the ownership of British colonial settlers, who accounted for 20 per cent of the population by the end of the seventeenth century (Howe 2000: 31). The civilizing rhetoric of British colonialism in Ireland has been well documented by historians, some of whom argue that the colonial project in Ireland sowed the seeds for British imperialism in the wider world, which would be accompanied by a similarly aggressive discourse of the cultural, moral and intellectual superiority of the colonizer and degradation of indigenous peoples and customs (Canny 1988; Montano 2011). By the time Máire Bhuí was born, the Gaelic court was no more, and the customs of the ruling classes were distinctly British.

The language and customs of the agrarian classes, on the other hand, were for the most part Irish, and Irish society was, as Morley describes: 'a bilingual and largely illiterate society in which oral and scribal means of communication played a decisive role in the formation of the popular mind' (2017: 313). British colonialism had succeeded in dismantling the traditional networks of court poets and harpists under the patronage of Gaelic nobles, and though formal training was no longer available to the Irish-language poet as had previously existed in bardic schools, a thriving oral tradition was still undiminished among the dispossessed Irish. Though Máire Bhuí would not have known the old Gaelic order from within, it is highly likely that she would have been exposed to poetry that recounted the trials and fall of Gaelic Ireland, such as the work of Aogán Ó Rathaille who was at the tail end of official poetic culture (Ó Buachalla 2007). Indeed, poetry had long been an important vehicle of political engagement in Irish society, from the praise elegies and satires of the bardic poets in Gaelic society (Knott 1960; Bergin 1970; O'Riordan 2007; McKibben 2010) to the political songs of Jacobite poets, which were committed to writing by scribal circles in the eighteenth century (Ó Buachalla 1996). The Jacobite movement supported the Catholic Stuart king, James II, who was deposed by William of Orange in 1688, and subsequently fled to France after the defeat of Jacobite forces in Ireland in 1690. The exiled Stuart king and his Catholic son, James Edward Stuart, and his grandson, Charles Edward Stuart, both pretenders to the throne in the eighteenth century, were passionately supported by the indigenous Irish for whom the Stuart lineage was synonymous with relief from persecution for Catholics (Simms 1969).

There was a proliferation of Jacobite discourses in Irish poetry and song well into the eighteenth century, most famously in the aisling form. In his comprehensive study of Jacobite verse in the Irish language, Ó Buachalla remarks that the context of performance for the Jacobite songs as participatory songs (and often drinking songs), rather than just texts in a manuscript, is key to their importance (1996: 414). The Jacobite songs described by Ó Buachalla not only recount contemporary political events and articulate political aspirations, thus constituting an important sphere of political discourse, but were *performed* in company. These were song forms that straddled both scribal and oral cultures. Indeed, the historian Vincent Morley argues that song and orality were of the utmost importance in the political discourse and culture of the indigenous population of Ireland during the eighteenth century, to the point that they were more influential than English-language print culture:

> To believe that a pamphlet in English could have propagated a message as efficiently as a song in Irish at any time during the eighteenth century is to succumb to anachronism, to anglocentricism, or to the combined effect of both maladies. (2017: 313)

In addition to the pervasive oral culture, and the scribal/oral Jacobite songs in Irish that would have been integral to the sound world of Máire Bhuí, street songs and printed political ballads in English were very numerous also, and the street singer or 'ballad monger', who performed for the public and then sold printed copies of the songs themselves, was a common sight in urban centres, at fairs and other public gatherings, particularly in nineteenth-century Ireland (Zimmerman 2002: 23). The combination of performing songs and peddling broadsheets, as practised by the street singer, testifies to the persistent centrality of song performance through societal change, language shift and increased bilingualism; it also attests to the manner in which the dominant practices of orality engaged with a burgeoning print culture in Ireland (Ó Ciosáin 1997). Thus poetry as a sphere of public political engagement was well established, and Irish society was awash with song. Thus Máire Bhuí Ní Laeire was born into a society where to sing was one of the most effective ways to engage the masses in political thought; and into a new era of anticolonial agitation in Ireland, one which sought not so much the return of the lost king as heralded by the Jacobite songs in which the song poet was undoubtedly immersed, but rather the destruction of the ruling classes and self-determination for the dispossessed. Therefore, the work of Máire Bhuí, though often echoing strongly of the old Jacobite struggle, heralds an era of new politics and anticolonial agitation in Ireland.

Máire Bhuí Ní Laeire: Nineteenth-Century Song Poet

Máire Bhuí Ní Laeire (Yellow Mary O'Leary) was born in 1774 and died during the Great Irish Famine (Ó Donnchú 1931: 20). She could neither read nor write, her famous skills in composition being acquired by ear in a culture steeped in oral verse. She is represented as quite the formidable character in the Irish-language oral tradition, on the one hand as a poet of high status with an unrivalled mastery in poetic composition, and on the other as a strong anticolonial and antiauthoritarian figure. She is referred to by a contemporary of hers, fellow song poet Donncha Bán Ó Luínse, as 'Bláth 's Craobh na nÚdar' ('Flower and Greatest of all Authors') in the song 'A Mháir' Ní Laeire' ('Oh Mary O'Leary'), a poetic dialogue ascribed to Máire Bhuí and Donncha Bán. This is no small accolade, and points to Máire Bhuí's prominence as a poet at that time in Muskerry, a strong Irish-speaking hinterland in mid-west County Cork that is still an Irish-speaking Gaeltacht district today. Indeed, Pádraig Ó Crualaoi, a song poet of note and famous informant for the Irish Folklore Commission, later recounts Máire Bhuí's amazing fluency in composition, clearly positing her as superior to Donncha Bán Ó Luínse, as demonstrated by this same song in which she composed twice as many verses as Donncha Bán:

> Bhí a lán daoine do shórd Dhonacha ann: d'fhéataidís véarsa dhéanamh go maith ach ní fhéataidís leanúint dò, ar chuma éigin. Ach ní raibh Máire Bhuí mar sin i n-aochor: bhí ana-ruille cainte aici. (Ó Cróinín 1982: 116)

> [There were many people of Donncha's sort: they could make a verse well but they couldn't continue it, for some reason. But Máire Bhuí wasn't like that at all: she had a great flood of speech.]

Pádraig Ó Crualaoi's own father (who was also a poet-composer) personally knew Máire Bhuí in her later years, and it is clear from his account that Máire Bhuí was considered to be a cut above the rest. Other stories give a similar impression of Máire Bhuí's superiority over other (male) poets – indeed this is implied in the very accolade 'Bláth 's Craobh na nÚdar' ('Flower and Greatest of Authors'), which literally means 'flower and branch of authors', the 'branch' being symbolic of the greatest poet of the company, with *craobh* also denoting 'trophy' or 'accolade' in modern Irish society. The combination of both poetic and political authority is perhaps best illustrated by the story collected by Áine Ní Chróinín for the Irish Folklore Commission from Diarmuid 'ac Coitir in Ballvourney in 1932, entitled 'Máire Bhuí agus an Fíodóir' ('Máire Bhuí and the Weaver'), in which Máire Bhuí, through the excellence and cutting of her verse-making, shuts up the weaver, a supposedly inferior poet, who expressed an unfortunate belief in the inevitability of persistent British dominance in Ireland, a sentiment that angered Máire Bhuí:

> I ndeire na hochtú haoise déag nú i dtosach an naoú haois déag, do bhí Máire Bhuí ní Laeire i réim in iarthar Paróiste Íbh Laeire. File dob ea Máire agus lena línn féin ní raibh aon fhile eile in Éirinn chô cliste léi nú chô bínn léi. Amhrá[i]n náisiúnta is mó do cheap Máire Bhuí agus is minic do cháin sí go dian na Sasanaig nú na Clanna Gall. Mar gheall ar í féin ' bheith chô maith d'fhile agus an mola muar do bhí uirthi, ní thaithnuíodh filí beaga eile léi do bhíodh ag ceapa rócán. Le línn na haimsire céanna do bhí fíodóir ina chónaí i mbaile ann go nglaotar Gort a' Phlodaig air. Do bhí smidireacht bheag filíochta ag an bhfíodóir, ach ní raibh aon mheas ag Máire Bhuí air ... (CBÉ 42: 348–51, Ní Shíocháin 2012: 245)

> [In the end of the eighteenth century or the beginning of the nineteenth century, Máire Bhuí ní Laeire was in her prime in the Western part of the parish of Iveleary. Máire was a poet and during her own time there was no other poet in the whole of Ireland as clever nor as melodious as her. National songs mainly is what she composed, and she strongly criticized the English or the 'Foreign Clans'. Because she herself was such a good poet and because of her being held in such high esteem, she used not like other small poets who used to be composing *rócán*s [inferior or trite compositions]. During that same period there was a weaver living in a place called Gort a' Phlodaig. He had a small smattering of poetry, but Máire Bhuí had no respect for him ...]

The weaver agrees to prioritize the weaving of cloth for a local girl so that she will have a dress in time for Pentecost Sunday and on receiving a basin of butter in addition to his usual payment for his troubles composes a verse in a state of giddy delight. The verse he composes irks Máire Bhuí, however, and the tale does not end well for the weaver – a superior verse from Máire Bhuí puts him in his place and silences him:

Shuig sé síos agus duairt sé rann di mar seo:

"A chailín bhig na luachra, beig gruaim ort is oighear go deó,
ag baint do bhirt gach uair mhoch go buartha agus ag aeireacht bó,
beig Sasanaig na muar-chorp go huasal a' gabháil an róid
'na gcóistí greanta ag luasca mar is dualgas é do cheapag dóibh."

Nuair a chuaig an scéal chô fada le Máire Bhuí, agus nuair a airi' sí an rann beag filíochta i ndiaig an fhíodóra do bhí sí ar deargb[h]uile. Níor mhaith le Máire B[h]uí na Sasanaig a fheiscint in uachtar i gcónaí agus seo mar ' duairt sí:

"A Fhíodóir gan fuaimeint, eighrig suas anis agus caith do spól,
agus ná hairím a thuille dot dhuanta mar ní[o]r dhual duit gur bhínn
    do ghlór.
Níor gheallag dóibh do réir thuairimeach cead buanaíochta d'fháil go
    deó,
agus a chailín bhig na Luachrach, beig na sluaite fear ag rith it dheóig."

Ní duairt an fíodóir a thuille.

(CBÉ 42: 348–51, Ní Shíocháin 2012: 245–46)

[He [the weaver] sat down and said a verse like this for her [the girl]:

'Oh little girl of the rushes, you will be forever despondent and depressed,
gathering your bunch of rushes worriedly early in the morning and
    herding cattle,
while big-bodied Englishmen will go nobly along the road
in their ornate carriages swaying because that is the divine duty that
    was their fate'.

When the story went as far as Máire Bhuí and when she heard the little verse of poetry from the weaver, she was fuming in anger. Máire Bhuí used not like to see the English always having the upper hand and this is how she spoke:

'Oh foolish weaver of little consequence, get up and employ your spool,
and let me not hear any more of your poems because you were not
    bestowed with sweetness of voice.
They were not, by all accounts, promised permanent rule for ever,
and oh little girl of the rushes, there will be crowds of men running
    after you'.

The weaver said no more.]

Máire Bhuí is clearly the winner in this tale that tells of her anticolonial zeal and her mastery of oral composition all at once. The eminence of Máire Bhuí is also touched upon in a late manuscript source containing the compositions of a minor poet from North Cork, Tadhg Ó Síocháin, in which it is related to the reader that the poet Tadhg Ó Síocháin sought out Máire Bhuí only to apparently have been rebuked in some manner:

> Do rugadh Taig i gCnoc-an-Chapaill agus is doigh liom go raibh sé meadhon aosta sar ar chum sé aon Amhrán. Thug sé cuairt aon uair amhain ar Mháire ní Laoghaire Ach níor chuir sise aon suim ann, & d'fhág sé í gan bheith ró-bhuidheach di. (Torna Collection, LS 101:10ro)
>
> [Tadhg was born in Cnoc an Chapaill and I think that he was middle-aged before he composed any song. He went to visit Máire ní Laire once, but she displayed no interest in him, and he left having no cause to be grateful to her.]

Máire Bhuí, though absent from most of the contemporary scribal literature at the time, is represented in the oral tradition not just as a poet of note but as a formidable poet-composer whose approval is not easily won. It is particularly interesting that Máire Bhuí is represented as being a superior poet in a poetic tradition dominated by male song composers: though the tradition of the *caoineadh* (keen), the ritual poetry of the traditional Irish wake, was predominantly a female tradition, the song poet was typically male, as previously discussed by Ó Crualaoich (1986: 63). It is clear also that the literary tradition of the scribe was dominated by men, and that women's compositions seemed to have been given limited attention within scribal circles. That said, there were a significant number of female song poets in the tradition that we know of, such as Máire Ní Chruadhlaoich, Máirín Ní Dhonnagáin, Máire Ní Dhuibh and Máire Ní Dhroma (Molly na Páirce), among others whose legacy survived in the oral tradition, including Nóra Ní Shúilleabháin, the sister of the famous poet Eoghan Rua Ó Súilleabháin (1748–1784) (Nic Eoin 1998: 283–84). Máirín Nic Eoin explains how women occupied an extremely marginalized position in the scribal tradition, with only a handful of women being mentioned as scribes per se, such as Máire Ní Riain and Mairéad Ní Chadhlaigh (Nic Eoin 1998: 257), but that in cases where the scribe had a particular interest in transcribing elements of the oral tradition references to women as sources become more frequent (Nic Eoin 1998: 257–58). References to women are very scant in scribal sources, however, in comparison to references to men, and the evidence seems to point to the oral tradition as the sphere par excellence in which women composed and practised poetry in Irish-speaking Ireland. Indeed, we can assert with some confidence that the indigenous women's tradition in Irish-speaking Ireland was an oral rather than a literate one. Indeed, the representations of Máire Bhuí's own prodigious talent at ex tempore composition in folklore accounts also support this picture of women as masters of oral verse-making. Her fluency in poetic composition was notable among tradition-bearers: 'filíocht ab ea ga'h aon fhocal a labhradh sí' ('every word she spoke was poetry') according to Pádraig Ó Murchú (Peatsaí Chit) from Ballingeary in 1942, in reference to her ability to respond in verse on the spot, such as the time when awaiting the outcome of her sons' trial in Cork city following the famed insurgency at Keimaneigh, when asked by a neighbour if she would take a drink. She responds in verse:

> Bhí Máire Bhuí i gCorcaig le línn na trialach – is dócha coicíos nó breis.
> Bhí fear – côrsa éigin – 'na teannta ann agus mar seo lá duairt sé le Máire,
> "Téanam ort agus ól traeit."
> "Tá mo chroí dá shlad" a duairt sí
> "mar a shnoífí an gad
> agus ná féadfainn ól aon traeit
> agus buíon mo scart fé luí na nglas
> agus a gcúis gan stad le glaoch."
> (CBÉ 45: 387–91, Ní Shíocháin 2012: 249)

> [Máire Bhuí was in Cork during the trial – I suppose a fortnight or more. A man – some neighbour – was with her, and one day said to Máire Bhuí 'Come on and we'll have a drink':
> 'My heart is being slain' she replied,
> 'like a rope being worn
> and a drink I cannot take
> while the sons of my womb in fetters lie
> their case being decided as we speak'.]

There are other women who are thus represented as having an authoritative command of verse-making within the Irish-language oral tradition, most famously Máire Ní Dhonnagáin, who said of her own linguistic and poetic prowess, '"Mise Máire, a bhfuil dhá thaobh ar mo theanga - /An taobh mín, is an taobh garbh"' ('I am Máire, who has two sides to her tongue – / the smooth and the rough') (Nic Eoin 1998: 263), and the aristocratic Máire Ní Dhuibh (mother to Eibhlín Dubh Ní Chonaill), of whom it was said that she used to impose her authority over her servants through verse (uí Ógáin 1981: 101; Nic Eoin 1998: 264). There are also numerous tales of verbal battles between the priest and the keening woman, with the keening woman generally being the victor (Nic Eoin 1998: 288). Therefore, though women certainly did not figure largely in scribal circles, their participation within the oral poetic tradition itself as singers, as keening women and, less often, as poets is highly significant. Unfortunately, many of the oral compositions of these women have been lost to us forever, due to the receding of the oral tradition in modern times, and due to the marginality of women's compositions as represented in the Irish manuscripts. Often, the poetry that does survive is fragmentary or limited. In this respect, Máire Bhuí stands out because of the number of her compositions that have survived, which amounts to fourteen in total, excluding shorter verses and fragments (Ní Shíocháin 2012). This is more than other female oral poets, whose surviving compositions often amount to fragments, or a much smaller number of songs, but even among male song poets this is a very high number comparatively to have survived in the oral tradition. When compared with the great Connacht poet Raftery, for example, of whom eleven songs survived into the twentieth century in the oral tradition, in comparison to over fifty songs that survived in manuscript form, we get an idea of just how much can be lost when the oral tradition is declining, and indeed when the linguistic culture that fostered that oral tradition is also in decline (Ó Coigligh 1987: 213). It is striking also that in representations of Máire Bhuí in folklore she was the equal (if not the superior of) male song poets – and the large number of surviving compositions attributed to her does suggest that she was unequivocally accepted by the community as a master oral poet, as a prodigy, as someone who was not the norm. This is most evident in the multiforms of the words of Donncha Bán in 'A Mháir' Ní Laeire':

Le grá 's le méinn duit thar mhnáibh na hÉireann
a bhláth 's a chraobh na n-údar. (Crothúr 'ac Coitir, LS Í Chuív)

[With love and respect for you over the women of Ireland
Oh flower and greatest of all authors.]

Le feabhas do thréithe thar mhnáibh na hÉireann
A bhláith 's a chraobh na n-úghdar. (*Irisleabhar na Gaedhilge,* 1896: 120)

[With the excellence of your traits over the women of Ireland
Oh flower and greatest of all authors.]

It is interesting that as a female poet she is revered among men as well as women, and that she is represented as the foremost poet of Muskerry in folklore sources. Yet the representations of her that survive give us only an impression, but nonetheless hint at a historical character who was larger than life and who left her mark on the collective imagination of the community. In order to explore the meaning and significance of the songs of Máire Bhuí and the oral compositional craft that she practised, one must look to the oral culture that fostered her song-making and that enabled her poetic voice.

Irish-Language Song-Making: Poetry as Performance and the Aesthetics of Orality

The question of oral formulaic composition has been discussed quite extensively in relation to the keening tradition, most notably in Bromwich's seminal formulaic analysis (1945) of the keen for Art O'Leary and later in the work of Ó Coileáin (1988) and Bourke (1991)[1], and more recently in the work of Nic an Airchinnigh (2010, 2013). However, the question of song poetry as composition in performance has not been discussed as extensively, and I believe that this is, in part, due to the construction of lines being markedly different when compared to the structure of verse in *The Singer of Tales,* in which whole-line formulas were often the norm. In this sense, the short lines of the traditional Irish lament are easily identifiable as formulaic when compared with the empirical basis of Lord's analysis. However, as I have argued elsewhere (2012, 2013b), if we look to the half line in Irish-language song-verse, and if we look for formulaic phrases rather than whole formulas, the oral formulaic character of the song tradition becomes more apparent. The keen lent itself more clearly to the oral formulaic debate on account of the keening women generally being illiterate and not committing their compositions to writing themselves, and because of customs of ex tempore composition being remarked upon in the works of English-language travel writers – the keen was accepted almost automatically as a bone fide oral tradition. Many Irish-language song poets, however, such as Eoghan Rua Ó Súilleabháin, Tomás Rua Ó Súilleabháin and Mícheál Óg Ó Longáin, were literate, and though I would argue that writing was not necessarily central to the predominant *mode of composition* in such cases, the survival of autograph copies of song transcriptions gives the impression of a literary tradition at first glance. The existence of illiterate song poets such as Máire Bhuí and Raftery, however, who practised the same themes as the likes of Eoghan Rua and Tomás Rua, and who seemed to have drawn from a related common stock of formulas, throws into question the assumption that scribes, such as Eoghan Rua, who practised an oral tradition, were in fact *literary* authors in the strict sense. Indeed, I would argue that in such cases as song poet-scribes, it is highly possible that writing was a means of recording rather than composing.[2] Such a situation was referred to by Albert Lord in arguing that literacy and oral composition are not mutually exclusive: 'The use of writing in setting down oral texts does not per se have any effect on oral tradition. It is a means of recording' (1960: 128). This is a statement he further clarifies in relation to literate oral composers in particular: 'We might ask whether those oral poets who write their own texts (for there are such) can under any circumstances produce an oral poem. The answer is affirmative' (Lord 1960: 129). In this respect, it is interesting that folklore representations of song poets in the Irish tradition frequently depict composition in performance, one of the most famous examples being of the Munster poet Diarmuid na Bolgaighe:

'Nach file tusa?' arsan sagart.
'An-fhile go léir is eadh mé,' arsa Diarmuid.
'An ndéanfá amhrán domh-sa?'
'Déanfad, má's toil leat é. Cad é an ceol a chuirfead leis?'
'Ceol an "Ghille Mear", arsa an sagart … Bíodh sé ullamh agat dom fé cheann seachtmhaine.'
Bhuail Diarmuid a chleith i dtalamh ar an láthair sin, á chur in iúl do'n tsagart ná raibh cairde an lae sin féin uaidh agus thug amach amhrán seacht bhéarsa fhichead d'aon chaise amháin.
(Ó Súilleabháin 1937: 10–11)

['Aren't you a poet?' says the priest.
'I'm a great poet', says Diarmuid.
'Would you make a song for me?'
'I will, if that is your wish. What music will I put to it?'
'The music of the "Gille Mear", says the priest … Let you have it ready for me within the week'.
Diarmuid struck the ground with his staff, indicating that he needed not even the grace of that same day, and produced twenty seven verses in one fell swoop.]

Such representations in folklore of the prodigious compositional skills in performance among song poets are not uncommon, as previously discussed at length by Dáithí Ó hÓgáin (1982: 5–22), and indeed the representations of Máire Bhuí's abilities at on-the-spot composition, as previously mentioned, are in a similar vein. Indeed, the composition of 'A Mháir' Ní Laeire' is reputed to have been composed precisely in such a manner, which, as previously mentioned, is what led Pádraig Ó Crualaoi to refer to her extraordinary 'ruille cainte' or flood of speech. Indeed, the song poet-scribe, Eoghan Rua Ó Súilleabháin, who penned his own compositions in manuscript form, is nonetheless described by another scribe, Dónal Mac Consaidín, in a contextual note to the lullaby 'Seothó, a Thoil', as having composed the song 'extempore':

> The above lullaby was composed extempore by the author to calm the sorrowful moaning of an illegitimate infant which the victim of his Crim[inal]. Con[duct]. had left him and retired to a place of concealment to watch the result, but who was soon afterwards urged by maternal feelings to return and claim the child. (Ó Conchúir 2009: 69)

Another famous tale recounts the first words spoken by poet Tomás Rua Ó Súilleabháin as being in verse, as well as a number of accounts of keening women giving an extempore poetic tongue-lashing to priests, as previously mentioned. In folklore, poetic 'flow' and the ability to compose verse on the spot is a hallmark of the great poet (Ó hÓgáin 1982: 5–22, 80–93). Though Ó hÓgáin mainly focuses on the otherworldly aspects of these representations of poets in folklore, it is also striking that this image of composition in performance, as later depicted by the fieldwork of Lord and Parry in a 'real world' context, would be central to folklore accounts of Irish-language song poets and their defining characteristics. Indeed, we have reason to believe that these representations were not wholly fictional, largely due to the important body of material gathered by the Irish Folklore Commission from poet-composer Pádraig Ó Crualaoi at the beginning of the twentieth century, in which he describes both the precompositional period during his own youth and also the process of composition itself:

> Bhínn-se ana-thapaig i gcónaí chun filíocht a dhéanamh. Níor ghá dhom aon stuidéar a dhéanamh air – do ritheadh sí chúm i gcónaí. Agus bhí mh'athair mar sin, leis. Agus an chéad rud adéarfainn, b'shiné an rud a b'fheárr: ní fhéatainn aon fheabhas a chuir air. Is amhlaig a loitfinn é le haon atharú a chuirfinn air. (Ó Cróinín 1982: 172)
>
> [I used to be awful fast always at making poetry. I used not to have to study it in any way – it used to run to me always. And my father was like that too. And the first thing I'd say would be the best: I couldn't improve upon it. I'd only ruin it if I were trying to change it in any way.]

The composition of poetry, here being described as something that 'runs to' the poet without any 'study' beforehand, strongly suggests that song composition in performance was a central custom. This idea of the sheer fluidity of composition is further supported by other descriptions by practitioners of song, for example, Seán Ó hAo, alias Hamit, another prolific contributor to the Folklore Archives who describes members of his own family as composing poetry profusely and with great ease: 'cheapaidís rann chomh tiubh is do shiúlóidís' ('they used to compose as thickly as they would walk' – i.e. they used to compose with the same ease as walking) (Ó hAo 1985: 645). The ease of song transmission as represented by practitioners of song is also significant, as we see in Pádraig Ó Crualaoi's account of how songs used to travel from person to person, from community to community:

> Na bacaig a bheireadh na véarsaí leo tímpal, agus na hamhráin. Bhí seó dosna bacaig ann an uair sin agus iad ag imeacht ó áit go háit. An rud adéarfadh file anso bheadh sé ag an gcéad bhacach a thiocfadh agus bhéarfadh sé leis é 'na cheann: gach aon bhlúire dhe. Bheadh sé mar scéal nó aige sa chéad tig eile, nú sa chéad ph'róiste eile. Agus ansan, do bhí suím ag gach éinne ins na véarsaí agus sa bhfilíocht, agus do bhí an ceann acu chun í thúirt leo agus í mheabhrú – ní hineann is anois.

Ansan do bhí táilliúirí agus siúinéirí agus gach aon saghas ceárdaí a'
dul ó thig go tig ag obair, agus do bhíodh an fhilíocht acu san, leis.
Agus do bhí an Ghaoluinn acu go léir agus do thuigidís an chrua-chaint.
(Ó Cróinín 1982: 162)

[The boccaughs used to bring verses with them and songs. There was a
load of these boccaughs once upon a time and they used to travel from
place to place. That which a poet would utter would be picked up by
the first boccaugh that would come, and he would take it with him in
his head: every bit of it. And then, everyone was interested in the verses
and in the poetry, and they had the head and intelligence to bring it with
them – unlike today.

Then there were tailors and carpenters and every sort of trades-person
going from house to house working, and they used to have the poetry
too. And they all had Irish and they understood the hard talk.]

This picture of the oral tradition in its heyday, as recounted by Ó Crualaoi, is of particular interest in that it suggests that the community was utterly
steeped in verse and song, but also that verse and song were so speedily transmitted. This also correlates with Mac Síthigh's description of song transmission
in West Kerry, in the passionate pursuit of songs among the community, the
sheer centrality of singing to everyday social life, and in the fluid transmission
of songs by travellers:

Bhíodh tigh áirithe ar an mbaile a mbítí ag bailiú isteach ann istoíche,
agus bhíodh amhráin ar siúl go tiubh ann. Bhíodh na mná ag amhrán
chomh maith leis na fir. Deirtí gurbh fhearr iad ná na fir. Bhíodh na
hamhráin ar siúl, leis, i dtigh na scéalaíochta. Théadh cuid de na daoine tamall ó bhaile ag triall ar an amhránaíocht. Théidís go dtí paróistí
eile ag triall ar na hamhráin ... Bhí tarrac le fáil ar amhráin ar fuaid na
háite. Thógaidís amhráin ó lucht siúil. Bhíodh seanamhráin mhaithe ag
cuid acu, agus guth maith acu chun iad a rá. Déarfadh an fear siúil an
t-amhrán sa tigh mar a mbíodh sé ag fanacht, agus mhúinfeadh sé an
t-amhrán do mhuintir an tí. (Mac Síthigh 1984: 120–21)

[There used to be a particular house in the area where people used to
gather in at night, and there used to be a load of songs being sung there.
Women used to be singing as well as the men. It used to be said that they
were better than the men. There used to be singing also in the story-
telling house. People used to travel far from home in search of singing.
They used to go to other parishes to fetch songs ... Songs were in great
demand all over and to be found all over. They used to get songs from
the travellers. They used to have good old songs, some of them, and a

good voice with which to sing them. A travelling man would say a song in the house in which he was staying, and he would teach the song to the people of the house.]

A picture emerges, not just of poets who were purported to have had the capacity to compose in performance, but of a community who 'took' songs with great ease, of songs that were transmitted fluidly from place to place, and of Irish-speaking communities who had a fanatical interest in songs. Hence Ó Madagáin's assertion that song was integral to almost every facet of Irish life in the nineteenth century (1985: 131). It is to be noted, also, that women were not excluded from singing occasions – and this exposure to the living tradition explains the very existence of the female song poet within the tradition. To prevent women becoming scribes is simple enough – do not teach them to read or write – however, if women are present during song performance, they cannot be entirely prevented from developing compositional skills by ear and through experience, as any man might. It appears, therefore, that though Máire Bhuí practised a poetic tradition that intermingled with scribal culture, the dominant mode of composition remained an oral process, and therefore it was still possible that within that tradition the illiterate female poet could come to prominence.

Multiformity and Oral Formulaic Techniques

An oral formulaic analysis of Máire Bhuí's poems (see Ní Shíocháin 2012, 2013b) show that the poetics she practised did indeed draw strongly from common formulas and themes, and that she is also represented as having had a great 'ruille cainte'/ 'flood of speech' implies that Máire Bhuí Ní Laeire practised composition in performance. Indeed, her poetics were strongly 'echoic', as Foley would put it (1991: 7), an aesthetic that is strongly associated with oral formulaic composition. The most salient example of Máire Bhuí's use of formulas is in the famous opening lines of 'Cath Chéim an Fhia' ('The Battle of Céim an Fhia') when compared with lines from the songs of Eoghan Rua Ó Súilleabháin:

A' machnamh seal liom féinig a' déanamh mo smaointibh
[Thinking a while to myself and making my ideas]
        by Máire Bhuí (Ní Shíocháin 2012: 212)

Ag machtnamh go faon is ag déanamh smaointe
[Thinking while languid and making ideas]
        from 'Ar Maidin Inné Cois Cé' by Eoghan Rua Ó
        Súilleabháin (Ó Foghludha 1937: 54)

Not only is it clear, in Lordian terms, that the first two lines when compared constitute formulaic phrases, but further analysis also suggests that they were part of what Lord termed the 'formula system' (1960: 35):

A'/ ag mach(t)namh: go faon/ seal liom féinig
[Thinking: while languid/ a while to myself]

This is even more apparent when compared with other lines from another of Eoghan Rua's compositions, namely:

Ag machtnamh dam féin ar thréithe an tsaoghail
[Thinking to myself on the traits of the world]
from 'Do rinneadh aisling bheag aerach' by Eoghan Rua Ó Súilleabháin (Ó Foghludha 1937: 74)

The above line would suggest that the formula system may have functioned as follows:

A'/ ag mach(t)namh: go faon/ seal liom féinig/ dam féin
[Thinking: while languid/a while by myself/ to myself]

Furthermore, another line attributed to Eoghan Rua' 'Gur casadh i gcéin me *ag déanamh smaointe*' ('I found myself afar *making my ideas*') would lead us to conclude that, at the level of the half line, 'ag déanamh (mo) smaointe' was indeed a formula (Ó Foghludha 1937: 74). This is an important point, because it helps us to understand that the beautiful and iconic opening to the song 'Cath Chéim an Fhia', a line associated so strongly with Máire Bhuí in particular, was oral formulaic and drew from a common stock of formulas that were re-created in composition and performance. This is further evident from a comparison of 'Seo Leó, ' Thoil' by Máire Bhuí, and similar compositions by Eoghan Rua Ó Súilleabháin and Diarmuid na Bolgaighe. Here we see three prominent Munster poets using a common lullaby theme for composition, and the re-creation of common formulas is also apparent. The use of the sub-theme of the Amadán Mór (the Big Fool) from the Fiannaíocht tradition in particular elucidates the re-creative impulse so central to 'new' compositions in the oral tradition:

(A)
Do gheobhair an corn *nár bh'fholamh mar sheoid*
Do-gheobhair an adharc is *gadhair chum spóirt*
Do bhí ag Gruagach Dhún an Óir
Cé gur dochma leis siúd a dtabhairt dod shórt.
Seothó, a thoil, etc.
                    Eoghan Rua (Ó Conchúir 2009: 14)

[You will get the cup that was never empty as a jewel,
you will get the horn and the dogs for sport

that the Enchanter of Dún an Óir used to have
even though he'd be reluctant to give it to the likes of you.
Seothó, my darling, etc.]

(B)
Gheóir a' clogad 's a' sciath ón Amadán Mór
'us gheó' tú an t-úll ón gcúillinn óig,
gheóir a' gadhar ba mheidhraí ceól
do cheangail a' laoch à héill 'na dhóid;
agus seo leó, ' thoil, agus ná goil go fóill ...

Gheóir a' corn fí dheochanna sóil
do chuireadh a' draíocht ar na mílthe sló,
do gheóir a' chathair úd Dhún an Óir
a bhí 'gen nGruagach Muar chun spóirt;
agus seo leó, ' thoil, agus ná goil go fóill ...
Máire Bhuí (Ní Shíocháin 2012: 206)

[You will get the helmet and shield from the Big Fool
and you will get the apple from the fair young lady,
you will get the dog of the merriest music
that the hero tied from a rope in his fist;
and seo leó, my darling, and don't cry...

You will get the cup of the sumptuous drinks
that used to enchant the thousands,
you will get that fort of Dún an Óir
that the Great Enchanter used have for sport,
and seo leó, my darling, and don't cry ...]

(C)
Dá gcuireadh an duan chun suain mo stór
Níor bhaoghal dó *Gruagach Dhúna an Óir*,
Mar a bhfaightheá an corn do shloigfeadh an bheoir
Is do bhainfeadh na cosa ó'n Amadán Mór.
Agus seo hó leo a thoil, ná goil níos mó.
Diarmuid na Bolgaighe (Ó Súilleabháin 1937: 41)

[If my poem were to put my beloved to sleep,
he would not be in danger from the Enchanter of Dún an Óir,
where you would get the cup to sup the beer
and which would remove the legs from the Big Fool.
and seo hó leo, my darling, don't cry anymore.]

Here we see the unfixity of the traditional theme in oral verse, as described by Lord: 'not any fixed set of words, but a grouping of ideas' (1960: 69). The Enchanter of Dún an Óir and an enchanted cup are central thematically, with the Big Fool being mentioned also by both Máire Bhuí and Diarmuid na Bolgaighe, yet each poet re-creates the theme in his/her own way. We see in particular in Máire Bhuí's rendition the elasticity of the theme in her development of it for a whole extra verse in comparison to the other two poets. The formulaic basis of these verses is also apparent:

(A) Do-gheobhair **an corn** nár bh'fholamh mar sheoid
[You will get the cup that was never empty as a jewel]

(B) Gheóir **a' corn** fí dheochanna sóil
[You will get the cup of the sumptuous drinks]

(C) Mar a bhfaightheá **an corn** do shloigfeadh an bheoir
[Where you would get the cup to sup the beer]

The meter remains constant, and the half line 'Do-gheobhair an corn'/ 'Gheóir a' corn' ('You will get the cup') appears to be a formula that can end either as 'fí dheochanna sóil' ('of the sumptuous drinks') or 'nár bh'fholamh mar sheoid' ('that was never empty as a jewel'). Furthermore, with an corn/ a' corn metrically remaining in the same position in each line, according to Lord's theoretical framework, these three lines constitute formulaic phrases. A similar structure can be seen with Gruagach remaining in the same position in the line, again strongly suggestive of the re-creation of formulas and creation of formulaic phrases indicative of oral formulaic composition:

(A) do bhí ag **Gruagach** Dhún an Óir (Eoghan Rua)
[that was held by the Enchanter of Dún an Óir]

(B) a bhí 'gen n**Gruagach** Muar chun spóirt (Máire Bhuí)
[that was held by the Enchanter the Great for sport]

(C) Níor bhaoghal dó **Gruagach** Dhúna an Óir (Diarmuid na Bolgaighe)
[he would not be in danger from the Enchanter of Dún an Óir]

Again, the half line 'do bhí ag Gruagach'/ 'a bhí 'gen nGruagach' ('that was held by the Enchanter) appears to be a formula that in one case concluded with 'Dhún an Óir', and in the other 'Muar chun spóirt' ('the Great for sport'), suggesting the existence of half-line formulas that also functioned as part of a larger formula system. Again, with 'Gruagach' (Enchanter) remaining in the same metric position in each of the three lines, they can be classed as formulaic phrases. I believe that the Irish-language song poet, be he a scribe like Eoghan Rua, or be she illiterate like Máire Bhuí, was adept at oral formulaic composition to which the half-line formula and the formulaic phrase were key, as well as common themes. Therefore, in the work of Máire Bhuí, we see that the echoic and 'intertextual' character of her poetry is distinctive. This 'pull' towards other uses of the same theme, like many other oral poets, is a hallmark of her compositional style (Lord 1960: 94).

Further to this 'intertextuality' when compositions of other poets are compared to songs by Máire Bhuí is the pronounced multiformity evident in different renditions of Máire Bhuí's songs by singers. It is for this reason that I have argued for the singer as re-composer, and indeed that the formulaic nature of the multiformity of traditional Irish songs shows significant crossover between compositional practices on the part of the poet and creative transmission on part of the singer (2012, 2013b). A comparative analysis of three versions of one of Máire Bhuí Ní Laeire's aisling (vision poem) compositions, entitled 'Maidean Mhoch 'us me ' Feighilth mo Stuic' ('Early One Morning as I Herded My Cattle'), shows that half-line formula substitution and the re-creation of formulaic phrases was part and parcel of the creative process of oral transmission. The following examples are drawn from the manuscript versions of Crothúr 'ac Coitir, and versions collected from singer Nóra Ní Chonaill from West Muskerry, and singer Seán Ó Muiríosa from the Waterford Gaeltacht.

Multiform 1:

(A) Maidean mhoch 'us me ' feighilth mo stuic/ 'us dá seóla chun an fhéir
    (LS141, Crothúr 'ac Coitir in Ní Shíocháin
    2012: 193)
[Early one morning as I herded my cattle/ steering them to grass]

(B) Maidean mhoch ar mh'eighrí dom/ a' múscailt mo stuic chun féir
    (CBÉ 47: 66–68, Nóra Ní Chonaill in Ní
    Shíocháin 2012: 195)
[Early one morning as I rose up/ stirring my cattle to grass]

(C) Ar maidin moch is mé i ndiaidh mo stoic/ á sheoladh tríd an bhféar
    (Seán Ó Muiríosa in Tóibín 1978: 55)
[Early one morning as I followed my cattle/ steering them through the grass]

Here, the formula system inherent on the level of the half line is evident as stipulated by Lord (1960: 35), and can be imagined thus:

Maidean mhoch/ Ar maidin moch + 'us me ' feighilth mo stuic
        ar mh'eighrí dom
        is mé i ndiaidh mo stoic

Early one morning/ Early in the morning + as I herded my cattle
        as I rose up
        as I followed my cattle

Of course, 'Maidean mhoch/ Ar maidin moch' is a repeated 'group of words' commonly found in traditional songs, and in other compositions such as 'Maidean Mhoch ar Leabaig Bhuig' (Early One Morning on a Soft Bed), also by Máire Bhuí (LS141 in Ní Shíocháin 2012: 177). In the same composition, we see the use of a formula that is shared with Nóra Ní Chonaill's rendition of the previous song 'Maidean Mhoch 'us Me ' Feighilth mo Stuic':

Do smaoiníos-sa gur chóir dom dul/ *a' múiscilt stuic chun féir*
[I thought that I should go/ stirring my cattle to grass]
    (from 'Maidean Mhoch ar Leabaig Bhuig' ['Early One
    Morning on a Soft Bed'] by Máire Bhuí)

Maidean mhoch ar mh'eighrí dom/ *a' múscailt mo stuic chun féir*
[One early morning as I rose up/ stirring my cattle to grass]
    (from a version of 'Maidean Mhoch 'us me ' Feighilth mo
    Stuic' ['Early One Morning as I Herded My Cattle'] from
    singer Nóra Ní Chonaill)

Therefore we see that these half-line formulas present themselves in numerous different arrangements, not just from composer to composer, but from singer to singer. Examples of these formulaic multiforms even just within three versions of this one song are numerous, for example:

Multiform 2: 'Maidean Mhoch 'us me ' Feighilth mo Stuic' ['Early One Morning as I Herded My Cattle']

(A) An tu Céarnait ghlic an bhé ' cheap muilthe/ amach à t'íntinn ghéar
        (LS144, scribe Crothúr 'ac Coitir)
[Are you clever Céarnait the lady who created mills/ out of her sharp mind?]

(B) An Céarnait tu na ráite suilth,/ nú an bhé thar lear i gcéin
        (CBÉ 47: 66–68, singer Nóra Ní Chonaill)
[Are you Céarnait of the happy utterances/ or the lady far away overseas?]

(C) An tú Céarnait shnoite, an bhé cheap muilte/ amach i dtuiscint ghéar
(Tóibín 1978, singer Seán Ó Muiríosa)
[Are you beautifully formed Céarnait, the beautiful woman who created mills/ out of sharp understanding?]

Again the basic line pattern is stable, with word substitution creating formulaic multiforms (Lord 1960: 36), with 'ghlic' ('clever') and 'shnoite' ('beautifully formed') easily interchangeable and likewise 'à t'íntinn ghéar' ('out of your sharp mind') with 'i dtuiscint ghéar' ('in sharp understanding'). This calls to mind Seán Ó Coileáin's analysis of the formulaic basis of the lines of the traditional keen:

> For example, *Rúmanna dá mbreacadh dhom* of the first piece becomes *Seomraí dá nglanadh dhom* of the second; *breacadh,* however, does not go astray and reappears in *Róst dá bhreacadh dhom*; referring back to Version 1 we find a corresponding *Róst ar bhearaibh dom*. Within the main theme one might describe the line as a binary unit, the parts of which are to some degree independent of one another: *rúmanna/seomraí* may be complemented by *breacadh/glanadh,* róst by *bearaibh/breacadh*. (Ó Coileáin 1988: 111)

Examples of this same sort of formulaic word substitution abound in the different song versions from the Máire Bhuí repertoire; for example, in 'Maidean Mhoch ar Leabaig Bhuig' ('Early One Morning on a Soft Bed'):

chuala 'mu na héin [I heard, outside, the birds] LS141
chuala ceól na n-éan [I heard the music of the birds] CBÉ TO649
chuala guth na n-éan [I heard the voice of the birds] UCC K68

fáth mo scéil [the reason for my story] CBÉ TO649
brí mo scéil [the import of my story] UCC K68

do ghluais tar muir [who travelled over the sea] LS141
do ghluais anuir [who travelled from the East] CBÉ TO649

Much like Ó Coileáin's analysis of word substitution in the keen, we find that ceól/guth (music/voice), fáth/brí (reason/import), tar muir/anuir (over the sea/ from the East) are interchangeable; likewise in multiforms pertaining to the more violent end of the spectrum, we find: 'stealla p'léar dhá ndúiseacht'/ 'cáithe p'léar dá rúsca'/ 'cátha p'léar 'gus púdair' ('pelting of bullets rousing them'/ 'spraying of bullets shaking them'/ 'spraying of bullets and powder') (from 'A Mháir' Ní Laeire' ('Oh Mary O'Leary')) (Ní Shíocháin 2012 124–25, 219–25). Here stealla/ cáithe/cátha (pelting/shaking) can be fluidly substituted for one another, and likewise dúiseacht/rúscadh/púdair (rousing/shaking/of powder) can interchange without disturbing the meter. It appears, therefore, that the interchangeability of short formulas and the re-creation of formulaic components to produce 'new' formulaic phrases was not just the stock and trade of the named oral poet, such as Máire Bhuí, but of the communities of singers who sung her songs. For example, when we compare two multiforms describing the hair of the spéirbhean from two different renditions of the same composition by Máire Bhuí with a similar line in a song attributed to Eoghan Rua Ó Súilleabháin, it is very clear that this re-creative impulse is shared by both the composers and those who transmit the songs:

Multiform 3: 'Maidean Mhoch 'us me ' Feighilth mo Stuic' ['Early One Morning as I Herded My Cattle'] compared with 'An Spealadóir' by Eoghan Rua

(A)
Ba chrothach scuabach dualach dubh a cuacha ' titim léi
[Wavy, sweeping, curly and black her tresses did flow]
> from 'Maidean Mhoch 'us Me ' Feighilth mo Stuic' (Máire Bhuí)
> (Ní Shíocháin 2012: 193)

(B)
Ba dualach, cluthar, scuabach, tiubh a cuacha ag titim léi
[Curly, cosy, sweeping and thick her tresses did flow]
> from 'Ar Maidin Moch is Mé i nDiaidh mo Stoic' (Máire Bhuí)
> (Tóibín 1978: 55)

(C)
Ba dréimreach dualach daithte tiubh/A craobhfholth cuachach camarsach
[Climbing, sweeping, colourful and thick/ was her winding twisting curly hair]
> from 'An Spealadóir' (Eoghan Rua)
> (Ó Foghludha 1937: 41)

The formulaic word substitution that is evident in the above formulaic descriptions of the beauty of the spéirbhean's hair is indicative of the multiformity that is found generally when different versions from within the Máire Bhuí repertoire are compared. In the above examples, it appears that a number of suitable formulaic adjectives are interchangeable – dubh/tiubh (black/thick), scuabach/dualach (sweeping/curly) – when the multiforms of the first half of the lines are compared. Common recompositional patterns can thus be seen when comparing songs across composers, or indeed different renditions of the same song by different singers. The following comparison of multiforms shows again the fluidity of line formation, however the same recompositional impulse pervades: one in which words are unfixed, but meter remains relatively stable.

Multiform 4: 'Maidean Mhoch 'us me ' Feighilth mo Stuic' ['Early One Morning as I Herded My Cattle']

(A)
Nú an bhé a tugag thar bhárr na tuinne/ do mhúiscil cath na Trae
[Or the woman who was brought over the top of the wave/ and who roused the battle of Troy]
(LS141, Scribe Crothúr 'ac Coitir)

(B)
Nú an bhean sa chnoc do thraoch na cuin/ lena ráinig cath na Trae
[Or the woman in the hill who tired the hounds/ for whom the battle of Troy was struck]
(CBÉ 47: 66–68, Nóra Ní Chonaill)

(C)
Nó an chúileann tugadh de bharr an tsrutha/ do mhúscail cath na Trae
[Or the fair lady who was brought over the top of the stream [ocean]/ who roused the battle of Troy]
(Seán Ó Muiríosa, Tóibín 1978: 55)

Here we see 'do mhúiscil/do mhúscail cath na Trae' ('who roused the battle of Troy') as a half-line formula of which 'lena ráinig cath na Trae' ('for whom the battle of Troy was struck') is but another rendition. The above comparison clearly outlines a multiform system in which formulaic elements are foundational to the reconstruction of lines, which illustrates the recomposition inherent in transmission and performance among singers. Indeed, this skill at creating phrases was posited by Albert Lord as being where the real skill lies for the oral composer:

> I believe we are justified in considering that the creating of phrases is the true art of the singer on the level of the line formation, and it is this facility rather than his memory of relatively fixed formulas that marks him as a skillful singer in performance. (1960: 43)

These examples tell us a great deal about the aesthetics of Máire Bhuí's poetic compositions: rooted in the traditional and richly echoic but, most crucially, inherently re-creative. Though there can be no original 'text', no urtext, but numerous performances, renditions and re-creations of her compositions through song transmission, this multiformity is the very poetic aesthetic and practice that formed Máire Bhuí as a poet. Therefore, rather than view the fluid, unfixed existence of the oral composition as a nuisance that obscures 'the original' and hinders the establishment of fact, rather these multiforms enlighten our understanding of the poetic world that Máire Bhuí herself inhabited. To try and fit Máire Bhuí into the constraints of our own textual world would be to do an injustice to the very art she mastered.

Local Agrarian Agitation and the Creation of the Poetic Radical

From the United Irish Rebellion of 1798 to the Rockite Rebellion of 1822

Máire Bhuí Ní Laeire grew up in the rich singing and oral narrative culture of West Cork and the oral tradition was a core formative influence. She also lived during a time of political turmoil and change, which would ultimately leave a lasting mark on her thinking. While still a young woman, the growing influence of the Jacobin French Revolution was beginning to be more acutely felt in Ireland, for example, and in 1796, when Máire Bhuí was twenty-two, a French fleet attempted to land in Bantry Bay near Whiddy Island only to be thwarted by a storm. This event left its mark on the local population, who could see the revolutionary fleet in the bay, unable to land (Ó Crualaoich 1997). The year 1796 marked the revolution that was so near and yet so far. It is unsurprising, given that Bantry Bay is a mere 22 km from Keimaneigh, that the earliest composition attributed to Máire Bhuí is a response to this very event in the form of the traditional vision poem, the aisling, in which the spéirbhean, the otherworldly woman of the aisling, says 'go bhfeaca-sa an *fleet* i bhFaoide 'na lánchumas tréan' ('that I saw the fleet in Whiddy in full strong might'), only to have her hopes dashed when informed that the fleet was dispersed by the storm: 'tháinig scaipe orthu ón ngaoith, fóraíor, ' chuir a lán acu ar strae,/ agus i nglasaibh 'sea do shuíd mar an ríbhean so ' thárlaig i gcéin' ('alas, they were scattered by the wind, which sent a lot of them astray, and they now sit in fetters, like this royal woman who came from afar') (Ní Shíocháin 2012: 175). Not only does this song explicitly refer to a real-life event that was part of Wolfe Tone's radical political campaign, but is most strikingly of a Jacobin hue, with the end of the song telling of an imminent future in which 'land will be without rent without payment without tax and without dispute': 'beig talamh gan chíos gan íoc gan cháin is gan phlé'. It appears, therefore, that Máire Bhuí's thinking, as expressed through the traditional idiom of the aisling, was engaged with some of the most pressing concerns of Jacobinism more widely.

Indeed, though the campaign of the United Irishmen is generally understood as a movement that had its greatest successes in English-speaking Ireland, there is also evidence to suggest that in counties that were predominantly Irish speaking, such as Cork, school masters read aloud radical literature and pamphlets, and discussed the French debates with locals. Kevin Whelan refers to one such schoolmaster, John Hurley, of whom it was said in 1794 that he 'used to read the French debates and other seditious publications to the multitude at the chapel of Toobane in Drinagh parish and at Ballygurteen village in Kilmeen parish next to Drinagh' (1996: 83), a mere 38 km from Máire Bhuí's home near Ballingeary. This suggests one context in which ideas from literate sources may have spilled into local oral culture, and indeed, through the language divide. Another example of the 'seditious schoolmaster' is of course the famous Cork poet and scribe Mícheál Óg Ó Longáin, who was a member of the United Irishmen, and we can assume that there were other such figures who engaged explicitly with international radical debates; who were educated mediators between political thought among literate circles and a rural population who practised a rich oral culture (Dunne 1998, 2004). It is highly probable, given the radical discourses in her songs, therefore, that Máire Bhuí, in her formative years, was exposed to mediated forms of European radical revolutionary thought, which she re-created through the creative processes of orality. What we can be certain of, however, is that she lived through this unprecedented period of dissolution of order, in which the very foundations of the social status quo were questioned and indeed shook to its core. The 'sheer potentiality' of the radicalism of the 1790s, particularly for a young woman for whom the imminent arrival of revolutionary forces from France spurred her to song, we must assume, was an experience that would prove foundational.

The revolutionary aspirations of 1796 gave way to open rebellion in 1798, particularly in predominantly English-speaking Antrim and Wexford, which ultimately is quelled and leads to the trial and death of Wolfe Tone, the charismatic leader of the United Irishmen. The schismatic end result of the United Irish revolution, in people's response to the bloodshed, and indeed the atrocities, of the uprising, is well documented, with Catholic leaders distancing themselves from the United Irishmen thereafter, and with politics becoming polarized along sectarian grounds as before. Indeed, the impetus of the United Irishmen, which was based on the ideal of non-sectarian unity and radicalism, died a death of sorts in official political culture from the beginning of the 1800s (Whelan 1996: 130). A new charismatic political figure took centre stage: the Catholic lawyer Daniel O'Connell, who enjoyed unprecedented success in politicizing the rural poor through his mass meetings. His political campaign of Catholic Emancipation, which sought to repeal the Act of Union, left an extraordinary imprint on the popular tradition, though often at odds with the official line of non-violence promoted by O'Connell himself (uí Ógáin 1985, 1995). It is during this political period of the 1820s, during which time the Rockite movement took flight, that Máire Bhuí emerges as the pre-eminent poet of Muskerry, and it is with this movement that she is most closely associated.

The Rockite movement, which originated in Co. Limerick, spread throughout all the counties of Munster and also Kilkenny, and their activities are considered by James S. Donnelly to have been 'a sustained outburst of agrarian violence greater than any that had occurred previously in Ireland' (2009: 5). The Rockites were most active, however, in Cork and Limerick. The origins of the movement appear to have been rooted in a conflict between local tenants and Alexander Hoskins, the notoriously oppressive chief agent of Viscount Courtenay's estates around Newcastle West in Co. Limerick, who was appointed to deal with the enormous rental arrears that had accumulated on the estates. Through a number of measures, including increasing the annual rental to the order of 40 per cent and through aggressively pursuing rental arrears, the disquiet among tenants eventually reached boiling point (Donnelly 2009: 26, 31–32). Of particular significance was the number of undertenants who came to the defence of middlemen, such as Robert Parker of Glenquin and William Brown of Rathcahill, who had been targeted by Hoskins. It was one such response to the perceived injustice of Hoskins' actions that saw the genesis of the first 'Captain Rock'. Following a period of bitter dispute between Hoskins and Parker regarding monies owed, in which Parker resisted vehemently and even assembled a group of undertenants to prevent his livestock being confiscated, Hoskins ultimately served Parker with ejectments from all his lands. The shocking saga included a party of armed police and estate bailiffs raiding the house of Robert Parker, arresting the family and parading them through the street, and also the destruction of Parker's house and all its contents by fire, believed to have been arson (Donnelly 2009: 35–46). Parker was also a road contractor, who employed a considerable number of people, and in 1821 held a county presentment for a road in the locality but had his horses and carts for work on the road seized by Hoskins. It was when Hoskins sent his own labourers to finish the job that the term Rockite was first coined: on seeing their own roles being usurped by others, the undertenants and employees of Parker drove Hoskins' men off the road with stones and sticks. One man in particular, Paddy Dillane, brought fame upon himself for his expert flinging of stones, to be Christened 'Rock', as described in *Old Bailey solicitor*:

> The peasantry about the hills, viewing the transaction of sending men to repair the road with an eye of jealousy, particularly as none of themselves were to be employed, rose up against the labourers and actually drove them from off the road with stones and sticks, and it was by the activity and exertions of Paddy Dillane on that day that he was called Carrigah or Rock, he being so expert in flinging stones from a gravel quarry at the invaders ... (cited in Donnelly 2009: 38)

From the outset, the Rockite agitation was one of rebellion against the architects of the landlord system, borne of a sense of grievance due to unfair rental demands, particularly when contrasted with the ostentatious living of those imposing austerity upon tenants (Donnelly 2009: 33–34). However, a sense of loyalty to and identity with the local middleman seems to have been central to the agrarian upset at the time, which also echoes of Whelan's analysis of the significance of the 'underground gentry' in agrarian politics (1996: 3–58). Though the Rockite movement drew significant numbers of the rural poor to its ranks, it did also include a number of middlemen and gentleman-farmers. Furthermore, it appears from the above account from *Old Bailey solicitor* that the term Rockite was initially coined in Irish, which would have been the indigenous language of the majority of the rural poor in Cork and Limerick: we might suppose that Carrigah on the part of the author of *Old Bailey solicitor* may have referred to 'Carraigeach' or maybe even 'Paddy na Carraige' in Irish. This suggests from the onset that Irish speakers were central to this particular agrarian movement. The initial foray that christened Paddy Dillane as 'Rock' was followed by a number of antiestablishment disturbances, and by October of 1821 this disquiet had spread to a number of other regions and, according to Donnelly, was showing all the signs of a 'supralocal agrarian movement':

> The robbery of arms and ammunition, the exaction of financial 'contributions' to the cause, the swearing of oaths, and the posting of threatening notices were all much in evidence, along with a striking amount of collective violence against the enemies of 'Captain Rock'. (2009: 51)

In Máire Bhuí's own locality of West Muskerry and Iveleary, local lore still testifies to the heavy involvement of locals in the secret society of the Rockites, known locally as 'na Buachaillí Bána' ('the Whiteboys'), which indicates a perceived continuity between the agrarian agitation of the early 1820s and the earlier Whiteboy movement of the eighteenth century. There were widespread disturbances throughout Co. Cork, most notably in the raiding of arms by Rockites from North Cork to as far as the western coastal regions of Bantry and Schull, and in January of 1822 there was widespread apprehension among landlords and the authorities that the area was on the verge of insurrection (Donnelly 2009: 65–66). There were a number of heated clashes between the authorities and Rockite supporters in Ballyagran in North Cork, Newcestown near Bandon, and in Ballinard in Clonakilty, which seemed to galvanize support for the Rockite cause. Donnelly believes, however, that the pre-insurrectionary clash that most directly affected the Rockite uprising in Co. Cork was the Battle of Keimaneigh, in which Máire Bhuí's brother and two sons fought, and which sparked a larger insurgency throughout the county but which was short lived, lasting less than a week (Donnelly 2009: 71).

It is arguable that, where the Rockite movement represents localized violent struggles for tenant rights and economic justice, it was the song poetry that symbolically radicalized and utopianized the political impetus of the Rockites, thus creating a larger web of compelling anticolonial thought. Máire Bhuí lived during a time of extreme hardship for the rural poor, and in a period in Irish history that was speckled with uprisings. This was a society almost constantly teetering on the brink of revolution or anarchy, in which anti-authoritarian activity and beliefs were persistently strong. Her songs sung of the ideas that emerge from both the experience of subjection and the experience of the dissolution of order associated with hunger, marginalization, persecution and economic crisis. Her songs also articulated a vision of anarchy and renewal that would speak to the multitudes for whom song constituted an integral part of their intellectual and emotional life. Her work epitomizes the dynamic re-creativity of the oral tradition and the pressing relevance of singing ideas to the development of anticolonial political consciousness, and her own direct involvement with the Rockites points to the pivotal role of prophetic song in agrarian politics.

Family Life, Local Violence and Agrarian Agitation

Máire Bhuí was born in Túirín na nÉan near Ballingeary in 1774, according to the local lore collected by Fr. Donncha Ó Donnchú in the early twentieth century (1931: 15–20). Her parents, Diarmuid Buí and Siobhán, had fifty acres of land, and therefore she was not of humble origins. She eloped in 1792 with a horse merchant, Séamus de Búrca, from Skibereen in West Cork. They later bought 150 acres of land near Keimaneigh in Co. Cork, where, according to Ó Donnchú, they became very wealthy, had a large livestock and both workhorses and racehorses. In their family home in Inse Mhór was where Máire Bhuí's nine children were born (Ó Donnchú 1931: 15–16). Though Máire Bhuí was well off for much of her life, her own parents were evicted from their house at Túirín na nÉan in 1820, and during the famine Máire Bhuí and all the Burkes were evicted from their holdings near Keimaneigh (Ó Donnchú 1931: 131; Brennan 2000: 27–29). In this sense, Máire Bhuí could be considered to be a member of the 'underground gentry' of the period, having accumulated significant wealth, only to lose it all (Whelan 1996: 3–58). However, despite her own wealth and standing, she was purported to have had huge sympathy for the poor, as indicated by Ó Donnchú's representation of Máire Bhuí, which was informed by local lore: 'Ach dá mhéid a gcuid saidhbreasa, níor chailleadar riamh an tseana-sprid, agus níor theip riamh ar éileamh an duine bhoicht iad do bhogadh' ('However much their riches, however, they never lost the old spirit and the want of the poor never failed to stir them') (1931: 15–16), but also by her references to the plight of the poor in her compositions, most notably 'Tá Gaeil Bhocht' Cráite' ('Poor Gaels Are Tormented') (Ní Shíocháin 2012: 226).

As well as being reputed for their involvement in revolutionary agitation, her brothers are represented in folklore accounts as being involved in faction fighting, an apolitical and highly violent recreational form of fighting among the indigenous Irish (O'Donnell 1975), as well as other local violent disputes, most notably one incident where a local man narrowly escaped death at their hands (Ó Cróinín 1982: 110). Indeed, Pádraig Ó Crualaoi (Ó Cróinín 1982: 110) refers to them as 'fiain' ('wild') and Ó Donnchú described them with a more measured yet insinuative 'aerach go leor' ('pretty high spirited/pretty mad') (1931: 12). The Yellow Learys are portrayed as being unruly and frequently finding themselves on the wrong side of the law, as depicted in oral verse by a nemesis of Máire Bhuí, Donncha Chruíd. Their animosity for each other was generally played out through poetry, and through which Donncha Chruíd chastises the O'Learys for their troublesome anti-authoritarian activity, referring particularly to a relative of Máire Bhuí, Cormac Buí, who was hanged for some reason unknown:

> Níor crochag riamh éinne dom mhuíntir
> is níor cuireag thar loíng i gcéin
> murab ionann is glamar na nÍnseach
> go bhfuil na Botanies líonta 'á bpréimh!
> (CBÉ 849: 438–39, Ní Shíocháin 2012: 254)

> [No member of my family was ever hanged
> nor sent abroad in a ship
> unlike that noisy lot of the Inches
> of whose roots the Botanies are full!]

'Glamar na nÍnseach' or 'that noisy lot of the Inches', which refers to the holdings of Máire Bhuí, is suggestive of the strong anti-authoritarian streak associated with the O'Learys and Burkes. Indeed, the O'Learys' general affinity with and interest in fighting is further reflected in one of Máire Bhuí's own compositions, 'A Bhúrcaig Bhuí ón gCéim' ('Oh Young Burke from Keimaneigh'), in which, through song, she attempts to exert motherly influence on her son's choice in marriage. Máire Bhuí urges her son not to rebuke his young love on account of her dowry being small, but points instead to the numerous excellent attributes of the young lady, including the added bonus of her family being formidable fighters:

> A Bhúrcaig óig ón gCéim,
> mar a dtéann a' fia chun strae,
> fíll thar n-ais 'us bheir leat bean
> do dhéanfaig beart dod réir.
> Ná fág í siúd id dhéig
> mar ghiúll ar bheagán spré;
> dá dtíodh a cleaing sa bhruín let ais
> go mbuafí leat a' *sway*.
> (LS139, Ní Shíocháin 2012: 189)

[Oh young Burke from Keimaneigh
where the deer strays,
come back and bring with you a woman
who will act in your interests.
Do not leave her after you
for having a meagre dowry;
if her clan were to join the fray by your side
you would win the sway.]

These accounts not only attest to the O'Leary clan's engagement with fights locally, but Máire Bhuí's own compositions also attest to the poet's own ease with the culture of faction fights and indeed, in other compositions, with violent insurgency. The O'Learys are certainly depicted as having a strong anti-authoritarian and violent streak in local lore, as well as possessing no small generosity and notable poetic skills – Máire Bhuí's two brothers were also poets, though not of her calibre. The O'Learys' fervour for faction fighting seemed to translate quite easily into anticolonial violent rebellion. Of Máire Bhuí's nine children, two of her sons were purported to have been heavily involved in Rockite activity in the area, as well as her brother Crothúr Buí Ó Laeire, all three of whom figure largely in the oral testimony that has been collected in the locality on the Battle of Keimaneigh. In some accounts, Crothúr Buí is reported to have killed John Smith, who fought on the side of the British authorities during the Battle of Keimaneigh, as represented by Ó Donnchú in the 1931 edition (1931: 26). However, this is generally believed to be false and that it was in fact Séamas Rua an Bhreathnaigh who delivered the fatal blow to Smith, with Crothúr Buí driving his pike through the belly of Smith after the fact:

Bhí fear éigin go nglaeidís Crothúr Buí air agus isé mo thuairim gur do mhuíntir Laeire é agus go raibh gaol aige le Máire Bhuí. Bhí sé i gCath Chéim an Fhia. Nuair a mhairbh Séamas Rua an Bhreathnaig Smith le buille dá ghunna sa cheann do tháinig Crothúr Buí agus píce aige agus rop sé Smith leis an bpíce: sháig sé síos trína bholg é. (CBÉ 849: 438–39, Ní Shíocháin 2012: 23)

[There was a man called Crothúr Buí (Yellow Conor) and I believe that he was one of the O'Learys and that he was related to Máire Bhuí. He was in the Battle of Keimaneigh. When Séamas Rua an Bhreathnaigh (red-haired James Welsh) killed Smith with a blow of his gun to the head, Crothúr Buí came with a pike and pierced Smith with it: he drove it down through his belly.]

Even so, the oral testimony on the Battle of Keimaneigh points to Crothúr Buí as a central figure. Indeed, the animosity between the Yellow O'Learys and the infamous landlord and County Sheriff, James Barry, is stuff of legend, with Máire Bhuí's two sons being pursued and targeted by Barry himself, following the Battle of Keimaneigh, to be subsequently tried by the authorities only to be successfully defended by Daniel O'Connell himself and released. Furthermore, their uncle, Crothúr Buí, reportedly stood on top of the marble slab that covered the tomb of the same James Barry when in attendance at the burial of an elderly woman from Keimaneigh being put to rest in the same graveyard at Inchigeelagh and exclaiming: '"Tánn tú ansan thíos inis go macánta, chô tréith leis an seana-mhnaoi do thugamair linn aniar ó Chéim an Fhia"' ('"You are now down there honestly, as weak as the old woman we took with us eastward from Keimaneigh"') (CBÉ 1527: 144, Ní Shíocháin 2012: 249–53).

From the oral testimony collected by the Irish Folklore Commission, and from the local knowledge that informed Ó Donnchú's 1931 edition of Máire Bhuí's songs, we can infer that the O'Learys and the Burkes were at the thick of seditious agrarian activity in Muskerry during the 1820s and that they held a particularly intense dislike for James Barry, who as both landlord and sheriff could be seen as being symbolic of both the oppressive landlord system, which was opposed so violently by the Rockites, as well as being the strong arm of a legal system synonymous with brutality and injustice. It appears also that no other Irish-language oral poet was so heavily embroiled with the Rockites as Máire Bhuí Ní Laeire – though both Tomás Rua Ó Súilleabháin and Raftery refer to the millennial prophecy of Pastorini,[3] which became central to the movement as a whole, for example, neither of them, that we know of, had such a direct link to the Rockites as did Máire Bhuí. The songs of Máire Bhuí, therefore, give us extremely valuable insight into the ideology and the key political concepts that motivated the Rockite movement, as a poet whose sons and brother had an immediate involvement with the rebellion, and in this sense, it could be said that she was personally invested in the rebellion. However, in saying this, I do not suggest that Máire Bhuí's songs were merely a passive reflection of the key ideas that were being developed among the men of the Rockite movement. Rather, I suggest that an analysis of her work gives us a picture of her role as being much more central: as an oral poetic parrhesiast who took on a prophetic role in moulding the very ideas and concepts that drove the movement. I therefore suggest that song played a crucial role in the development of the very ideas by which the Rockites and their sympathizers and supporters would live, the very ideas that would justify the Rockite call to arms.

In the sections that follow, I offer an analysis of the songs of Máire Bhuí Ní Laeire that makes a claim for the sheer centrality of orality and song both to the generation of ideas and their impact. In doing so, I will argue that Máire Bhuí was a prophetic charismatic figure who, through her oral poetic craft, generated ideas and visions that would answer to an acute experience of crisis among the community, and that these ideas would be foundational in the creation of an anticolonial political consciousness. Máire Bhuí was a singer of ideas of no small consequence, and it was in the act of singing that her ideas would take hold both among contemporaries and subsequent generations. Rather than view Charles Walmesley, literate author of the infamous Pastorini's prophecy, as the key prophet of the millenarian Rockite movement, therefore, I argue that it was the song poet in fact who moulded the political vision that would spur 'a fanatical pursuit of the millennium' (Cohn 1970: 314). Though there are others who spoke of the day or year of reckoning in 1820s verse, no other poet engaged with the millenarian prophecy as vehemently as Máire Bhuí did. In this case, our pure type of the ecstatic millennial prophet is a woman who could neither read nor write. That an illiterate farmer's wife should take such a crucial role in idea-making potentially puts a serious dent in the usual male-dominated textual construction of official history. That this illiterate female singer of ideas would play such a visionary role in 'unofficial' Ireland at the same time that highly educated Daniel O'Connell was making such an astonishing (and well-documented) headway as one of Ireland's great parliamentarians is a tale worth telling, and a history worth reimagining.

Crisis and Charisma: The Song Poet as Prophet and Truth-Teller

The connection between prophecy and poetry in the Irish tradition has long been established. That the prophetic overtones of poetry can be considered to be much more 'real' than just a literary trope has been suggested by Ó Buachalla, who identifies certain categories of people as being particularly associated with prophesizing in the Irish tradition by virtue of being specialists in *fios* (otherworldly or supernatural knowledge) and magic, these being druids, prophets, poets and saints (1983: 77). Joseph Nagy also highlights this connection between prophecy, profession of 'truth' and poetico-musical forms in the Irish tradition, which is demonstrated by the case of the famous Finn of the Fenian sagas, who when prophesizing always does so in poetic verse (1985: 21). Poetry can therefore be considered to be the language of prophecy in the Irish tradition. The supernatural connotations of poetry and poets persisted down to the twentieth century, according to Dáithí Ó hÓgáin, in his study of the poet persona in the Irish tradition, and the persistent relevance of prophetic poetic forms in Irish down to the nineteenth century has also been discussed by Vincent Morley in his study of the construction of Gaelic history (2011: 20–21). Indeed, as both Ó hÓgáin and Nagy have argued, the etymology of the Irish word for poetry, *filíocht*, is literally 'to see', and representations of the poet from early Irish to modern Irish sources attest to these seer-like qualities of the poet as an in-between figure who mediates between the mortal world and the supernatural (Knott 1960: 7; Ó hÓgáin 1982: 15; Ó Buachalla 1983: 82; Nagy 1985: 24–25). For the song poet of the nineteenth century therefore, the poetic language that he/she has mastered is not just held in the highest esteem aesthetically, but is in itself a symbolic marker of otherworldly truth. In this sense, the poet is a 'transmitter' of *fios* or supernatural knowledge (Nagy 1985: 36). The semiotics of Irish-language poetry venture into otherworldliness, therefore, and indeed it can be argued that this is integral to the experience of song performance itself as ecstatic and indicative of some higher meaning. Máire Bhuí, in taking on the mantle of the song poet, therefore, also took possession of the traditional medium of truth-telling and of prophecy.

Indeed, Max Weber identifies the cultural form of song, as well as dance, drama and prayer, as part of the orgiastic ecstasy-inducing culture of prophecy historically (1978: 422). The prophet, according to Weber, 'exerts his power simply by virtue of his personal gifts' (1978: 440), the gift that is at the core of the 'ecstatic abilities' of the prophet in this case being a prodigious fluency in oral composition. Though the literate Pastorini, who is so closely associated with the Rockite movement of the 1820s in Ireland, was a prophet from within an educated literary Catholic tradition, Máire Bhuí, though also a Catholic, had inherited an alternative prophetic tradition with its roots in pre-Christianity: that of verse-making. Máire Bhuí, just like Weber's prophet (1948: 280, 1978: 445), stands 'in the face of the world', a bearer of 'vital emotional preaching' through song, and the sheer immediacy of her political discourses and the intensity of her compositions can still be felt today. Lines that occur at the high point of the music that display this sense of 'vital emotional preaching' in the most popular of her compositions, 'Cath Chéim an Fhia' ('The Battle of Keimaneigh') include: 'Is acu 'thá 'n tslat, is olc í ' riail' ('It is they who hold the cane, terrible is its rule'), 'Beig na sluaite fear a' teacht gan chiach' ('Hordes of men will joyfully arrive'), and 'bíodh 'úr bpící glan' i gceart i ngléas' ('let your clean pikes be at the ready'). Likewise in the other most popular of her songs, 'A Mháir' Ní Laeire' ('Oh Mary O'Leary'), the sheer intensity of the violent antiestablishment 'preaching', in Weberian terms, fused with the climax of the air is striking:

> beid siad faonlag fí spalla gréine
> gan neach sa tsaol 'na gcúram,
> a gcuin 's a m*béagles* 's a gcapaill traocht[a]
> gan dúil i ngéim ná ' liú 'co.
> (Ní Shíocháin 2012: 220)

> [they will be exhausted and weak under scorching sun
> with no one in the world to care for them,
> their hounds and beagles and their horses exhausted
> with no desire for game or shout.]

This emotive intensity of her work lies in the discourses of social injustice and of the plight of 'Gaeil bhocht' cráite' ('Poor tormented Gaels') as contrasted with images of the opulence and comfort of the nobles and seems to be what drives her songs. Indeed, her attack on symbols of the nobility and the ruling classes are particularly strong; for example, in 'beig a leathaireacha geárrtha 'na gc'ráistíochaibh uaisle' ('the leathers in their noble carriages will be cut'), or in her proclamation of a time fast approaching in which the community will have 'cead ráis ar na huaisle' ('permission to send the nobles racing') from 'Maidean Álainn Ghréine' ('One Sunny Morning') (Ní Shíocháin 2012: 197–98). The performance context of traditional song also resembles the ecstasy-inducing prophetic experience as outlined by Weber (1978: 422) – an element that is seemingly absent from the culture of printed prophecy. Not only do the ritualistic traits of song provide, as discussed in the previous chapter, an effective forum for ecstatic truth-telling, but the very discourses of Máire Bhuí's songs, in which she clearly represents herself as a 'transmitter' of a higher truth, point to a distinctly prophetic role:

'Do chualag scéal duit anis go déanach/ ó fhiodóg slé ' bhí i nDiúchuil ...'
['I heard a tale for you of late/ from a mountain plover in Diúchuil ...']
('A Mhair' Ní Laeire' ['Oh Mary O'Leary'])

'Is é ' chuala ó fháigibh go ndúirt Naomh Seán linn/ go raibh deire an cháirde caite leó ...'
['What I heard from prophets is that St John has told us/ that their time is up ...']
('Tá Gaeil Bhocht' Cráite ['Poor Gaels Are Tormented'])

'Go b'é ' deir gach údar cruínn liom ...'
['As every accurate author [prophet] tells me ...']
('Cath Chéim an Fhia' ['The Battle of Keimaneigh'])

The above lines are suggestive of the song poet being privy to some special message or truth beyond the capacity of a normal person. As Foucault has argued, the 'mode of veridiction' of the prophet is one of mediation in which he/she 'addresses a truth to men which comes from elsewhere' (2011: 15). Similarly, Szakolczai argues that the prophet *transmits* truth and communicates it to his/her following: 'The prophet receives a message and develops a following that "receive" this delivery. The prophet is therefore an in-between figure, a mediator, even a "transmitter"' (2001: 380). Through her frequent references to the year of reckoning fast approaching 'an bhliain seo chúinn ...'/ 'this coming year ...', and likewise her predictions of the annihilation and downfall of the ruling classes and the subsequent reordering of the social reality of her listeners, it can be said that Máire Bhuí *performs* this intermediary role of prophet:

Sa bhliain seo 'nis atá 'gainn beig rás ar gach smíste ...
[This coming year every good for nothing lump will be sent racing ...]
('Cath Chéim an Fhia' ['The Battle of Keimaneigh'])

Is an bhliain seo atá againn 'sea ' bheig rírá againn/ tar éis búir do thnátha
is do charta i ngleó …
[And this coming year we will have uproar/ having exhausted and cleared
out boors in noisy battle …]
('Tá Gaeil Bhocht' Cráite' ['Poor Gaels Are
Tormented'])

'us ná caill do ch'ráiste – insa bhliain seo lámh linn/ a bheig ochalán ar
bhúraibh
[and don't lose courage – in this coming year/ boors will be groaning …]
('A Mháir' Ní Laeire' ['Oh Mary O'Leary']

'us ar a' mbliain seo chúinn beig búir go lag …
[and next year boors will be weak …]
('Maidean Mhoch 'us Me ' Feighilth mo Stuic'
['Early One Morning While Herding My Cattle'])

'Ar a' mbliain seo chúinn beig búir fí bhrón'
[Next year coming boors will be sorrowful …]
('Seo Leó, ' Thoil' ['Seo leó, My Darling'])

Máire Bhuí's predictions of the year of apocalypse fast approaching, which are found in her aisling compositions, in her lullaby, as well as in her three 'big' songs of prophetic millenarianism, 'Cath Chéim an Fhia' ('The Battle of Keimaneigh'), 'A Mháir' Ní Laeire' ('Oh Mary O'Leary') and 'Tá Gaeil Bhocht' Cráite' ('Poor Gaels Are Tormented'), are frequently accompanied by graphic images of violent apocalypse. Máire Bhuí articulates a vision of violent anarchy, of revolution, of the overturn of the colonial system, in graphic detail, such as we find in the following verse from 'A Mháir' Ní Laeire' ('Oh Mary O'Leary'):

Beig stealla p'léar agus pící géara
dhá gcuir 'na méadail bhrúidig,
beig cloch 'us craobh orthu ó láimh gach éinne
'gus mùllacht Dé ar a' gcúmplacht …
(Ní Shíocháin 2012: 220)

[There will be pelting of bullets and sharp pikes
being driven through their brutish paunches,
a stone and branch down upon them from every hand
and God's curse on the company …]

The wilderness theme of the poet thinking in isolation, which we encountered earlier and is symbolic of the 'in-between' status of the poet between this world and the other world, is also utilized by Máire Bhuí in both the aisling form with which it is usually associated, but also in her famous and prophetic 'Cath Chéim an Fhia', and is another symbolic marker of her prophetic mediation (see this volume, pp. 30–31). Therefore, even through its themes, song poetry symbolically performs the medium through which ecstatic truth is relayed, and thus the ideas that Máire Bhuí sings are imbued with the prophetic authority of some higher 'truth' that can only be transmitted by such an extraordinary charismatic figure as the poet. In the 1820s, therefore, it is possible the traditional song poet, inheritor of the traditional medium of prophecy, might fulfil the role of millenarian prophet in contemporary politics. The manner in which Máire Bhuí moulds and articulates her radical millenarian vision through song suggests that she did just this, and that she communicated her vision with absolute conviction and intensity brings Cohn's depiction of the millenarian prophet to mind:

> It is the prophet who carries out this adaptation of traditional lore and who becomes the bearer of the resulting ideology. If in addition the prophet possesses a suitable personality and is able to convey an impression of absolute conviction, he is likely in certain situations of emotional tension to become the nucleus of a millenarian movement. (1970: 42)

Máire Bhuí injects her political prophetical discourses with the sting of the 'real' colonial experience of hunger, injustice and state brutality, thus electrifying the contemporary political discourse and conveying a sense of absolute conviction that not only was violent rebellion justified, but that the day of reckoning was fast approaching, as we see in the song 'A Mháir' Ní Laeire' ('Yellow Mary O'Leary'):

> Do chualag scéal duit anis go déanach
> ó fhiodóg slé ' bhí ' nDiúchuil,
> go suífeadh téarma gan moíll in Éirinn
> a chuirfeadh béir ar gcúlaibh;
> go mbeadh *repéalers* 's a bhfórsaí tréana,
> agus cúnamh Dé 'co á stiúra,
> 'gus buín a' Bhéarla gan fíon gan féasta,
> 'gus stealla p'léar dhá ndúiseacht.
>   (Ní Shíocháin 2012: 219)

> [I heard a tale for you of late
> from a mountain plover in Diúchuil,
> that a term would reside shortly in Ireland
> that would send bears retreating;
> that there would be repealers and their strong forces,

and the help of God steering them,
and that English-speaking crew without wine without feast
and pelting of bullets starting them.]

Máire Bhuí, therefore, appears to perform the role of millenarian prophet through song, and her songs also embody the parrhesiastic drive of being compelled to speak out. The conditions of emergence also match Cohn's schema: the 1820s in Ireland was a time of hunger and evictions, a period of great uncertainty and severe marginalization, such as would result in a liminal existence that would provide a fertile ground both for the development of a millenarian movement and the emergence of a charismatic prophetic leader that would develop the ideas and values that would define the milieu. That Máire Bhuí was referred to by her contemporary, Donncha Bán, as 'Bláth 's Craobh na nÚdar' / 'Flower and Greatest of Authors' whereby *údar* (author) also denotes prophet in Irish, would suggest that Máire Bhuí was recognized by her peers as fulfilling such a prophetic poetic role in the community at that time.

As a young woman who grew up during a time when the prospect of a liberating French invasion was imminent, when radical change was afoot, and in which popular print culture was awash with contemporary political discourses, it is of particular interest how central the indigenous prophetic idiom of oral poetry would be to her own political expression. In this sense, Máire Bhuí is not entirely dissimilar to the educated British women of the Romantic era, who consciously sought out prophecy as a way to contribute to political discourses during their own lifetime and who were drawing on 'a rich tradition of female prophecy', including political prophesizing of the 1790s in England and the work of sectarian female prophets during the English Civil War (Smith 2013: 1). Though there can be a tendency to categorize the revolutionary culture of late eighteenth-century European thought in the wake of the French Revolution as distinctly secular and 'rational', it appears, to the contrary, that Europe was awash with popular prophecy during that same period and that countries such as England experienced a huge resurgence in millenarian prophecy after 1789 (Smith 2013: 4). That these educated English-speaking women drew from what Smith terms 'a matrilineal genealogy of female authority', that the female tradition produced significant millenarian thinkers in England at the same time that Máire Bhuí was articulating her political voice through the traditional Irish idiom of prophecy, is highly interesting, and points to a larger role being played by women in the development of political ideas during this period than is generally acknowledged. Though Máire Bhuí differed from the corresponding English-speaking literate prophetess in the medium of her thought and composition, she is comparable in that she utilized prophetic discourse as a political response to crisis and also in that her work was *visionary* in nature. Indeed, much like the English-speaking prophetess, she had a distinctly parrhesiastic quality, in Foucauldian terms: this was 'fearless speech', an intervention of truth-telling during a time of dissolution of order, crisis and uncertainty. Indeed, following the work of Weber, I argue that Máire Bhuí generated a certain charismatic authority, which was connected to her role as a prophetic poet through which she would articulate a vision of the world that would electrify the agrarian movement. This radical anticolonial 'image of the world' was a potential game-changer in the history of agrarian political thought, much like Weber's paradigm of the 'switchmen', who can send ideas and society in one direction rather than another at any given time:

> ... very frequently the "world images" that have been created by "ideas" have, like switchmen, determined the tracks along which action has been pushed by the dynamic of interest. "From what" and "for what" one wished to be redeemed, and let us not forget, "could be" redeemed, depended upon one's image of the world. (Weber 1948: 280)

Charisma, for Weber, is the very core of societal renewal and creates important junctures of change in society (be it good or bad). The very ideas sung by Máire Bhuí in her performance of charismatic authority, the very vision she articulated, thus had the capacity to prove central to the direction of political life, thought and unrest thereafter. Therefore, much more than her work being a mere reflection of the 'serious' discourses of the political world of men, it is rather a dynamic parrhesiastic political engagement of song with the thoughts and minds of the people. Though the evidence of printed and written sources is important (and furthermore it is highly convenient to scholars in that it has survived), it is important not to underplay the cultural significance of the traditional idiom of Irish-language truth-telling that coexisted with print. In this sense, the political pamphlet or printed prophecy did not supplant the potent indigenous expressive medium of song (see Morley 2017). Indeed, I argue that what song poetry had to say was of such pressing relevance for the agrarian classes that it fulfilled a role beyond the capabilities of the written word at that time. For the medium of song was a message in itself: one of prophetic authority imbued with parrhesiastic intensity, one through which 'new' ideas could be reconfigured as integral to the identity of the community. It is particularly because the song poet practised a performance-based verbal art that would create a liminal ludic space in which the very ideas that people live by would 'tremble in the balance' that song must be considered as a central transformative medium in the development of ideas historically.

Máire Bhuí was a parrhesiast, a charismatic figure that emerged during a liminal period of crisis to create a meaningful 'image of the world' through singing. Though Foucault outlines four distinct modalities of truth-telling (prophet, sage, technician/teacher and parrhesiast), these modalities have frequently been combined by historical truth-tellers (2011: 25–26). We see, with Máire Bhuí, that parrhesia and prophecy co-existed through her song-making – she articulates both a sense of divine or otherworldly truth and inspiration in her songs, at the same time as engaging the 'telling all' of the parrhesiast. The parrhesiast has a duty to speak with insuppressible urgency, has something that *must* be said. The parrhesiast 'unveils what is' and is compelled to intervene (2011: 16). Máire Bhuí's songs represent the challenge to authority of the parrhesiast and also demonstrate the sense of danger and the imminent threat of rupture that Foucault associates so closely with the modality of parrhesia. This 'courage in the face of danger' is integral to Máire Bhuí's call to arms and legitimization of violence. Indeed, the intensity of Máire Bhuí, this sense of sheer urgency she portrays, is a hallmark of her songs – there is no denying the sense of belief that she communicates in her depiction of bloody insurgency. It is these very traits that suggest that as a real-life historical figure Máire Bhuí played a central role both in the development of anticolonial political consciousness, and in the mobilization of a radical agrarian movement. For, crucially, it was the 'image of the world' that she sung of that had the capacity to create the world anew, to create a way of thinking that would perpetuate and legitimize the anticolonial movement. To understand the ideas that formed the 'image of the world' put forth by the song poet, we must look in the first instance to her most famous composition on the Battle of Keimaneigh, a song that connects the poet explicitly to local Rockite agitation but that also is suggestive of the prophetic role of the song poet in agrarian agitation.

'An liú gur lean i bhfad i gcian ...'/ 'The shout that resounded afar ...': Singing Revolt and the Battle of Keimaneigh

An integral part of the Rockite campaign was the raiding of gentry houses for arms, and the Cork branches of the secret society also pursued this tactic. Rockite activity was strong in Máire Bhuí's own hinterland of Iveleary and Muskerry, with reports of up to 2,000 men in active service of the Rockites in the area of Keimaneigh, and 5,000 in Rockite camps between Millstreet and Macroom (Ó Gráda 1989: 42; O'Leary 1993: 13). On 11 January 1822 the Rockites raided Bantry House, taking off with what arms they could find, only to be pursued by Lord Bantry himself and the local police. The Rockites held them off at the pass of Keimaneigh (Céim an Fhia) near Ballingeary. Unsuccessful in thwarting the Rockite group, Lord Bantry and his followers turned back, only to return on the 21 January with additional yeomen and armed soldiers from the 39th regiment. After a day of fighting, Lord Bantry's troops had failed to apprehend a single Rockite. The following day on the 22 January 1822, the reviled landlord and collector of tithes from Inchigeelagh, James Barry, was sent for and promptly arrived with reinforcements from the Muskerry Yeomanry (Ó Donnchú 1931; Ó Gráda 1989; O'Leary 1993). The conflict that ensued became known by locals as Cath Chéim an Fhia or the Battle of Keimaneigh, and though only one of Lord Bantry's men was killed, the foray incited an uprising of Rockites throughout the county. The Battle of Keimaneigh was a massive symbolic victory for the local Rockites, most of whom were armed not with guns, but with pikes and shovels, or indeed rocks for throwing (much like the original 'Captain Rock') (Ní Shíocháin 2012: 251). Two Rockites were killed – Amhlaoibh Ó Luínse and Barra Ó Laeire – in comparison to one soldier of the 39th regiment, John Smith. Only four of the Rockites were captured, however, and much like the symbolic storming of the Bastille, in a movement saturated with millenarian aspirations, the news that agrarian rebels could resist the might of the authorities excited a call to arms that quickly spread throughout Cork (Katsuta 2003: 282–84).

Máire Bhuí's most famous composition recounts the events of Cath Chéim an Fhia, and Ó Donnchú was of the opinion that the central importance of the song was that it kept the memory of the battle alive (1931: 28). However, I argue that Cath Chéim an Fhia did much more than keep the story of the Battle of Keimaneigh alive, though undoubtedly it did that too: on analysing the discourses of the song, we see that it was as much a prophetic battle cry or a visionary call to arms as it was a commemorative tale of a local event. Both Donnelly (2009: 68–70) and Katsuta (2003: 282–85) imply that the Battle of Keimaneigh sparked this larger and more widespread insurgency, and I argue that the song 'Cath Chéim an Fhia' in the immediate aftermath of the battle itself could have been a key factor in inspiring 'a sudden fanatical pursuit of the millennium' (Cohn 1970: 314). Indeed, I believe that the millenarian compositions of Máire Bhuí point to her fulfilling an important visionary role in the Rockite movement, and that as a singer of ideas she articulated concepts that wrought a radical political worldview from the shared lived experience of colonization among the rural Irish-speaking population.

The song 'Cath Chéim an Fhia' begins with the beautifully serene imagery of the poet pondering her thoughts in the woods while listening to the sweet singing of the birds, a paradigm closely associated with the aisling theme and a symbol of the sacred liminality of the wilderness, as discussed earlier. This repose is soon disturbed by the sound of battle and the poet proceeds in giving an animated account of the battle itself:

Cois abha Ghleanna 'n Chéama i nUíbh Laeire 'sea ' bhímse
mar a dtéann a' fia insan oíche chun síor-cholla sóil,
a' machnamh seal liom féinig a' déanamh mo smaointibh,
ag éisteacht i gcoíllthibh le bínn-ghuth na n-eón;
nuair a chuala 'n cath a' teacht aniar,
glór na n-each a' teacht le sians,
le fuaim an airm chrith a' sliabh …
                    (Ní Shíocháin 2012: 2012)

[By the river of the glen of Keimaneigh in Iveleary that I frequent
where the deer goes at night to sleep soundly,

thinking a while to myself and making my ideas,
listening in woods to the melodious voice of the birds;
when I heard the battle coming from the West,
the symphonic sound of the horses coming,
with the noise of the army the mountain shook …]

Though the song recounts the battle in detail, from 'an liú gur lean i bhfad i gcian' / 'the shout that resounded afar', which summoned the Rockites to arms, to specific names of people who fought and died on the opposing side, the prophetic hue of 'Cath Chéim an Fhia' is also apparent. Though the poet depicts the events of that fateful day itself in the song, the final three verses explicitly speak of what is yet to come, thus re-creating the Battle of Keimaneigh not merely as an event that was over and done with, but as a symbol of a revolution fast approaching, most markedly in the fourth verse:

Sa bhliain seo 'nis atá 'gainn beig rás ar gach smíste,
cuirfeam insa díg iad, draoib orthu 'us fóid;
ní iarrfam cúirt ná stáitse, beig árd-chroch 'na suí 'gainn,
's a' chnáib go slachtmhar sníte le díolthas 'na gcóir.
    Is acu 'thá 'n tslat, is olc í ' riail,
    i gcóistíbh greanta is maith é ' ngléas,
    gach sórd le caitheamh, flea 'gus féasta,
      ag béaraibh ar bórd.
Go b'é deir gach údar cruínn liom sara gcríochnaí siad deire an fhôir
insa leabhar so Pastorína go ndíolfaid as a' bpóit.
          (Ní Shíocháin 2012: 213)

[This coming year every good for nothing lump will be sent racing,
we will bury them in the ditch, covered with mud and sods;
we will seek neither court nor stage, we will have a high hanging,
with the noose neatly taut in vengeance.
    It is they who hold the cane, terrible is its rule,
    in ornate coaches of fine gloss,
    every good thing to consume, feast and banquet,
      laid out for bears.
What every accurate author [prophet] tells me that before they finish the end of harvest-time
that in this book of Pastorini that they will pay for their drunkenness.]

Here Máire Bhuí re-creates the very meaning of Pastorini's prophecy such as would surely appal the original author. Though the man who initially penned the prophecy was an anti-Jacobin conservative Catholic bishop, his name is now used to strike a blow against the establishment, as a sign of the imminent overthrow of the Protestant English-speaking nobility in Ireland. As Niall Ó Ciosáin pointed out, the foretelling of the demise of Protestantism in Pastorini's prophecy was akin to the foretelling of a massive social revolution in the eyes of the Irish poor (1997: 196). The Jacobin sentiment that precedes the mention of Pastorini is striking: that the will of the people is pre-eminent, and to it everything must submit – they will seek no court or stage, but they themselves, the people, will mete justice upon their overlords through a 'high hanging'. Máire Bhuí's intense distain for the finery of the nobles is articulated here again in her ire against the ornate glossy polished coaches of the nobility and the plentifulness of their food and drink; but most importantly she problematizes their use (or misuse) of power: 'Is acu 'thá 'n tslat, is olc í ' riail' ('It is they who hold the cane, terrible is its rule'). This goes to the heart of her justification of violent revolt, a theme which is developed in many of her compositions from the revolutionary movement of the 1820s. This is followed in the second half of the fifth verse by outright prophesizing:

> Beig na sluaite fear a' teacht gan chiach,
> ar longa mear' is fada é a dtriall,
> 's a' Franncach theas nár mheathlaig riamh
>   i bhfaor agus i gcóir.
> Beig catharacha á stríoca agus tínteacha á lasa leó –
> tá 'n cáirde fada díoltha 's a' líonrith 'na gcóir.
>   (Ní Shíocháin 2012: 214–15)

> [Hordes of men will joyfully arrive,
> in swift ships they travel from afar,
> and the Frenchman to the south who never waned
> in blades and arms (or zeal and justice).
> Cities will submit and be set ablaze,
> long have we been owed, and terror is in store for them.]

Máire Bhuí shows her mastery of poetic resonance in her articulation of this vision of the future, whereby the theme of deliverance that was so central to Jacobite aisling poetry is now re-created as Jacobin (see Ó Buachalla 2003; Morley 2017: 242). Her song speaks acutely of the here and now, of the current agrarian agitation, but is deeply evocative of themes of former struggles, both of the Jacobite saviour who will travel from over the sea and of the more recent Frenchman as a symbol of radical revolt. Though her song echoes of Jacobitism, her vision of anarchy and renewal is distinctly anti-nobility – Máire Bhuí seeks not the reinstatement of a rightful king as did her predecessors Eoghan Rua Ó Súilleabháin and Aogán Ó Rathaille; rather, she seeks the mobilization of the community and the establishment of the authority of the people themselves. Furthermore, the air to the song also belongs to a famous 1798 song 'Cath Bhéal an Mhuighe Shailigh' recounting the tale of the Battle of the Big Cross near Clonakilty in West Cork, and therefore the very air resonates with the United Irish Rebellion. When we consider that 'a' Franncach theas'/ 'the Frenchman to the south' features at the climax of the air in all its explosive and connotative might, we might imagine the resonant meaning felt by audiences and singers for whom the Battle of the Big Cross was still within living memory. Thus the current Rockite event is fused with a reimagined collective narrative of successive resistance, and imbued with radical antiestablishment concepts of the will of the people. Thus Pastorini is transformed and radicalized by the song poet, and the printed prophecy is born anew through song. In this sense, it cannot be said that the singing tradition merely transmitted or reflected the printed prophecy of Pastorini, but rather that song dynamically engaged with and re-created the millenarian vision that would be the nucleus of the Rockite movement. The song is not just about commemoration, but is an active visionary engagement with contemporary politics. Indeed, not only does the song articulate a vision of revolt that sends the blood racing, but it is explicitly a millenarian call to arms, an incitement to rebellion with the surety of supernatural intervention that is often synonymous with millenarian movements:

> 'S a Chlanna Gaíol na n-árann, ná staonaig 'us ná stríocaig,
> is geárr anis gan moíll go mbeig crích ar 'úr ngnó …
>   bíodh 'úr bpící glan' i gceart i ngléas,
>   téig 'on chath, ná fanaig siar,
>   tá an chabhair a' teacht le toil ó Dhia,
>   agus léiríg na póirc …
>   (Ní Shíocháin 2012: 214)

> [And oh beloved Gaelic clans, do not desist and do not submit,
> it will not be long now before your work is done …
>   let your clean pikes be at the ready,
>   go forth to battle, don't hold back,
>   help is coming with the grace of God,
>   and subdue the swine (or show the swine) …]

Not only does the song refer to 'the shout that resounded afar' – that of the local Rockites shouting from hilltop to hilltop to summon their troops, a shout that was said to have travelled with great rapidity from Bantry as far North as Carraig an Ime before it stopped (Ó Suibhne 1932: 149) – but in many ways the song itself can also be considered to be a shout that resounded afar, a visionary battle cry that we can suppose spread with great rapidity through the rich oral culture of Irish-speaking Cork in the 1820s.

Máire Bhuí is here the voice of the rebellion: it is she who moulds the political vision that impresses upon the community the immediacy of the current crisis and the legitimacy of violent uprising. It is not the literate Pastorini, in the true sense, therefore, that is the prophet of the Rockite rebellion, but the oral poet, for it cannot be said that Pastorini himself actually moulded the millenarian vision of the Rockites. It is Máire Bhuí who gives a sense of immediacy to the movement; it is she who melds the prophetic millenarian vision to the collective narrative and identity of the people; it is she who radicalizes the millenarian impulse, weaving it into a shared narrative of oppression and social injustice. The prophetic and supernatural associations with the Battle of Keimaneigh are not limited to the discourses of the songs alone, of course. The lore that survived on the battle is in itself representative of apocalyptic millenarian thought (see Ó Tuairisg 2009). The common belief in prophecy is indicated by tales of other prophecies that circulated among the people, including that 'a battle will be waged in Keimaneigh in which a man that was never born will be killed'/ 'Buailfar cath i gCéim an Fhia agus marófar ann fear nár rugag riamh': Barra Ó Laeire, who was born by caesarean section was killed in the fight, and the prophecy therefore was deemed true (Ó Tuairisg 2009; Ní Shíocháin 2012: 250). Another prophecy was supposedly from the mouth of a local priest, Diarmaid Ó hUallacháin, who was saying mass as battle raged, and who at one point said: 'No more of our people will be killed today but those who are already dead'/ 'A dhaoine, ní marófar a thille dár muíntir iniubh, ach pé méid atá marbh fé láthair' (Ní Shíocháin 2012: 250). Furthermore, Diarmuid 'ac Coitir (1880–1959), a storyteller of note and song composer who was born in Ballingeary, recounted his grandmother's memory of the Battle of Keimaneigh to the Irish Folklore Commission. She was but a few years old when one day in the absence of her father, her mother and another woman got down on their knees praying, while she was left to her own devices in the cabbage patch, but recalls a red hue coming over their faces, which is a possible reference to the red sky of apocalypse: 'Do mheas sí go raibh a gcnitheàcha dearg nú a' féachaint dearg'/ 'She thought their faces were red or looked red' (Ó Tuairisg 2009; Ní Shíocháin 2012: 252). Prophecy was an integral part of the oral tradition of the Irish-speaking community, and it is clear that the supernatural prophetic connotations of the battle were still alive when Diarmuid 'ac Coitir was visited by folklore collectors in 1959. Because of the cultural beliefs that proliferated among the Irish-speaking population in the 1820s, in which otherworldly truth in the form of prophecy was both a time-honoured trope and contemporary belief, the medium through which Máire Bhuí expressed her political vision could scarcely have been more appropriate or effective. Indeed, there is evidence to suggest that Máire Bhuí's song-making was very much the thorn in the side of the infamous James Barry, who featured so prominently in the Battle of Keimaneigh, of whom Ó Donnchú, collector and editor of local lore on Máire Bhuí and the battle, said: 'They say the raison d'être of the battle was that Barry was roused by the song of Máire Bhuidhe' (Ó Donnchú 2012 [1917]: 38–39). By this account the songstress was the formidable enemy of the local authorities to the point that her radical verse-making went so far as to provoke an armed response! Whatever the ins and outs of this clear animosity between Barry and Máire Bhuí and her family, this particular piece of local lore certainly suggests that Máire Bhuí was in the thick of anticolonial agitation and had a prominent role, though perhaps not one from within the Rockite organization in the strict sense.

Singing Prophecy: Máire Bhuí as a Radical Visionary

Of all Máire Bhuí's songs, 'Cath Chéim an Fhia' is perhaps most easily identifiable with the contemporary agrarian political movement itself, and, indeed, though transmitted orally from 1822 in various multiforms, it recounts with striking accuracy the events of the day and correlates with contemporary newspapers and other written accounts (Katsuta 2003: 282–85; Donnelly 2009: 68–69). However, a number of other songs also deserve our attention if we are to attempt to understand the radical millenarian vision espoused by the song poet. In all her songs, Máire Bhuí draws heavily on the paradigms, themes and formulae of oral culture. In this sense, her work is not 'schismatic', her radicalism does not openly profess a sudden break with tradition, unlike her educated English-speaking male counterparts in the United Irishmen (Whelan 1996: 61; Ó Giolláin 2000: 11). Though her songs are borne of the immediacy of crisis and speak of a radical future, they echo richly of the past and of tradition: from former rebellions to the saviour over the seas, to the formulaic classical allusions of the spéirbhean motif. In this sense, it could be argued that Máire Bhuí achieved what few literate political thinkers could boast in imbuing the 'new' Jacobin politics of crisis with the timelessness of the oral tradition and with the emotive resonance of collective memory. Máire Bhuí's vision is one of extreme violence and revolt – but ultimately is not one of schism, but one of imagined continuity and renewal.

The politics of power feature largely in her songs, and her portrayal of the stark contrast between rich and poor is intense. Though she can be compared to the United Irishmen in her politicization of poverty, Máire Bhuí does more than merely recount radical concepts that seeped into the oral tradition through the reading aloud of newspapers and other publications. Máire Bhuí speaks from within the colonial experience and produces a penetrating depiction of the plight of the colonized and the injustice of the colonial system as she sees it. The prophetic 'Tá Gaeil Bhocht' Cráite' / 'Poor Gaels Are Tormented', which was composed in the aftermath of the Battle of Keimaneigh and recounts the reprisals of hangings and transportation that took place soon after, epitomizes this politicization of poverty and of the colonial experience:

> Tá Gaeil bhocht' cráite go céasta cásmhar
> agus cúirt gach lá orthu mar dhúbailt bróin,

clanna sáirfhear dá gcrocha i n-áirde
's dá gcur síos láithreach sa *chroppy-hole,*
tá na loingeas lán díobh dá gcur thar sáile,
mo chú go brách sibh faoi iomad *yoke* …
          (Ní Shíocháin 2012: 226)

[Poor Gaels are tormented, troubled and in sorry plight
and court every day upon them as a double sorrow,
sons of fine men being strung up (hanged)
and being thrown immediately into the croppy-hole,
the ships are full of them being transported overseas,
my eternal sorrow that you are under the yoke …]

The law that criminalizes and punishes the Rockites is here problematized and represented as inherently unjust. Everything is wrong with the status quo of the colony – men of fine families are being hanged and not even afforded the dignity of a proper funeral or burial; instead they are thrown into the croppy-hole, a mass rebel grave, again echoing of the fate of the revolutionaries of the United Irish Rebellion. Indeed, the use of English words here, croppy-hole and yoke, indicate an interaction between Irish-speaking and English-speaking political discourses, and the ebb and flow between the oral tradition and the reading aloud of printed sources that was associated with the 1790s. Máire Bhuí's response to this tragedy of reprisals against her community in which local men are being killed and transported in retribution for the Rockite rebellion is to prophesize of an ever bloody uprising:

Is é ' chuala ó fháigibh go nduairt Naomh Seán linn
go raibh deire an cháirde caite leó,
's go dtiocfadh *slaughter* ar gach piara másach
nár ghéill don Pháis is do chaith an phóit;
aon chaonaí fánach ná túrfar bás do
ag iompar mála agus é 'na dhóid,
's gan déirc sa láimh sin a thúrfadh náid do
ach buala is cáine dá mbrú go deó.
          (Ní Shíocháin 2012: 226)

[What I heard from prophets is that St. John has told us
that their time is up,
and that slaughter will befall every fat-arsed peer
who didn't submit to the Passion and who engaged in drunken excesses;
any poor wandering loner that isn't given death
while he carries nothing but a bag in his fist,

and with no charity in that hand that would bestow him nought,
but beating and disparagement forever pressing on him.]

The prophecies of John are referred to here by Máire Bhuí in her attack on the nobility, with their well-fed figures and false authority. Again these printed prophecies that have made their way into the popular oral tradition are being sung by Máire Bhuí as predicting the fall of the gentry, much like the re-creation of the meaning of Pastorini's prophecy. The poet marries the imminent doom that is to befall the ruling classes to the mistreatment of the poor by the wealthy – that the destitute receive neither pity nor charity but instead have to endure unending degradation and oppression. This ultimately spurs Máire Bhuí to profess of a time fast approaching in which the colonial system as they know it will be upended:

> Is an bhliain seo atá againn 'sea ' bheig rírá againn
> tar éis búir do thnátha is do charta i ngleó;
> beig tínte cnâ againn ar na mullaíbh árda
> agus adharc le háthas ag seinm ceóil;
> mná agus páistí go mbeid dá dtnátha
> is le clochaibh an bháin 'sea do leagfaid póirc
> is le leônú an Árdmhic go dtitfid lánlag
> chô tiubh le báistig ar chnoc lá ceóig.
>   (Ní Shíocháin 2012: 226)

> [And this coming year we will have uproar
> having exhausted and cleared out boors in noisy battle;
> we will have bonfires on high summits
> and the horn joyfully playing music;
> women and children will wear them down
> and with the rocks of the plain they will defeat swine,
> with the permission of the High-son that they will fall full-weak
> as thick as rain on a hill on a misty day.]

The levelling impulse of liminal millenarianism is here felt with the melting of distinctions of gender and status within the community – that the women and children will also join the fray and beat down the oppressor with the rocks of the plain. Máire Bhuí's vision of the revolution is ruthlessly violent and punishing – but adheres to the foundational principle of the will of the people and the undeniable authority of the community. Though she invokes a higher power that will be instrumental in bringing about the day of reckoning, in the mortal world it is the ordinary people who will take the mantle of power unto themselves:

Tá mo shúil lem Mháistir gur geárr an cáirde
go bhfeiceam lá orthu agus tamall spóirt,
is go mbeid dá dtnátha gan chúirt gan stáitse
gan fallaí bána gan fíon gan beóir;
                        (Ní Shíocháin 2012: 227)

[My hope is with my Master that it will not be long now
'til we shall see the day and have sport at their expense,
and that they will be ground down without court without stage
without white walls without wine without beer;]

It is to be noted, also, that the concept of 'gan chúirt gan stáitse' ('without court without stage'), which can be considered to be the articulation both of a rejection of the laws of official colonial culture and the establishment of the ultimate authority of the people themselves, can be identified as a compositional formula in the poet's work, as we find in the related 'ní iarrfam cúirt ná stáitse'/ 'we will seek neither court nor stage' in 'The Battle of Keimaneigh'. The formula being rooted in 'a given essential idea' as described by Lord is of particular interest here when we see that the essential idea was a radical Jacobin idea of the will of the people as sovereign. Rather than view oral composition as hopelessly clichéd or stagnant, therefore, we see that the very foundation of oral composition, the formula, can act as a medium through which contemporary ideas can be generated. Likewise, the formulaic 'hallaí bána'/ 'white halls' and 'fíon ná beóir'/ 'wine nor beer' serve to denigrate the opulence of the ruling classes, a key symbolic element of Máire Bhuí's political vision, as previously mentioned. In 'A Mháir' Ní Laeire', which she co-composed with contemporary song poet Donncha Bán Ó Luínse, but which was primarily composed by Máire Bhuí, the traditional formula of the white halls of the ruling classes is again contrasted with the plight of those who are saddled with oppressive rents and taxes:

Tá dram an áil seo go céasta cráite
'ge cíos 'us cáin á dtúrna,
'gus búir go táchtmhar in allaí bána
'gus deire ' gcáirde túrtha.
                        (Ní Shíocháin 2012: 220)

[Our people are tormented and troubled
by rent and tax which defeat them,
and boors (self-)importantly in white halls
and their time is running out.]

Thus traditional formulaic composition, including all its intricacies of formula creation and re-creation, can be seen as enabling the emergence of a radical contemporary political vision of immediate relevance. This central theme of class conflict, of the problematization of the status and wealth of the gentry and the destitution of the poor is central to many of Máire Bhuí's visionary prophetical tracts. In the following prophetical excerpt from 'A Mháir' Ní Laeire' we are told of a people's violent revolt in which the subduing and silencing of hounds and beagles, core symbols of the Anglophone aristocracy, is key to her millenarian vision:

> Beig stealla p'léar agus pící géara
> dhá gcur 'na méadail bhrúidig,
> beig cloch 'us craobh orthu ó láimh gach éinne
> 'gus mùllacht Dé ar a' gcúmplacht;
> beid siad faonlag fí spalla gréine
> gan neach sa tsaol 'na gcúram,
> a gcuin 's a mbéagles 's a gcapaill traocht[a]
> gan dúil i ngéim ná ' liú 'co.
>   (Ní Shíocháin 2012: 220)

> [There will be pelting of bullets and sharp pikes
> being driven through their brutish paunches,
> a stone and branch down upon them from every hand
> and God's curse upon the company;
> they will be exhausted and weak under scorching sun
> with no one in the world to care for them,
> their hounds and beagles and horses will be exhausted
> with no desire for game or shout.]

The times that the poet sees fast approaching are of the downfall of the colonial rulers in which the fate of the aristocracy will be the inverse of their real-life status: they will lose it all, totally enweakened and abandoned, and the everyday markers of their dominance such as their hunting dogs will be mute. Indeed, they will get a taste of the sheer destitution experienced by the real-life poor. Through her weaving of these themes of illegitimate authority, injustice, poverty and suffering with a millenarian vision of supernatural intervention, Máire Bhuí forges political concepts that resonate with *lived experience*. Thus the poet communicates an incredible immediacy to her politics: she does not merely peddle abstract political ideals of equity, but forges her politics from the grim reality of life for the rural poor. Though her songs echo of the tropes of the older Jacobite struggle, it is newer anticolonial politics she sings. She communicates through the traditional idiom of oral formulaic song, thus generating ideas that are borne of tradition at the same time as heralding a new future. Thus the politics that Máire Bhuí sings are as much the politics of identity as they are the politics of revolt. Oral formulaic composition, though strongly echoic and resonant, is inherently re-creative and regenerative. It is this regenerative dynamic that serves the visionary song composition of Máire Bhuí so well in rooting violent radicalism so deeply within the shared identity of the community and in the naturalization of a radicalized collective narrative, enabling the radicalism she sung not only to be a major formative force, but to become a core paradigm that would persist through the generations.

Identity and the Aesthetics of Orality: New Ideas and the Narrative of Belonging

As we have seen, Máire Bhuí practised a style of composition that drew heavily on common formulas and themes. The compositional craft she mastered was acquired by ear and honed through exposure to songs and verse composed by others and transmitted orally in the community. The poet-composer is therefore inextricably linked to both the practices of the wider community of poets and of generations of singers. This traditional 'intertextuality' defies many of our most cherished modern literary concepts of 'author' and 'original'. As Albert Lord once put it, 'In a traditional poem, therefore, there is a pull in two directions: one is toward the song being sung and the other is toward the previous uses of the same theme' (1960: 94). The sometimes schismatic originality associated with literary endeavours, therefore, is not usually a hallmark of oral poets. With Máire Bhuí, though she had a definite style of her own, she composed songs that were richly echoic of a time-honoured tradition, and she spoke from within that tradition. In a period of great change in Europe in the aftermath of the French revolution, and with historical discourse being awash with the great literate Enlightenment thinkers of the age, it would be easy to discount the traditional arts or to assume that a compositional approach that was based on common formulas and themes could not have the capacity to engage with 'serious' political thought. Perhaps one would assume that a literate author who would consciously defy tradition and boldly go forth into a brave new world would be the vital thinker in a liminal period of transition. However, in doing so, one would be seriously underestimating the cultural authority of the oral tradition and the centrality of song performance to intellectual life more generally. I argue that it is precisely the echoic and traditional character of Máire Bhuí's songs that made them such a potent medium for the development of anticolonial thought, and that the ecstatic liminal space that song performed would enable new ideas to be reconfigured as integral to the identity of the community. Though some Irish scholars consider the Irish-language poetic tradition of the nineteenth century to have been a dying tradition full of 'hackneyed' themes no longer relevant,[4] the work of Máire Bhuí shows the absolute vibrancy and contemporary relevance of the oral tradition. Máire Bhuí practised a method of composition that created the old anew (Foley 1991: 57). It was this re-creative dynamic that enabled the generation of new forms of thought, through concepts that could be almost seamlessly introduced to the poetic idiom.

Máire Bhuí's poetic play on identity is explicit in the use of strong we-images (Elias 1994) in her songs, and through the castigation of the colonial oppressors, the 'other', which clearly distinguish Máire Bhuí's audience from powerful English-speaking society. Derogatory and sectarian insults against the English-speaking ruling classes abound, for example: 'Galla-phuic' / 'Foreign pucks', 'Fanatics', 'an t-ál so Chailbhin choîthig'/ 'this clan of foreign Calvin', 'búir'/ 'boors', 'na póirc'/ 'the swine', 'buín a' Bhéarla' / 'the English-speaking crew', 'buín na mbolg mór' / 'the crew of the big bellies', which serve to demarcate and perform boundaries of identity between the indigenous and the colonizer, between Catholic and Protestant, between Irish-speakers and English-speakers (Ní Shíocháin 2012: 75). However, her play on identity is also implicit in the way she employs echoes of former rebellions to create a meaningful contemporary radical impulse, as previously discussed, but also in her handling of traditional themes and formulas, through which she naturalizes some of her most radical concepts. The idea that oral formulaic composition cannot create 'new' concepts is wrong, though these 'new' ideas may appear to be deeply embedded in the tradition. The most salient example of this is the song poet's articulation of the traditional aisling theme. Though she does not depart from the premise of the theme as a compositional trope – the poet is alone set apart from society and the spéirbhean appears and speaks of the political fortunes of Ireland and of a saviour who will come from over the seas – the message of the aisling has changed and is now radicalized. In one of her aisling compositions 'Maidean Álainn Ghréine', for example, the song begins in a most traditional manner with the usual evocative description of the beauty of the spéirbhean, including hair so long that it sweeps the dew off the grass, and finishes with a common formula often used to close a verse:

> Maidean álainn ghréine 'us me ar thaobh chnoc na buaile
> 'sea ' dhearcas cúileann mhaorga 's a bréid fliuch ón luachair;
> bhí gile 'us finne ' n-aonacht go gléineach 'na gruanna,
> d'fhúig sí m'íntinn léanmhar 's is baolach nách buan ' bhead –
>   'us gheóm arís a' crúiscín 'us bíodh sé lán.
>   (Ní Shíocháin 2012: 197)

> [One lovely sunny morning on the side of the booley hill
> I saw a stately fair maid whose braid was wet from the rushes;
> there was brightness and fairness combined radiantly in her cheeks,
> she left my mind sorrowful and I fear I may not last long –
>   and let us get the jug again and let it be full.]

In every respect there is a pull here towards previous uses of the same theme, as described by Lord, and when Máire Bhuí's aislingí are compared with the works of other poet-composers, such as Eoghan Rua Ó Súilleabháin, the commonality of sub-themes and related formulae becomes apparent (Ní Shíocháin 2013b). However, it is through the dialogue of the spéirbhean that we see the re-creation of the aisling tradition. Rather than predicting the return of the rightful king, she now speaks of the destruction of the ruling classes, albeit with the familiar formulaic close of verse:

> 'Beig Sasanaig á thnátha 'us ní cás liom a gcruatan,
> a dtithe geala bána go láidir á gcuardach,
> a leathaireacha geárrtha 'na gc'ráistíochaibh uaisle
> 'us siúlóig Gaeil go rábach ar a lán-chorpaibh muara' –
>   'us gheóm arís a' crúiscín 'us bíodh sé lán.
>   (Ní Shíocháin 2012: 197)

> ['Englishmen will be worn down and I care not their plight,
> their bright white houses will strongly be ransacked,
> the leathers in their noble carriages will be cut
> and Gaels will walk with gusto over their fat fulsome corpses' –
>   and let us get the jug again and let it be full.]

The prophetic overtones of the vision-poem remain just as strong, but the import of the prophecy has changed. The aisling now foretells of the overthrow of the landed classes and heralds a radical new dawn. This 'contemporaneity' of the oral tradition is also apparent in Nóra Ní Chonaill's version of 'Fáinnín Geal an Lae'/ 'The Dawning of the Day' by Máire Bhuí, in which references in the dialogue of the spéirbhean to the political campaign of Daniel O'Connell re-creates the saviour figure so strongly associated with the aisling paradigm. Though O'Connell is given the role of the rightful king, he is of course not a royal, but an educated politician trained in the legal profession: 'O'Connell clúmhail, plúr na bhflaith,/'tá a' d'iarr' ár gcirt a phlé'/ 'reputable O'Connell, flower of men, who is trying to negotiate our rights' (Ní Shíocháin 2012: 196). Be it anarchic anti-nobility rhetoric or contemporary references to politicians, when articulated through the rich echoic fabric of oral verse alongside mythical figures such as Céarnait, Helen and Venus these new elements become deeply embedded – enveloped, as it were, by traditional referentiality. O'Connell is depicted as having gone over seas (to the British Parliament, no doubt) and yet to return: 'do chua' sé 'núnn i gcúrsaí fear/agus slán go dtigig sé …'/ 'he went abroad for the causes of men/and may he return safely …' (Ní Shíocháin 2012: 196). This is just like the theme of exile and imminent return of the Jacobite pretender – but the political context has changed completely and hence the meaning and import of the saviour figure has also changed. In another of her aisling compositions, 'Go Moch Ruimh Lúra Phoébus' / 'Early Before Phoebus Shone', references to O'Connell as the great political saviour who could not be bought off show the response of the tradition to contemporary political culture. The spéirbhean tells us how she has suffered grave brutality at the hands of her oppressors until good tidings of 'an priúnsa fónta' / 'the good prince' came to her from England:

> 'dtí go bhfuaras scéal ó Shasana
> go raibh ministrí gan deachuithe
> agus na cléirig a chaimeadh dhóibh
> gur leagag iad i bpá;
> mo ghrá mo bhráthair Dónall, an priúnsa fónta nár breabag riamh,
> do dhein bóthar doilbh dóite go deó trína gcliabh.
> (CBÉ 47: 73–75, Ní Shíocháin 2012: 228–29)

> ['til I got word from England
> that ministers were without tithes
> and that the corruptly complicit clergy
> have been knocked in pay;
> my love to my brother, Daniel [O'Connell], the good prince who was never bribed
> but who forever burnt a desperate hole through their chests.]

This is no longer the world of kings, but of the murky dealings of politics and politicians with all its associated pitfalls of injustice and corruptibility. O'Connell is professed as the prince by the spéirbhean, but this is not the Jacobite prince we used to know, but a flesh and blood elected representative, and one who cannot be bribed. That a song poet practises old sovereignty traditions in her compositions, forms that once were central to the expression of Jacobite aspirations through poetry in the eighteenth century, does not mean that the meaning of the discourse itself is not capable of change, as we see here. Therefore, when saying that oral formulaic composition is inherently re-creative and echoic, it must be pointed out that this is true of meaning just as much as it is of structure. The sovereignty figure of the spéirbhean, which roots the poetic form of the aisling, remains central and evocative of a higher truth – but this higher truth speaks of a new political consciousness; one that echoes of a lost nobility but that professes the burgeoning identity of a colonized collective. As is typical of the aisling form, the spéirbhean is questioned as to who she is in another song of Máire Bhuí's, 'Maidean Mhoch ar Leabaig Bhuig', with the usual appendage of a formulaic list of famous mythological women, including Helen, Déirdre, Clíona, Aoibheall and Cuileann, but to which the spéirbhean replies that she is none of these women but rather a true 'native' of Iveleary:

> ní stuaire me do ghluais tar muir
> gur thúrnaig cath ná plé –

do *natives* chirt Íbh Laeire me
'us do shío'rach mhaithe Ghael …
(Ní Shíocháin 2012: 178)

[I am not a beautiful woman who moved over the sea
and caused battle or dispute –
I am of the rightful natives of Iveleary
and descended from Gaelic nobles …]

Here the otherworldly figure of the spéirbhean is still very much the royal sovereignty queen, but her identity is now with the indigenous people of the colony, even borrowing the English term 'natives' from contemporary colonial discourse, a term generally used when referring to the lowly multitudes (see Ó Laoire 2012: xxi–xxii). Here we see how both political discourses and identity are 'alive' through song, neither stagnant nor predetermined, but liquid and changeable, despite any appearance of unstinting continuity. This vibrant contemporary potentiality of the aisling theme is aptly described by Ó Buachalla:

> Irish Jacobite rhetoric does not constitute a received canon of derived themes which was passively transmitted from generation to generation, but rather a dynamic and vibrant discourse which could accommodate and respond to changing circumstances, both locally and nationally. (2003: 78)

The aisling is not an ossified form, therefore, but rather is an evocative paradigm that creates meaning out of the contemporary, despite its antiquity. Ó Crualaoich (1983, 1997) and Dunne (1998) also identify this contemporary relevance and re-creative potential of the aisling in the Irish tradition, with the most striking example perhaps being the re-creation of the aisling theme in Brian Merriman's humorous yet cutting poem 'Cúirt an Mheon Oíche', which challenges gender discourses and social norms at the end of the eighteenth century (Ó Murchú 1982). In Máire Bhuí's compositions, it is precisely the combination of this traditionality with the articulation of political ideas of acute contemporary relevance that makes song such an effective medium for thought. Rather than erudite political abstractions, therefore, we have radical ideas that feel like they are at the root of communal identity. The medium of song poetry, so meaningful in itself, is part of the message: these ideas are integral to who we are. The songs perform the story of these people, the narrative of 'us'; they perform the consciousness of the colonized. Indeed, for a people whose own nobility was dispossessed, whose systems of governance and learning were dismantled, the idea of a poetic tradition and shared past stretching back to antiquity would have given a sense of stability and continuity lacking from many other aspects of colonial existence. The very language of traditional poetry that was symbolic of that antiquity added a powerful force to the generation of new politics, or as Cohen argues, 'Myth confers "rightness" on a course of action by extending to it the sanctity which enshrouds tradition and lore. Mythological distance lends enchantment to an otherwise "murky contemporary view"' (1985: 99). These key ideas in Máire Bhuí's songs of the legitimate authority of the people, and the problematization of power and poverty, are given the sanctity and authority of the native poetic tradition. Traditional oral aesthetics 'confer rightness' upon radical thought as a response to colonial experience. These political ideas that engage with contemporary existence also emerge in other received themes employed by Máire Bhuí, such as her famous lullaby 'Seo Leó, ' Thoil' ('Seo Leó, My Darling'), which develops the traditional theme of promises to soothe a fretting infant, but which Máire Bhuí radicalizes by promising a millenarian uprising to the baby:

Ar a' mbliain seo chúinn beig búir fí bhrón
'us cathair 'us dún gan smúit gan cheó ...

Ná goil a thuille 'us ná ficim do dheóir,
mar beid siúd scriosta shara dtigig a' fôr,
beig a súile ' sile agus briste ar a nglór,
'us a gcóistí againne 'na ngliugaram spóirt;
agus seo leó, ' thoil, agus ná goil go fóill ...
           (Ní Shíocháin 2012: 207)

[Next year coming boors will be sorrowful
and city and fort will be without blemish without mist ...

Don't cry anymore and let me not see your tears,
for they will be destroyed before harvest-time,
their eyes will be weeping and their voices will be broken,
and we will make joyous wreckage of their coaches;
and seo leó, my darling, and don't cry yet ...]

In each articulation of these songs, we see how the traditional theme is elastic; it can be extended or shortened and still be wholly intact, and it can even develop new sub-themes (such as radical millenarian predictions as part of an old lullaby form in this case) without detracting from the integrity of the theme as 'traditional'. Máire Bhuí therefore both conserves the tradition and creates it anew, and this is key to her importance as a singer of ideas. For it is one thing for a new concept to emerge in public discourse at any given time, but it is another thing entirely for that concept to take off or to be incorporated with such ease into the shared identity of the community and to become part of the central ideas through which people interpret the world. It is thus that singing ideas constitutes a core formative force in the creation and performance of the colonized self. Traditionality, therefore, is not the enemy of thought, but its enabler. The oral tradition does not just echo of the old in a nostalgically pleasing way, but the echoic resonances of orality engage vibrantly with contemporary experience, ploughing new furrows in the development of ideas. The formula itself is essentially idea-based (Lord 1960), and thus oral formula-based composition is akin to oral idea-based composition. Oral composition is at once conservative and transformative, and traditional song is at its core a vehicle of thought.

Framing the Revolution: Performing Antistructure and the Vision of the Revolution through Song

The above analysis demonstrates, I believe, that the act of song composition involved re-creation not repetition, and that Máire Bhuí succeeded in creating anti-colonial ideas of acute contemporary relevance out of an age-old tradition. I have also argued that Máire Bhuí was a prophetic truth-teller imbued with the sacred authority of the traditional oral poet, a seer of communitas, a master of liminal performance. Tradition, in this instance, did not hinder developments in political ideas, but enabled them. I should stress, however, that I do not mean to suggest in any way that the work of Máire Bhuí marks a rupture with tradition; rather the re-creative ludic dynamic of oral formulaic composition is the very essence of traditionality, as is the liminal experience of performance itself. Indeed, it is time to return again to that all important moment of performance, that special space that is inaugurated by the combination of verse, rhyme and melody in the lives of people.

As demonstrated by the work of Ó Laoire and Ó Madagáin, singing was and is an intensely emotive experience in traditional Irish society. This deep transcendental experience of singing is also described by Becker (2004) in her theoreticization of 'deep listening' and trancing in different musical cultures, as previously mentioned. Song was, as has been argued, a moment of sheer potentiality with an almost sacred power to it. It created a powerful sense of communitas that had, as Turner described, something 'magical' about it: 'Subjectively there is in it the feeling of endless power' (1969: 139). Also striking in the work of Máire Bhuí is the sheer sense of immediacy she communicates, a true mark of a seer of communitas according to Turner (1969: 142). Because of the antistructure created by song, it was possible for these new ideas to come to the fore, and, arguably, the experience of communitas generated through singing was highly conducive to many of the proto-egalitarian concepts in the songs that were discussed earlier. Her verses abound with symbolic we-images (Elias 1994), as already discussed, and accounts of shared experience under colonial rule. It is not hard to imagine how the communitas of shared colonial experience combined with the communitas of the moment of song performance itself could be cathartic. Song, as a symbolically performed period of antistructure, just like a rite of transition, can be seen as a formative experience. Indeed, the egalitarian democratic concepts of the French Revolution are theorized by Turner and Thomassen as being experientially based, derivative of the levelling experience of the liminal dissolution of order and communitas during the Revolution, as Thomassen remarks: 'the slogans of the French Revolution might as well have been heard shouted by a cohort of Ndembu neophytes: liberty, equality, fraternity' (2014: 212). Similarly, Wydra argues that the 'social spirit of democratic communities' emerges in liminal transitions, a symbolic expression, as it were, of the communitas of liminality (2009: 89). As argued by both Wydra and Thomassen, liminality is a moment of becoming, a period of transformation of immediate relevance to our understanding of the anthropology of social and political revolutions. Liminality is where order is suspended, where the unthinkable can become a reality. A revolution is in itself a period of transition, therefore, of dissolution of order, during which time the ultimate outcome is unknown, as Thomassen outlines:

> Revolutions evidently represent clear-cut instances within the political history of liminal figurations: drastic moments in which previously existing structures crumble and collapse, where norms and hierarchies are turned upside down. (2014: 191)

Thomassen also discusses the importance of town squares as spaces that frame the social drama and ritualistic performance of the revolution, noting that anthropologists 'are keen to insist on the importance of the concrete spaces in which social action takes place, whether in the household, the village square, or political assemblies' (2014: 205). Here Thomassen argues that revolutions take on 'highly ritualized forms', often appropriating public places such as squares as their 'ritual stage' (2014: 207). I argue that song, though not a physical space like a square, or a room, is of equal importance in framing revolt. Song is a *symbolic* space where social action takes place; it is a symbolic space through which the experience of revolt, oppression and subversion are ritualized, much like the public spaces described by Thomassen. This ritualized framing of revolt, which also involves the generation of liminal communitas through singing, not only plays with the new emergent ideas of transition, but creates an important sense of the collective. Through song, not only do new ideas and forms emerge, but they become integral to collective identity also, a symbiosis that is particularly prominent in the songs of Máire Bhuí, as discussed. In her songs, the impetus to violent revolt is strongly woven to a strong sense of identity and shared history. Therefore, in the narrative of sustained colonial oppression articulated by Máire Bhuí – the strong anticolonial anti-authoritarian message she put forth, her concepts of the ultimate authority of the will of the people themselves, her outrage at social injustice, her distain for the nobility – in the liminal sphere of song, those same concepts would have a feeling of intense potentiality and possibility, of immediacy and truth, but also would themselves be imbued with an overwhelming sense of communitas. To sing, because of its liminal nature, is transformative, but it also reaffirms the collective bonds of the community. This sense of conviction and belief in the possibility of ending colonial rule through song echoes of Wydra's reading of the living political processes of liminal experience that are central to the contestation of authority and power:

> The radical reorientation of political purpose requires the mobilization in people's minds and hearts of a belief, if not of a cult, of the impossible. The crucial point is that models of authority often have invisible bonds tying its members together. (2009: 98)

It was through song that the 'invisible bonds' that tied the community together were socially performed, through the combined experience of the liminality of the singing occasion and the meaning of the words. Indeed, the legacy of the song 'Cath Chéim an Fhia' was indeed 'a cult of the impossible', in Wydra's terms, in which men with pikes would send armed British soldiers fleeing. The song in itself was a moment of becoming, a symbolic space that enabled the very idea of political change and mobilization. Song here is the crucial space that frames the experience of violent rebellion and generates the vision of the revolution. Much like a rite of transition enabling social death and rebirth, song enables a burgeoning political consciousness; it enables a new world image and political ethos (Weber 1948). Indeed it is in thinking and feeling as combined in the fulsome experience of song where its importance in the history of political thought lies, as Turner said of the power of liminal experience: 'persons will desire and feel as well as think, and their desires and feelings impregnate their thoughts and influence their intentions' (1982: 63). Song could generate and perpetuate the 'collective effervescence' that would be the driving force behind violent political activism (Thomassen 2014: 196). Indeed, it is likely that song itself could play a key role in transforming an ordinary member of the community into a radical who would either engage in violent rebellion or be part of a secret network that would shield those involved from the authorities. The liminality of song would be central to the very processes at play in the establishment of a new vision of legitimate authority. As a charismatic leader figure in the Rockite rebellion, who, as I have argued, moulded a radical millenarian vision through song, Máire Bhuí can be seen as similar to revolutionary leaders who produce foundational texts for the new order that emerges (Thomassen 2014: 196). This persuasive world image through song was one where the nobility were beyond neither blame nor retribution, in which the subjected and the poor were elevated, and in which the right of the community to pursue its own interest, despite the power of hierarchical colonial structures in the 'real world', would assume a sacred authority (Wydra 2009: 93). Thus Máire Bhuí's songs can be understood as what Thomassen terms the 'condensed symbolic struggle over the legitimate right to power' that is central to social revolutions (2014: 209).

From Generation to Generation to Regeneration: The Legacy of Ideas through Song

Máire Bhuí composed songs that were, as John Miles Foley (1991: 7) would say, 'explosively connotative' and deeply echoic of themes and formulas to which the song poet was exposed throughout her life. The 'old song', therefore, is foundational in the composition of a 'new song'; the creativity of the poet is deeply engaged with traditional paradigms and modes of expression. Máire Bhuí's compositions attest to the contemporaneity of the oral tradition, to the extraordinary cultural force that old echoes can have as part of singing experience as it relates to contemporary politics, and to the inherently regenerative dynamic of oral formulaic composition. The Irish tradition, as I have discussed elsewhere, distinguishes between song poet and singer, both of whom have a hand in the compositional process. We might describe the song poet as composer and the singer as re-composer, however there is much common ground between the two in that the singer re-composes using formulas and formulaic phrases, much like what the song poet does when composing 'anew' (Ní Shíocháin 2013b). Furthermore, much like the poet who composes in performance, the singer has a central role in creating the ecstatic context of song. I have argued for the importance of song as a liminal ludic space and the centrality of singing experience to play and the generation of new forms through oral composition; I now wish to turn to the import of singing old songs, even after the song poet who composed them has passed. For these formula-based ideas (or idea-based formulas) that are articulated by the poet continue to live through and be re-created by generations of singers. One might suppose that the singer who performs Máire Bhuí's songs during the time of political upheaval and agrarian disturbance she refers to may have experienced a particular immediacy in the political discourses they sang; however, what of the singer who sings of these events such as the Battle of Keimaneigh that have long passed? Why do they sing of the past? How do they hear the politics of song? And what happens when they sing?

The liminality of song creates what Turner termed 'the regenerative abyss of communitas', and this is not just confined to the initial moment of song-composition (1969: 139). The singer can also take on an ecstatic role in the community, much like our song poet, in performing the musico-poetical liminal juncture that gives a regenerative rhythm to human life. One such example is the famed Ballingeary singer, Cáit Ní Mhuimhneacháin (1918–1949), who was particularly known for her renditions of the songs of Máire Bhuí, but also for her extraordinary ability to perform and communicate the meaning of what she sung. Cáit Ní Mhuimhneacháin, though not the composer of the songs, makes an extraordinary impact upon the listener. Another such singer famed for his renditions of Máire Bhuí's songs is Pádraig Ó Tuama (1893–1968), best known as Peáití Thaidhg Pheig, born in Baile Mhic Íre but who lived most of his adult life in Cúil Aodha, a man also credited with the ability to cure animals, and who was also an active member of the Irish Volunteers (1916–1922) (Ó Tuama 2011). Similarly to Ní Mhuimhneacháin, it is his intense and engaging song performances that grip the listener and the community, and that create the regenerative antistructure of singing that gives meaning to political struggles. The singer creates the intense experience through which the 'old' political discourses of Máire Bhuí feel to the listener as being of deep significance, even at over one hundred years' remove from the political milieu of the composer, even after the former colony has established its independence. The singer is therefore central to the legacy of ideas through song, for the singer performs ideas that create an 'image of the world', in Weberian terms, that determines the route of both ideas and political action that the individual and the community may take. Indeed, this is much like what happens even during Máire Bhuí's own lifetime, when her songs rip through the Irish-speaking countryside from singer to singer. It was this deeply rooted tradition of song transmission and performance that both Peáití Thaidhg Pheig and Cáit Ní Mhuimhneacháin inherited from generations of singers before them who sung the songs of Máire Bhuí.

Song demarcates an important time outside of ordinary time, a period of antistructure that regenerates meaning; the moment a song is sung, something happens. Song, even old song, will still semiotically perform the essential vitality of 'truth' and create an experience of some kind of higher meaning. Indeed, the demand for hearing certain songs again and again and again is characteristic of a certain search for 'experience', of a desire to relive the penetrating experience of song. 'Cath Chéim an Fhia' ('The Battle of Keimaneigh') is one such song, which, even in contemporary Irish-speaking Cork, is requested repeatedly, and in my experience, one which never fails in intensity or emotional resonance. Both contemporary and historical ethnographic accounts of the Irish-language singing tradition speak of the ecstatic and highly emotive (almost sacred) tenor of song performance and reception (Ó Madagáin 1985; Ó Laoire 2002). Thus the singer, hugely invested in the song being sung, has the task of conveying with intensity and conviction what the song means. It is in this ecstatic context that song performs the very ideas by which the contemporary interprets the world. Thus the ideas of song are ideas of ecstasis – rather than ideas of cold rationality. The ideas of song are experiential ideas, ideas that you feel as well as think. Steve Coleman theorizes this experience of singing of events past as 'if we are momentarily thrown into the actual events themselves through the magic verisimilitude of sound' (2010: 28). This brings to mind the account of Ó hAnnracháin of an old man who sang a song entitled 'Cath Bhéal an Mhuighe Shalaigh' or 'The Battle of the Big Cross' for him in 1944, which recounted the defeat of the United Irish Rebellion near Clonakilty, Co. Cork, in 1798:

Bhí a lámh ar mo ghlúin aige, á fásgadh, uaireanta, nuair a deireadh sé cuid den chaint. Mheasfadh duine air gur le n-a linn féin do thuit sé amach agus go raibh aithne aige ar na daoine do thuit sa chath. (Ó hAnnracháin 1944: 289; Ó Madagáin 1985: 135)

[He had his hand on my knee, clenching at times, when he spoke. You would think that it was during his own time that the battle occurred and that he knew the people who were slain in battle personally.]

The 'semiotic nature of music itself', according to Coleman, is what makes it so compelling, and in which 'performances weave together fragments of "other times and places" – the persons and occasions of a piece's performance history as well as the multiple "stories" alluded to therein' (2010: 28). Song, though of long ago, is always of the 'now'. A song is always a liminal space where new meaning can emerge, where the boundaries of time itself can feel like they have temporarily disappeared. This is how it is to this day when 'Cath Chéim an Fhia' is sung in the Muskerry Gaeltacht. Though it was composed almost two hundred years ago, there is an incredible immediacy felt when it is sung as though, like Coleman describes, one has been *projected into the scene* that song represents' (2010: 26). And of all the 'big' songs in the repertoire of Muskerry singers, 'Cath Chéim an Fhia' feels like the biggest of them all: when it is sung, time stands still, and singers and listeners become completely immersed in the air and words and meaning of the song performance. Henry Glassie argues that in song 'timeless meanings matter more than temporal sequences' and it is those 'timeless meanings' in the songs of Máire Bhuí that the singer seeks out, and it is those timeless meanings that can excite, energize and impassion the community not just in the direct aftermath of the Battle of Keimaneigh in 1822, but during subsequent revolutionary periods, and later as part of the burgeoning postcolonial state in Ireland, all the way through to the present day. In his study of 'The Swad Chapel Song', Glassie argues that song 'reverses the norms of academic history, being spatially precise, and temporally vague' (2012: 205). This particular spatial quality of song, which for Glassie is 'tight about space, loose about time' is what creates the sheer sense of 'up close and personal' relevance of the song for the listeners: 'Dates distance people from events, but exact locations drive events into insistent relevance. This happened here, right now, where tonight we are hearing and singing this song' (2012: 205). This idea of 'old song' as generative of deeply felt meaning is further supported by Nagy's theoreticization of the concept 'mimesis', which he takes in the word's archaic meaning of 'to re-enact' or 'to re-produce' in his study of Archaic Greek Sympotic Songs (2004: 27). Nagy understands the 'I' of song to be 'not so much a historical I but a re-enacting I', suggesting that song performance constitutes a re-enactment of meaning (2004: 27), an imagining of the historical in terms of the present in the ritual context of performance (2004: 31). The mimesis of song, not in the sense of copying, but in the sense of re-enacting, meant that the subject of song could be relived. This idea of the subject of song, even something that happened long ago, as being reborn in the present through song, also relates to the formulations of both Coleman and Glassie on the contemporary moment of meaning generated through singing old songs, and also Ramey's conceptualization of the 'perpetual present moment' of oral performance and re-creative transmission that 'operates within a timeframe that is uniquely present' (2012: 450). The 'perpetual present moment' of Ramey's Caedmon's Hymn and the 'mimetic I' of Nagy's sympotic songs can equally be applied to traditional song in modern Irish society – that song enabled the past to be framed in an intensely contemporary way. The mimesis of song means that song is not just commemorative, but flows into and animates the present moment. The 'mimetic I' in singing the anticolonial ideas of Máire Bhuí would involve a reliving of the experience of colonial subjection, of social injustice, of the delegitimization of imperialism and the legitimization of violent revolt, and of the sacred authority of 'the people'. This means that in the case of the songs of Máire Bhuí, their performance and reception long after the death of the poet could be central to the ideas that govern our lives and actions, that create our image of the world, and that act as a catalyst in political activism.

In the intervening period between Máire Bhuí's death and the Easter Rising of 1916, the particular ideas that she articulated continued to be sung and re-sung, and her songs continued to be in strong demand. The widespread circulation of her songs during the decades leading up to the 1916 rising and subsequently the Irish War of Independence is reflected in the collection of her songs by Crothúr 'ac Coitir from the end of the nineteenth century, the songs and lore collected by Fr. Ó Donnchú dated 1917, and also the transcription of songs from the living tradition, which were published in revivalist journals such as *Irisleabhar na Gaedhilge* (1896/7) and *An Claidheamh Soluis* (1915). It is therefore clear that her core concepts of the problematization of power and class, her distain and outrage at the opulence of the ruling classes, her scathing depiction of the illegitimacy of colonial rule, her belief in the legitimacy of the will of the people, her unyielding demand for the violent establishment of self-determination, and, perhaps most importantly, her representation of colonial subjection, continued to live on as part of an evolving tradition of anticolonial thought and action. In essence, she wrought political concepts from an experience of extreme marginalization and precarity that would continue to be sung. It was through song that these concepts became core ideas, central tenets of identity and deeply embedded cultural forms, just as Weber described the fate of the dynamic creative impulse of charisma, which ultimately will generate forms that become central to the structure of life:

> When the tide that lifted a charismatically led group out of everyday life flows back into the channels of workaday routines, at least the 'pure'

form of charismatic domination will wane and turn into an 'institution', it is then either mechanized, as it were, or imperceptibly displaced by other structures, or fused with them in the most diverse forms, so that it becomes a mere component of a concrete historical structure. (1978: 1121)

Therefore the ecstatic concepts of the powerful and the weak, of subjugation and subversion, of the mobilization of the people for the people, can eventually go beyond being newly radical, and become reaggregated into the very ideas we live by and take for granted. However, the radicalism of these ideas so thoroughly embroiled in the 'collective excitement produced by extraordinary events' of the 1820s would never wane entirely, not while song continued to create an ecstatic time outside of time through which those experiences could be relived (Weber 1978: 1119). Indeed, I believe that song was one such tide, described by Weber, that lifted a charismatically led group out of ordinary life and into the risky and precarious world of revolutionary thought and activity. However, perhaps song differs from other media of charismatic authority that melt imperceptibly into the status quo, in that a song that lives on has the capacity to reignite or reperform the charismatic moment, the experience of crisis past, with an intensity that can renew or reconfigure the contemporary. As Eisenstadt has argued, there is a symbiosis between the order-maintaining and order-transforming dynamics of culture such that the meaning of song performance maintains a fluidity that can reignite the potentiality of liminal experience.

We know little more of the reception of Máire Bhuí's songs since her death during the Famine, other than that they were in significant demand and to this day continue to form an integral part of the repertoire of major Cork singers, such as Nell Ní Chróinín, Iarla Ó Lionáird, Eilís Ní Shúilleabháin, Máire Ní Cheocháin, Eibhlís Uí Thuama, Áine Uí Chuill, and Máire Ní Chéilleachair, among others. We can deduce from that that Máire Bhuí's ideas continued to be sung because they meant something – they could have, like many other songs, merely melted away into oblivion. Her songs continued to engage the consciousness of the people long after her own demise. We also know that from the end of the nineteenth century Gaelic revivalists took a particular interest in collecting and editing the songs of Máire Bhuí for publication in Gaelic League journals, something that marked a notable politicization of the language movement, a development that its founder, Douglas Hyde, had sought to avoid. This attests not just to the popularity of the songs in the living tradition from which they were collected but also to how they now had a new relevance in politicizing the language movement among revivalists, many of whose mother tongue was English. It is worth noting that many of the men and women involved in the 1916 uprising were committed language activists and regular readers of *Irisleabhar na Gaedhilge* and *An Claidheamh Soluis*, and it is highly likely that they knew the songs of Máire Bhuí. Furthermore, the Muskerry Gaeltacht was a mecca of sorts for both cultural nationalists and republicans, with Máire Bhuí's home area of Ballingeary being visited by prominent republicans, such as Pádraig Pearse, Terence McSwiney and Liam Lynch (Ó hÉalaithe 2014: 69–73). Indeed, Piaras Béaslaí, who fought in the 1916 rising, was a prominent Gaelic Leaguer who frequently visited Ballingeary, where he would have undoubtedly been exposed to the work of Máire Bhuí through Siobhán an tSagairt (Ní Chróinín) and Diarmuid 'ac Coitir, two renowned oral practitioners and exemplars of the Cork dialect who had songs of Máire Bhuí in their repertoire, both of whom were central figures in the Irish language movement in Ballingeary at the time (Béaslaí 2010 [1953]: 11; Ó Cuív 1915). Not only do Máire Bhuí's songs continue to have a regenerative resonance in the living tradition, but as published texts form part of the public discourses that created the seedbed of contemporary radicalism. This is not surprising, of course, when one considers that song was an enduring cultural practice and vehicle of political engagement among young revolutionaries, and the British authorities were still confiscating seditious songs in English at this point, as documented by Moylan in his anthology of over 1,000 revolutionary songs from 1887–1926 (2016). Song was an integral part of revolutionary culture and discourse at that time. Indeed, it is interesting to compare some of the core concepts of Máire Bhuí with those of The Proclamation of the Irish Republic, most notably in arguing for the absolute authority of the will of the people, though Máire Bhuí, of course, does not broach the question of suffrage in her songs. The document of The Proclamation of the Irish Republic, much like the songs of Máire Bhuí, however, can be considered to be part of a visionary tradition that stands 'in the face of the world' (a term used both by Weber and the authors of the proclamation itself); it also conjures up a powerful we-image based upon an imagined collective narrative, much like what Máire Bhuí achieved through echoic oral verse; it draws heavily from old sovereignty traditions, but, like Máire Bhuí, imbues them with contemporary significance. Where in the songs of Máire Bhuí we have the otherworldly female sovereign, the spéirbhean, proclaiming the imminence of radical political change, The Proclamation of the Irish Republic evokes the image of Ireland as the female sovereign figure in whose name they rebel: 'In the name of God and of the dead generations from which she receives her old tradition of nationhood, Ireland, through us, summons her children to her flag and strikes for her freedom'. Where Máire Bhuí evokes the indisputable authority of the people themselves in 'beig talamh gan chíos gan íoc gan cháin is gan phlé' ('we will have land without rent without payment without tax and without dispute') and the more violent 'ní iarrfam cúirt ná stáitse, beig árdchroch 'na suí 'gainn' ('we will seek neither court nor stage, we will have a high hanging'), Pearse and his comrades 'declare the right of the people of Ireland to the ownership of Ireland and to the unfettered control of Irish destinies, to be sovereign and indefeasible'. Much like Máire Bhuí, who performs a penetrating narrative of sustained colonial oppression as a justification for violent revolt, the proclamation performs the legacy of colonial oppression that justifies the contemporary violent struggle:

> The long usurpation of that right by a foreign people and government has not extinguished the right, nor can it ever be extinguished except by the destruction of the Irish people. In every generation the Irish people have asserted their right to national freedom and sovereignty; six times during the past three hundred years they have asserted it in arms.

Máire Bhuí evoked both the older Jacobite conflict and the Jacobin figure of the Frenchman in her songs, and in doing so re-creates the contemporary as integral to the shared identity and history of the collective. The rebels of 1916 make a similar play on identity, evoking the generations who came before them who suffered under the yoke of British imperialism. Thus echoes of Máire Bhuí-style radicalism can be read in one of the most influential anticolonial documents of the twentieth century.

The commonality between the tenets of The Proclamation of the Irish Republic and the political discourses we find in the songs of Máire Bhuí is suggestive of the proliferation of the ideas of song in the anticolonial movement in post-Famine Ireland. Therefore, in the history of anticolonial thought, the very ideas sung by Máire Bhuí seem to be part of a larger development in the formation of the consciousness of the colonized. The Proclamation of the Irish Republic, indeed, though very much part of the literate English-language culture of the time, nonetheless seems to resonate with the visionary Irish-language tradition, and therefore draws not just on the rational Enlightenment tradition of thought, but on the ecstatic tradition of thought also, such as that practised by our song poet. We know that her songs continued to exist and be sung as part of the oral tradition proper in the twentieth century, but also to have another life also as part of the public sphere of urban radicalism. Though this is not to suggest a direct causality between the songs of Máire Bhuí and the Proclamation of the Irish Republic, it can be said that the songs of Máire Bhuí were in the ether, and were an important part of the web of ideas that informed anticolonial thought into the modern age. Indeed, the politics of the 1916 rebels, though resonant of the politics of the United Irish Movement, do not owe their radicalism to the literate men of 1798 alone. These young radicals, most notably Pádraig Pearse, who was steeped in the Irish-language literary and cultural traditions, sought to engage rather than break with the indigenous tradition (Ní Ghairbhí 2008: 164, 168; Morley 2011: 279–81). By the time we reach the beginning of the twentieth century, therefore, the we-image of the indigenous people and the Weberian 'world image' of the colonial self as told through song has become integral to anticolonial thought. The vision of the 1916 rising is one of heated parrhesiatic ecstasis, rather than one of cold calculation. It is a vision wherein the experience of 'truth' spurs political action, not dissimilar to the ecstatic nature of singing experience: thus, according to Yeats, a 'terrible beauty is born', a phrase connotative of the ecstatic and dangerous potentiality of the revolutionary moment.

Not only do we find discourses similar to those of Máire Bhuí in the public sphere of Irish republicanism in the early twentieth century, but also significant paramilitary activism in the countryside in which the Irish-language oral tradition still thrived, in the immediate catchment area for her songs. The areas in which Máire Bhuí's songs continued to be sung, from Ballingeary to Inchigeelagh to Baile Mhic Íre to Cúil Aodha, continued to be a hive of anticolonial resistance into the early twentieth century, with both active battalions of the Old IRA, branches of Cumann na mBan, as well as numerous safe houses for rebels on the run (Ó Súilleabháin 2013; Ó hÉalaithe 2014). It is interesting, for example, that the famed rebel leader in the Irish War of Independence, Jamie Moynihan (Séamus Ó Muimhneacháin) (1893–1970), was a native Irish speaker who grew up in Gort na Scairte, the same townland so often frequented in later years by the aforementioned singer Peaití Thaidhg Pheig, from the neighbouring townland of Ráth, and who is associated so closely with the song 'Cath Chéim an Fhia'. It is particularly interesting, for example, that this legendary Muskerry singer, who has been mentioned a number of times already, sung the two great revolutionary songs of Máire Bhuí that are most popular in the living tradition – 'Cath Chéim an Fhia' and 'A Mháir' Ní Laeire' – and was also an active member of the Irish Volunteers 1916–1921 (Ó Tuama 2011), and therefore undoubtedly was closely acquainted with Moynihan. Given where Moynihan was reared, therefore, he is highly likely to have been well acquainted with lore about Máire Bhuí and the Battle of Keimaneigh from home, but furthermore it is most probable that Moynihan himself was directly exposed to the poetic radicalism of Máire Bhuí through song, given that the renowned singer Peaití Thaidhg Pheig was literally a comrade in arms. When we consider A.M. Freeman's description of singing occasions in the Ballyvourney area at that time and the proliferation of song among inhabitants of the Irish-speaking districts (1920), it is not hard to imagine that the songs of Máire Bhuí could have been a feature of the lives of local members of the Irish Volunteers. It is highly likely, therefore, that the songs of Máire Bhuí continued to be part of the fabric of anticolonial radicalism through to the Irish War of Independence, not just among rebels, but among members of the community who put themselves at significant risk in providing safe houses.

The songs of Máire Bhuí not only told the story of anticolonial activism past, but, most importantly, legitimized violent resistance and delegitimized colonial authority. The 1916 rising was famously coined a rising of poets and playwrights. In Co. Cork the Irish War of Independence could also be seen as a rebellion of singers and Irish-language activists. Jamie Moynihan's father, Conchubhar, for example, was an active member of the Gaelic League, and contributed to revivalist publications such as *Fáinne an Lae* and *An Claidheamh Soluis* (www.ainm.ie), which were an integral part of the contemporary cultural nationalist movement, which was becoming increasingly radicalized. Indeed, Jamie Moynihan's own words illustrate the connection between the revivalist roots of anticolonial agitation in the period leading up to the Irish War of Independence in his remarks on the influence of Irish-language revivalist Dr Ó Loingsigh in Muskerry:

> There is little doubt that his example and inspiration started the gradual process of national and cultural reawakening in Baile Mhúirne that reached its peak in the Volunteer movement during the War of Independence, a period which produced over 300 Volunteers in our parish, 152 in Baile Mhúirne, 143 in Cúil Aodha and 24 full-time Cumann na mBan members, believed to be the highest number of Volunteers in any parish in Mid-Cork. (Ó hÉalaithe 2014: 19)

Likewise, the singer Cáit Ní Mhuimhneacháin's family were centrally involved in the revivalist movement, with her brother taking a particularly active role in revivalist print publications, and her father having been taught to read and write Irish by a collector of Máire Bhuí's songs, the schoolmaster Crothúr 'ac Coitir (www.ainm.ie). It is also interesting that former generations of the family of Cáit Ní Mhuimhneacháin, the great singer of the Máire Bhuí repertoire, initially hailed from the same Gort na Scairte of Jamie Moynihan, from a community that, generations before, had been involved in the Battle of Keimaneigh in 1822. It is highly significant, also, that many of the families who were involved in the Cúil na Cathrach ambush, which took place in February 1921 during the Irish War of Independence, were the same families that had fought in the Battle of Keimaneigh all those many years ago.[5] It is clear, therefore, that Máire Bhuí's songs continued to be of huge significance for the local community, and that the story of the Battle of Keimaneigh continued to figure large in the contemporary imagination. The songs that reached the ears of young Cáit Ní Mhuimhneacháin, who won the gold medal at Oireachtas na Gaeilge in 1942, had been sung by generations before her. The community had continued to sing of key ideas that problematized colonial power, such as 'is acu 'thá 'n tslat, is olc í ' riail'/ 'it is they who hold the cane, terrible is its rule'; ideas that castigated the opulence of the English-speaking ruling classes such as 'buín na mbolg mór' / 'that big bellied lot' in contrast with the sorry plight of the rural poor; ideas that targeted the nobility 'beig a leathaireacha geárrtha ina gc'ráistíochaibh uaisle'/ 'the leathers in their noble carriages will be cut'; ideas that spoke of the legitimization of the authority of the people themselves, and of violent uprising. Indeed, in the memoirs of old IRA member Mícheál Ó Súilleabháin, who was from Kilnamartyra, Máire Bhuí and the Battle of Keimaneigh are mentioned specifically in the introductory section in which he explains his rationale for engaging in armed revolt. The collective narrative of colonial oppression and successive attempts to overthrow colonial rule is central to the revolutionary rationale, as described by Ó Súilleabháin, and the Battle of Keimaneigh figures as an important part of the genealogy of colonial resistance that informed the contemporary revolutionary outlook: 'In the year 1822 our people took up arms again' (Ó Súilleabháin 2013: 18). It is evident that the songs of Máire Bhuí made no small impression on this particular revolutionary, and he goes into some detail in explaining the significance of the meaning of her song 'Cath Chéim an Fhia'/ 'The Battle of Keimaneigh':

> The heavy harmony of the cavalry and the general vibration of the whole army seemed to shake the mountain. The terror of the women and children as they ran from their homes bewailing the fate of their fathers, brothers and husbands who they thought would be encircled and whose utter destruction seemed imminent. The sight of other brave men hurrying to the scene to help their neighbours or die with them. The rolling volleys of musketry. The fierce charge with the steel of our men. The immediate break and utter rout of the well-equipped and numerically far superior enemy. The joy at the seemingly impossible victory. The praise for her great men of the Gael. The return of hope. The exhortation to stand firm with the good steel always ready. The vision of the day when Irishmen would be back in the good land of Ireland which they had had to yield. The final verse where she admitted harbouring a good deal of ill-feeling for the pot-bellied Planters. (2013: 20–21)

For Micheál Ó Súilleabháin, Máire Bhuí's concept of 'buín na mbolg mór'/ 'that big bellied crew' or 'pot-bellied Planters', which encapsulated a deep distain for the reckless opulence of the ruling classes while others go hungry, was foundational to his world view, and formed part of the web of ideas that informed political and paramilitary activism, and a narrative of oppressed Gaels overcoming the might of the empire through sheer bravery that resulted in 'the joy of a seemingly impossible victory' would inform the 'world image' that would fuel the contemporary revolutionary zeal of the 1920s. Indeed, he further elaborates on the inspirational presence of Máire Bhuí in his own hinterland, her influence on the men of previous generations and her compelling uncompromising anticolonial fervour, once again echoing the discourses of 'The Battle of Keimaneigh':

> Hers was no mere huckstering spirit that would recommend patience and politicians as a remote cure for Ireland's ills. The present was ever and always the time to deal with tyrants, she had declared. She did not want courts or other useless machinery for their trial, but a high gallows and a good rope. She counselled the young men to be always ready with service-

able pike and gun to meet the enemy. She exhorted them, over a hundred years ago, boldly to retake possession of the lands and homes of their ancestors. We understood how right she was. (Ó Súilleabháin 2013: 123)

The immediacy of Máire Bhuí's parrhesiastic voice, therefore, held sway long after her passing, and her anticolonial vision and 'world image' were of enduring significance. Indeed, in Jamie Moynihan's own words 'the Irish demand for independence was the result of British attempts to control, dominate and penalise our country, politically, socially, economically and culturally, over seven long centuries' (Ó hÉalaithe 2014: 19). These identity-laden political discourses of the colonized collective are much like Máire Bhuí's, bringing to mind her famous plea of 'sáigh isteach go dána in áitreabh a dtáinig róibh'/ 'boldly push in to the holdings that came before ye'. In many ways, 'Cath Chéim an Fhia' was the shout that resounded afar beyond its immediate context, recounting a battle that not only sparked a Rockite uprising in Cork in the 1820s, but also created a persuasive narrative of sustained oppression, injustice and shared history that would spur anticolonial paramilitarism for generations after. Integral to this anti-imperial narrative is the claim to the integrity and self-determination of the common man and woman found in both Moynihan's and Ó Súilleabháin's memoirs, in which the heroism of the ordinary Volunteer and Cumann na mBan member is celebrated. Indeed, this heroism of the ordinary people, akin to the bravery of David against Goliath, was sung of in Cath Chéim an Fhia, when despite the well-armed 'gárda a' teacht láidir 'na dtíompall'/ 'guard closing in strongly around them', the Rockite men arrive with pikes and against the odds get the upper hand on the authorities. It was the Bastille moment of the Rockite movement, and, as we see in the memoirs of Ó Súilleabháin, was still an important symbol of anticolonial resistance 100 years later when the people of Irish-speaking Muskerry took up arms in the Irish War of Independence.

There was a marked interest in Irish-language songs as part of the anticolonialist cultural nationalism that came to the fore from the end of the nineteenth century onwards. Though Máire Bhuí did not figure largely in the traditional scribal culture of the nineteenth century, her work enjoyed a new prominence as part of the cultural nationalist revival, not just as published texts, but as living song performances, which the young Gaelic League activists sought out in the their search for rediscovering authentic Gaelic culture. Her songs seemed to speak to the contemporary political situation; her songs performed the plight of the colonized and a long history of suffering and injustice, and seemed to meet the combined interest in Irish-speaking traditions and contemporary radical politics. Singing of a revolution past, even a revolution that had dissipated, as in the case of the Rockite uprising, would be an important part of the ideas that would spur future action and configure the identity of the community.

Notes

1. This analysis of the keen as a performance genre was later opposed by Breandán Ó Buachalla (1998); however, it is still generally accepted among scholars that the keen was a female oral formulaic tradition. See Nic an Airchinnigh (2013, 2010), Nic an Airchinnigh and Ó Laoire (2015), Nic Eoin (1998), Ní Shíocháin (2012).
2. See Ní Shíocháin 2013 for a comparative formulaic analysis of compositions ascribed to Eoghan Rua (song poet-scribe) and compositions of song poets Máire Bhuí and Diarmuid na Bolgaighe.
3. Charles Walmesley, whose pen name was Signor Pastorini, was a conservative English Catholic bishop, whose reading of the Book of Apocalypse was published in 1771 in his work entitled *The General History of the Christian Church from Her Birth to Her Final Triumphant State in Heaven, Chiefly Deduced from the Apocalypse of St. John the Apostle* (Scott 1985). It was a well-known text, excerpts from which were widely distributed in Ireland from the 1790s onwards. In the text, Pastorini predicts the downfall of Protestantism by the year 1825 and also the waning of Jacobinism by that same date. Scott argues that that distribution of the text in Ireland from the 1790s was 'undoubtedly encouraged, if not actually engineered, by the British government' (1985: 602) in an attempt to quell revolutionary fervour among the indigenous Irish because of the anti-radical leanings of the author. However, Pastorini's prophecy has been identified by historians as fuelling millenarian revolutionary aspirations in the 1820s (Donnelly 1983; Ó Ciosáin 1997: 192–97).
4. See Morley (2017) for a critical appraisal of this and related issues in Irish historical and literary scholarship over recent decades.
5. Local knowledge; see also Ó Súilleabháin (2013: 168–69).

Conclusion

Singing Ideas in Society
Experience, Song and 'Passing Through'

When Máire Bhuí Ní Laeire sung ideas of colonial subjection, social injustice, violent rebellion and self-determination in the first part of the nineteenth century, she was part of a maelstrom of political thinking that was generated by the liminal experience of dissolution of order throughout Europe from the French revolutionary period onwards (Thomassen 2014: 113–40, 191–214). Many of the thinkers we associate with that same period were literate men, who partook actively in official politics, such as Thomas Paine and Theobald Wolfe Tone. However, there were also other spheres in society where influential political ideas were coming to the fore, such as song and popular prophecy. The thought generated by these other media constitute an alternative history of ideas often overlooked by the mainstream. In the case of Máire Bhuí, song was the medium through which she articulated her ideas, much like her counterparts in Scotland and England, where songstresses and prophetesses were also responding to the socio-economic crises of the 1790s and 1820s (McCarthy 1990; McLane 2011). Unlike her male literate counterparts, however, Máire Bhuí's songs did not mark a rupture with tradition; they did not conjure up the image of a brave new world quite in the same sense, but rather were woven from the deeply echoic fabric of oral tradition. This is not to say that ideas such as 'talamh gan íoc gan chíos gan cháin is gan phlé' ('land without payment nor rent nor tax nor dispute') were not 'new' in indigenous Irish political discourse, but that the authority of tradition bestowed by the song form was an important part of their force. Likewise, Máire Bhuí's compelling 'is acu 'thá 'n tslat, is olc í ' riail' ('it is they who hold the cane, terrible is its rule') was a radical problematization of colonial power, and yet it was enabled by a most traditional song craft. In this sense, Máire Bhuí displays an incredible mastery of ideas, echoes, memory and evocation, even if the medium of traditional song composition does not conform to our usual conception of European intellectualism. In many ways, it is this very nonconformity when compared with the culture of mainstream literate thought that makes the ideas that were sung by such singers and song composers as Máire Bhuí so crucial to our formulation of the development of ideas in society. As Glassie has previously argued (2012), the traditions of vernacular intellectuals enable us to avoid an overly linear view of Western history, such as that described by Palmer in his summary of Jean Gebser's analysis of the modern mentalité:

> God places his blessing on the individualistic, competitive person (implicitly male) who exercises restraint and represses desires in the interest of more 'rational' goals: power and control … History perceived as a straight line that never circles back on itself, becomes the story of man's gradual self-improvement through the exercise of reason. (Palmer in Turner 1987: 73)

The work of Máire Bhuí is almost the opposite of such a linear 'rational' conceptualization of history as Palmer describes – not only was she a woman, but she certainly did not exercise restraint when singing of violent apocalyptic rebellion (e.g. 'go mbead á n-áireamh i bpollaíbh báite' ('I will be counting their dead bodies drowned in bog holes')) but rather was a master of ecstatic thought. She did not perform detachment, and she did not perform 'rationality' as a male literate thinker might. Furthermore, the force of her songs drew precisely on a history that 'circled back on itself', articulating a tapestry of echoes of former rebellions from Jacobite to Jacobin, of age-old sovereignty traditions, of old song airs, of received formulas and themes that would engage the collective imagination and social 'effervescence' of the community, rather than pursuing a trajectory of linear advancement and enlightenment favoured by literate political circles. Máire Bhuí eludes any clear-cut authorship, and is inextricably bound to the voices of the community who sung her songs and told stories of her for generations. Thus Máire Bhuí the 'author' cannot be compared to Thomas Paine the 'author'. And yet Máire Bhuí sung ideas that would have a lasting impact on anticolonial thought in Ireland, even though the very lifeblood of her history is borne of oral aesthetics and creativity and bordering on the mythical. In every respect the songs of Máire Bhuí pose a trouble all of their own to the story we tell of the past – in eluding 'easy' classification, in their inherent multivocality and in thus demanding of us that we reimagine the development of ideas historically. As Bruner has argued, there is an inherent advantage to studying such expressions of thought and experience among indigenous people:

> The anthropology of experience turns our attention to experience and its expression as indigenous meaning. The advantage of beginning the

study of culture through expressions is that the basic units of analysis are established by the people we study rather than by the anthropologist as alien observer. (1986: 9)

Therefore in studying the rich multivocal expressions of the Irish-language song and narrative traditions we are engaging with the interpretations of the community itself, the way in which they engaged with historical reality and experience and subsequently how they re-created their shared history and related it to their contemporary world. This is every bit as important as formulating history based on discernible 'fact'. Thus Bruner argues that 'the anthropology of experience sees people as active agents in the historical process who construct their own world' (1986: 12). This is precisely what I argue here in relation to the importance of song in the development of anticolonial thought: song was integral to the construction of a world image and of ideas that would inform the lives, thoughts and actions of ordinary people. I believe that this was the case with Máire Bhuí's immediate community during her own lifetime, when ordinary people chose to risk it all and take on the might of the British Empire, and also in subsequent generations; for example, in the modern Irish revolutionary period 1916–1922, when ordinary men and women cast themselves into the great uncertainty and personal risk of revolutionary activity.

Having argued that song performs a liminal ludic space, a time outside of ordinary time in society, and that song is inherently processual, not a mere text but utterly 'alive' in the moment of performance, I would like to return once again to the idea of song as 'an experience' in the Turnerian sense of 'passing through', a concept that has been further elaborated on by Szakolczai and Thomassen more recently. Turner has argued that the etymology of the word 'experience' indeed implies a 'passing through', and that experience itself is transitory and transformative. He also drew from the work of Wilhelm Dilthey who understood experience as 'thought structuring' (1976: 35), an analysis developed in later years by Arpad Szakolczai, who argued that 'the formative power of experience is inseparable from the formative power of thought' (2004: 82). Szakolczai further elaborates on the processual and transformative qualities of experience, through which identities and subjectivities are formed and reformed: 'Such identities are continuously in the process of formation and transformation, as life experiences generate fluid, liminal situations where the transformation of previous stabilities becomes possible' (2008: 28). Bruner also elaborated on the relationship between experience and expression in *The Anthropology of Experience,* which he co-edited with Turner, arguing that performance is *constitutive,* and that expressions 'are the people's articulations, formulations and representations of their own experience' (1986: 9). I believe there are two ways in which such a concept of experience is of relevance to our understanding of thinking and singing, as exemplified by the songs of Máire Bhuí. Firstly, Máire Bhuí's concepts are deeply *experiential,* drawing from the lived experience of existence under colonial rule. Her songs interpret and frame colonial experience; she gives expression to those experiences. Her political ideas through song are what Szakolczai would call 'experiential meanings' (2008). Just as Harald Wydra has argued for the liminal origins of democracy, the political ideas of Máire Bhuí are also borne of the liminality of colonial transformation and revolutionary turbulence, ideas that came into being during the profound antistructure of Irish life in the 1820s, ideas that would imagine a renewed society in which the poor would no longer have to endure the injustice, indignity and cruelty inflicted upon them by an uncaring nobility. Therefore ideas of the inherent injustice of poverty in contrast with wealth, such as 'Tá dram an áil seo go céasta cráite 'ge cíos 'us cáin á dtúrna, 'gus búir go táchtmhar in allaí bána …' ('Our people are tormented and troubled by rent and tax which defeat them/ and boors (self)importantly in white halls'); ideas of the inversion of power in society and derivative concepts of the authority of the people themselves, such as 'beig a súile ' sile agus briste ar a nglór,/ 'us a gcóistí againne 'na ngliugaram spóirt' ('their eyes will be weeping and their voices broken/ and we will make joyous wreckage of their coaches') and 'ní iarrfam cúirt ná stáitse, beig árd-chroch 'na suí 'gainn' ('We will seek neither court nor stage, we will have a high hanging'), or the levelling impulse of 'mná agus páistí go mbeid dá dtnátha is le clochaibh an bháin 'sea do leagfaid póirc' ('women and children will be wearing them down and with the rocks of the plane they will defeat swine'), are borne of the transformative passing through of lived experience. Likewise, the compelling prophetic justification of merciless anticolonial revolt in the following verse from 'A Mháir' Ní Laeire', which attacks symbols of wealth and nobility, but also incorporates a graphic image of a mass grave, an image rooted in real-life reprisals for revolutionary activity, must be understood as a discourse not only that resonated with the lived experience of the community but that was also *re-experienced* through singing:

> Tá mo shúil lem Mháistir gur geárr an cáirde
> go bhfeiceam lá orthu agus tamall spóirt,
> is go mbeid á dtnátha gan chúirt gan stáitse
> gan fallaí bána gan fíon gan beóir;
> go mbeig na mílthe lánphoc i n-aon pholl amháin acu
> ar a dtárr i n-áirde gan chloch gan fód,
> agus Gaeil ar chlár glan ag ól mo shláinte
> is me féinig láithreach dá chnaga leó.
>   (Ní Shíocháin 2012: 227)

[My hope is with my Master that it will not be long now
'til we shall see the day and have sport at their expense,
and that they will be ground down without court without stage
without white halls without wine without beer;

that thousands of those fat pucks will be in one hole
face down without stone nor sod,
and Gaels at a clean counter drinking my health
and I in the middle of them knocking it back.]

These political ideas smack of the 'free for all' of the liminal axial moment – of that time of change, where 'anything goes', where the powerful are in danger of losing it all and established hierarchies of power can be reversed. This 'power reversal' synonymous with liminality and transition is strongly felt in the words of Máire Bhuí – for in reality Máire Bhuí never saw nobles thrown with indignity into mass graves, but she did see the indigenous Irish meet such a fate, as is evident in her reference to the 'croppy-hole'. Her image of such brutality to be meted upon the ruling classes is a mirror image of the mistreatment of the rural Irish-speaking poor at the hands of the authorities. Here, experience, which Szakolczai would term 'a dangerous passage', is articulated in the songs of Máire Bhuí, and it is through this 'passing through' of experience that the subject and the community construct new identities and new ways of seeing the world. Song ritualizes this 'passing through' of colonial experience, creating meaning out of crisis.

Though we can see how Máire Bhuí's political concepts are also articulations of shared colonial experience, those same concepts frame the experience of colonization for the community. As Bruner writes, 'that experience structures expressions and expressions structure experience was for Dilthey a hermeneutic cycle ...' (1986: 6). The song 'Cath Chéim an Fhia', for example, recounts the tale of the battle, imbued with an anti-authoritarian radicalism borne of colonial subjection, as previously discussed. In turn, the song constructs the meaning of the battle itself, making meaning out of the conflict that would be sung and re-sung for generations. 'Cath Chéim an Fhia' performs the meaning of the battle, performs prophecy, performs identity, performs the impetus for the Rockite movement and indeed performs the rationale for sustained anticolonial activity over generations: 'It is in the performance of an expression that we re-experience, re-live, re-create, re-tell, re-construct and re-fashion our culture' (Bruner 1986: 11). Singing ideas, therefore, is akin to what Turner would term 'socio-processual thought' (1987: 97): song was literally 'history in the making', the very site in which ideas and identity would come into being.

Secondly, the concept of experience as developed by Turner, inspired by Dilthey, also tells us much of the importance of singing experience. Rather than being a mere text, song can also be considered to be a ritualized 'passing through'. Not only is song a form of 'cultural subjunctivity', where everything trembles in the balance, where 'the low are exalted and the mighty abased', from which a new radicalism can emerge, but much like a transition rite, song has the capacity to create the subject and the world anew. Song, through the enactment of the liminal play sphere, also can enact new forms of post-liminal existence, of new ways of seeing and being in real life. For it is this genesis and rebirth that is the essence and raison d'etre of liminality. For the contemporaries of Máire Bhuí, this means that song could enact a 'passing through' for the subject: from an ordinary member of society to a rural radical, from a rural community to a colonized collective conscious of oppression and injustice, now in 'fanatical pursuit of the millennium'. Singing the songs of Máire Bhuí was potentially transformative in creating a new politicized image of the world, in performing the oppressed colonial subject, and inaugurating a collective that seeks emancipation through violent means. Singing songs verges on the terror trembling of 'the experience of the sacred' (Turner in Szakolczai 2008: 14), and in itself constitutes a full-bodied formative experience. The importance of the highly charged liminal experience of singing goes beyond the immediate contemporary setting, however, and song can also be seen as performing liminal antistructure to great effect long after the times told of through the songs are long past, in such a way that the transformative dynamic of song carries on through the generations. Similar to Nagy's conceptualization of the mimetic 'I' in singing, for Dilthey, understanding involved 'a rediscovery of the I in Thou' (1976: 208). Integral to such understanding was the process of *re-experiencing,* that involved the 'projection of the self into some given expression', in this case, song (1976: 226). This empathy through reliving and re-experiencing was integral to the generation of thought for Dilthey, and is epitomized by the communitas of singing experience. Though the reality of colonized life for the marginalized rural poor was, in Dilthey's terms, an experience that transformed the meaning of the world, similarly singing was also an experience that was integral to the birth of new ideas and the rebirth and renewal of collective identity during a time of intense uncertainty and upheaval. These ideas and images were experienced through singing, and in that sense the formation of thought is inseparable from the formative power of song performance.

When theorizing the experience of song performance, therefore, orality again poses a challenge to our own construction of history: that the performative sphere of the oral tradition, even in an era where literacy and orality coexisted, constituted an important liminal ludic space that was at the crux of thought formation in society. Perhaps, therefore, through our engagement with song composers such as Máire Bhuí Ní Laeire, a woman who could neither read nor write, we cannot so easily perpetuate our fantasy of a neatly categorized linear history of male literary thought and advancement as the foundations of European intellectual culture. Rather the singer of ideas teaches us that to think is to ritualize experience through the rich tapestry of tradition; that thinking can be ecstatic not just rational; and that the moment of reckoning may not be on a page at all, but rather in the moment of liminal song performance wherein everything – thought, identity and human action – trembles in the balance.

Appendix of Songs and Lore

List of Songs and Lore

1. Ar Leacain na Gréine [On the Sunny Side of the Hill]
2(a). Maidean Mhoch ar Leabaig Bhuig [Early One Morning on a Soft Bed]
2(b). 'S ar Maidin Moch is Mi 'r mo Leabain Bhuig [And Early One Morning While on my Soft Bed] (Seán de hÓra)
2(c). Maidin Mhuch ar Leabaig Bhuig [Early One Morning on a Soft Bed] (Máire Ní Cheocháin)
3(a). A Bhúrcaig Óig ón gCéim [Oh Young Burke from Céim]
3(b). A Bhúrcaig Bhuí ón gCéim [Oh Yellow Burke from Céim] (Cáit Ní Mhuimhneacháin)
4(a). Maidean Mhoch 'us Me ' Feighilth mo Stuic [Early One Morning as I Herded my Cattle]
4(b). Fáinnín Geal an Lae [The Dawning of the Day] (Nóra Ní Chonaill)
5(a). Maidean Álainn Ghréine (An Crúiscín Lán) [One Lovely Sunny Morning (The Full Jug)]
5(b). Maidin Álainn Ghréine [One Lovely Sunny Morning] (Seán de hÓra)
5(c). Maidin Álainn Gréine [One Lovely Sunny Morning] (Áine Uí Chuíll)
5(d). Maidin Álainn Gréine [One Lovely Sunny Morning] (Cáit Ní Mhuimhneacháin)
6(a). Seo Leó, ' Thoil [*Seo Leó,* my Darling]
6(b). Seo Leó, ' Thoil [*Seo Leó,* my Darling] (Maighréad Uí Luínse)
7(a). Cath Chéim an Fhia [The Battle of Keimaneigh]

7(a). Cath Chéim an Fhia [The Battle of Keimaneigh] (Peáití Thaidhg Pheig Ó Tuama)
8. Tá Gaeil Bhocht' Cráite [Poor Gaels are Tormented]
9(a). A Mháir' Ní Laeire [Oh Mary O'Leary]
9(b). A Mháir' Ní Laeire [Oh Mary O'Leary] (Cáit Ní Mhuimhneacháin)
10. Máire Bhuí agus Donncha Chruíd [Máire Bhuí and Donncha Chruíd]
11. Máire Bhuí agus an Fíodóir [Máire Bhuí and the Weaver]

Note on Orthography

The songs below attributed to Máire Bhuí Ní Laeire are edited using a specially tailored orthography that sounds out the words to resemble oral performance and dialect forms as closely as possible and therefore differs somewhat from the Official Written Standard for Irish *(An Caighdeán Oifigiúil)*. The aim of the editorial methodology is to bring the reader as close to the sounds of the oral tradition as possible. It follows the editorial methodology of Donncha Ó Cróinín (1919–1990) for publishing transcriptions in Irish from oral tradition, but was further developed under the direction of Dr Seán Ua Súilleabháin at University College, Cork during my doctoral studies. Sources include late nineteenth-/early twentieth-century manuscripts from the hand of Crothúr 'ac Coitir housed in Special Collections of the Boole Library, UCC; additional manuscripts by the same scribe from the private collection of the late Professor Brian Ó Cuív, copies of which are now housed in the Irish Traditional Music Archive; materials from the National Folklore Archive; and archival, field and commercial sound recordings. Even with the manuscript sources, the sound-centred editorial methodology was used because the orthography used by Crothúr 'ac Coitir was itself phonetically guided, using a mixture of English and Irish orthography, and gave an incredibly accurate description of the living forms of the dialect as sung or spoken. All songs below were previously published in *Bláth 's Craobh na nÚdar: Amhráin Mháire Bhuí* (Ní Shíocháin 2012), which contains a detailed description of the editorial methodology used (2012: 321–65). Below is a list of some of the key differences between this orthography and standardized Irish spelling:

1. The use of the circumflex denotes a long vowel sound that historically was spelled with an *mh* and that in the Irish of Muskerry was indicated in speech by the nasalization of the long vowel sound. For example, chô = chomh, raî = raimhe, côcht = comhacht (cumhacht), côirle = comhairle, tâch-lag = támhach-lag, côir = comhair and so forth. Such words are pronounced with the long vowel sound usually denoted by a *síneadh fada*, but which in Muskerry Irish may also include nasalization. Therefore chô

is pronounced chó, but some speakers and singers will distinguish between words such as cóir and côir (comhair) by using nasalization in the pronunciation of the latter (Ó Cuív 1944: 54–56).

2. Elision of vowels and consonants is illustrated throughout with the use of apostrophes. For example, what would be depicted in standardized Irish as 'ag machnamh seal liom féinig' is here written as it would be sung (or indeed spoken): 'a' machnamh seal liom féinig'; likewise what in standardized Irish is written 'ar an ngarda' is here written as 'ar a' ngarda'; 'A Mháire Ní Laoire' in standardized Irish is here written exactly as it is sung– that is, 'A Mháir' Ní Laeire', et cetera (Ó Cuív 1944: 60–61).

3. Verb endings are written as they are pronounced in sung or spoken Irish; for example, where standard Irish would have 'gluaisigí', in this edition the dialect form of 'gluaisíg' is used; where standard Irish would have 'beidh', here 'beig' is preferred to denote the exact pronunciation (Ó Cuív 1944: 37); where the Irish standard has 'daoradh' or 'fágadh', here we have 'daorag' or 'fágamh', the two forms common to Muskerry Irish. The use of the *–dh* ending of verbs denotes the sound /x/ (i.e. the broad *ch* sound of Irish).

4. Broad and slender consonants are specified in the orthography as they would be sung or spoken as illustrated in sound recordings and manuscript sources; for example, *i nÍbh Laeire* denotes a slender *n*, but *i nUíbh Laeire* denotes a broad *n*.

5. The broad sound of /e:/: the spelling *ae* is used instead of the usual *ao*, to distinguish between /e:/ amd /i:/. For example, Máire Bhuí Ní Laoire/ Ní Laoghaire is here spelled as it would be pronounced in the dialects of West Munster – that is, Máire Bhuí Ní L*ae*ire (Ó Cuív 1944: 15–16).

6. Historical and dialect forms of the personal pronouns *me, mi* and *tu* are given where standardized Irish would have *mé* and *tú*, except in cases where the meter demands the standardized forms. The more unusual form of *túsa* from the dialects of Cairbre and Cléire is also given where standardized Irish would have *tusa* (Ua Súilleabháin 1994).

6. All dialect forms as represented in manuscript sources and sound recordings are represented as accurately as possible.

Note on Musical Transcriptions

Every effort was made to give as detailed a description as possible of the rhythm, pitch, contours and ornamentation as performed by singers. The notation was specially tailored to this end, using broken bar lines and time signatures in brackets to denote a freer 'elastic' pulse, and with changes of time signature used where appropriate. However, these transcriptions should not be considered as an exact representation of the oral performances, as it is beyond the capacity of Western musical notation to represent the rhythmic complexity of the free-rhythm seannós singing tradition. Therefore the reader is urged to refer to the sound recordings cited in the accompanying discography rather than transcriptions alone. A more detailed description of the methodology used for musical transcriptions can be found in *Bláth 's Craobh na nÚdar: Amhráin Mháire Bhuí* (Ní Shíocháin 2012).

Note on Translations

All translations are my own and endeavour to represent the meaning of the original Irish as accurately as possible as a reading aid to song texts.

1. Ar Leacain na Gréine [On the Sunny Side of the Hill]

Source: the Ó Donnchú papers, Ballingeary Historical Society. Previously published in *Filíocht Mháire Bhuidhe Ní Laoghaire* (Ó Donnchú 1931) and *Bláth 's Craobh na nÚdar: Amhráin Mháire Bhuí* (Ní Shíocháin 2012); previously published and translated in *Máire Bhuí Ní Laoire: A Poet of Her People* (Brennan 2000).

Singer: Diarmuid 'ac Coitir, na Corraithe Thiar, Ballingeary. Collected by Donncha Ó Donnchú in the early twentieth century. This song no longer survives in the living tradition and we have no record of the air of the song.

Ó Donnchú (1931) dates this song as being composed in 1797, assumedly based on the clear references in the song to the attempted landing of the French fleet in Bantry Bay in 1796. Diarmuid 'ac Coitir attributes the song to Máire Bhuí. The fleet in the bay was seen by locals, but a storm prevented the French revolutionaries from landing, thus thwarting local revolutionary efforts significantly. The song is an aisling or vision poem in which an otherworldly female figure brings a message of import to the song poet and listeners. The Jacobin hue of the song's political discourses are apparent particularly in the final verse.

1.
Ar leacain na gréine inné is me ag múscailt mo bhó,
'sea ' dhearcas-sa lem thaobh an spéirbhean mhodhail mhúinte dheas óg;
do bhí lasa na gcaor 'na gné agus a gnúis mar an rós,
agus a cúl carnfholt péarlach léi go dúnaibh a bróg.

2.
Níor dhanaid liom féin teacht féna déin lena fáilte is lena póig,
ach ar eagla nárbh aon bhean tsaolta a thárlaig im threó;

níorbh aithnid liom féin dá mhéid é a trácht insa chóig',
ach a pearsa agus a méinn, a scéimh, a cáil is a cló.

3.
Is 'na haice siúd do shuíos is do luíos ar phlámaireacht léi,
is is gairid arís gur shíleas ' bheith páirteach seal léi:
'Má taoi tuirseach ón slí, dein moíll is go lá tar liom féin
is gheóir leabaig nách tuí ar feag mí más áil leat gabháil léi'.

4.
'Tá maga ort, a mhaoin,' a duairt sí, 'is ní hábhar duit mé,
agus ná feadar cá luíonn do thíos ná t'áitreabh féin;
mar caithfead dul síos go híochtar Clár Luirc lem scéal
go bhfeaca-sa an *Fleet* i bhFaoide 'na lánchumas tréan'.

5.
'A mhascalaig mhín, thar an bh*Fleet* ná trácht liom go héag,
mar is le hanacra do chím-se na mílte i ngátar 'na déig;
tháinig scaipe orthu ón ngaoith, fóraíor, ' chuir a lán acu ar strae,
agus i nglasaibh 'sea do shuíd mar an ríbhean so ' thárlaig i gcéin'.

6.
'Gach duine acu ' chífir, mínig dóibh brí mo scéil,
go bhfuilid ag tíocht go buíonmhar fí ghrán is fí philéar –
geárrthacaig ghroí, an Laoiseach, 's an Spáinneach dá réir,
go Banba ag tíocht gan mhoíll le grásta mhic Dé'.

7.
'Go deimhin más fíor do laoithe, a stáidbhruinneall shéimh,
beig talamh gan chíos gan íoc gan cháin is gan phlé,
beig cruithneacht is ím is saíll ar an gclár againn féin,
agus gasra an ghrínn ag díoga na gcárt agus dá nglaoch'.

English Translation

1.
On the sunny side of the hill yesterday as I herded my cattle,
I saw beside me the young gentle fair lady;
her appearance had the radiance of berries and her cheek was like the rose,
and her curly pearly tresses flowed to the ties of her shoes.

2.
I did not hesitate in going to her with her welcome and kiss,
but for fear that it was not a worldly woman that had come my way,
I was not acquainted with her, despite her fame in the province,
but her person and mind, her beauty, her reputation and her form.

3.
I sat down beside her and started to talk softly to her,
and it was not long before I decided to share her company for a while:
'If you are tired from the journey, tally a while and come with me
and you will receive a bed not of hay for a month if you so wish'.

4.
'You are fooling yourself, my treasure', said she, 'and I am not for you,
and I don't know where your household lies or where your abode is;
because I have to go down to the South of Ireland with my story
that I saw the Fleet in Whiddy in full strong might'.

5.
'Oh fine gentle strong one, do not talk to me about that Fleet until I die,
because it is with distress that I see thousands in want for lack of it;
they were scattered by the wind, alas, it sent many of them astray,
and in fetters they now lie like this regal woman who travelled from afar'.

6.
'Everyone you see, explain to them the meaning of my tidings,
that they are coming in masses with grain and powder –
young strong soldiers, commanded by Louis and the Spaniard,
coming to Ireland without delay with the grace of the Son of God'.

7.
'Indeed if your lays are true, oh stately fair lady,
we will have land without rent without payment without tax and without dispute,
there will be wheat and butter and bacon on our own table,
and the joyous company drinking quarts and calling for more'.

2(a). Maidean Mhoch ar Leabaig Bhuig [Early One Morning on a Soft Bed]

Scribe: Crothúr 'ac Coitir.

Source: LS141, Special Collections, UCC Library, University College, Cork. Previously published in *Filíocht Mháire Bhuidhe Ní Laoghaire* (Ó Donnchú 1931) and *Bláth 's Craobh na nÚdar: Amhráin Mháire Bhuí* (Ní Shíocháin 2012); previously published and translated in *Máire Bhuí Ní Laoire: A Poet of Her People* (Brennan 2000).

An aisling or vision poem attributed to Máire Bhuí Ní Laeire.

1.
Maidean mhoch ar leabaig bhuig
   do chuala 'mu na héin;

do smaoiníos-sa gur chóir dom dul
 a' múscailt stuic chun féir;
do bhuail umam, 's a ciabh 'na hucht,
 's í a' cíor' a fuilt go réig,
an chúileann ghlic ba bhreátha cruth
 ná 'n eala ar sruth an éisc. 8

2.
Mo chroí gur chrith á fhiarthaí dhi
 gudae 'n tír gurbh as a' bhé:
'An tu péarla an tsuilth ón nGréig do rith
 'us d'fhág 'na raic a' Trae,
nú Déirdre ' thug grá cléibh 'us cion
 do Naois' a cailleag léi,
nú an bhean do riug le áilleacht cruth
 an t-úll ó iomaig géar?' 16

3.
'An tu Clíona ghlic ' chuir draíocht 'us bruid
 ar Aoibheall dheas gan chlaon,
nú stuaire an tuir do ghluais tar muir
 'us d'fhág na mílthe tréith,
nú an bhean sa chnoc do thraoch na cuin
 go nglaeidís Cuileann tSéimh
' chuir Fiúnn sa tsruth gan chrí' gan chion
 d'fhúig deórach fliuch an Fhéinn?' 24

4.
Do labhair sí liom, 'a shéimhfhir, suig,
 go n-ínsead fáth mo scéil:
ní stuaire me do ghluais tar muir
 gur thúrnaig cath ná plé –
do *natives* chirt Íbh Laeire me
 'us do shío'rach mhaithe Ghael,
'us mo chôra din mara bpósair me
 go moch le fáinne an lae'. 32

5.
'A bháb a' tsuilth is breátha cruth
 ná sneachta ar chnoc le gréin,
d'fhágais-se tinn breóite me,
 'us ní muar mo shos ó phéin;
do phósfainn-se gan feóirling thu
 'us ní iarfainn ba ná spré

ach tá móid orm le óigmhnaoi dhis
   don chôrsanacht ruim ré'.   40

English Translation

1.
Early one morning on a soft bed
I heard the birds outside;
I thought that I should go
herding my cattle to pasture;
she met with me, her tresses flowing down her bosom,
combing her hair smoothly,
the clever fair maiden of the finest shape
surpassing even the swan on the stream of fish.

2.
My heart trembled as I enquired of her
what land the beautiful woman was from;
'Are you the pearl of joy who fled Greece
and left Troy in chaos,
or Déirdre who gave affection and the love of her heart
to Naoise who died because of her,
or the woman who won with beauty of form
the apple from stiff competition?'

3.
'Are you clever Clíona who put enchantment and bonds
on lovely Aoibheall without vice,
or the beauty of the tower who moved over the sea
and left thousands in weakness,
or the woman in the hill who tired the hounds
who they used to call gentle Cuileann
who put Fionn in the stream in a terrible way without affection
and who left the Fianna wet and teary?'

4.
She spoke to me, 'oh gentleman, sit,
'til I tell you the import of my story:
I am not a beautiful woman who moved over the sea
and caused battle or dispute –
I am of the rightful natives of Iveleary
and descended from Gaelic nobles,
and make my coffin if you don't marry me
early with the break of day'.

5.
'Oh joyous babe of the most beautiful form
surpassing snow on the sunny hill,
you left me sore and sick,
and I scarcely get any respite from my pain;
I would marry you without a farthing
and I would look for neither cattle nor dowry
but I have pledged myself to a fine young woman
in the neighbourhood already'.

2(b). 'S ar Maidin Moch is Mi 'r mo Leabain Bhuig [And Early One Morning While on My Soft Bed]

Singer: Seán de hÓra (1908–1989), Cloichear, the Dingle Peninsula, Kerry.

Source: National Folklore Archive, sound recording CBÉ TO649, collected in 1973 by Breandán Breatnach. Previously published and released in *Bláth 's Craobh na nÚdar: Amhráin Mháire Bhuí* (Ní Shíocháin 2012).

Figure A.1 'S ar Maidin Moch is Mi 'r mo Leabain Bhuig [And Early One Morning While on My Soft Bed]

1.
'S ar (a) maidin (a) moch is mi ar mo leabain bhuig
   'sea ' chuala(ing) ceól na n-éan;
mar 'sea ' smaoiníos-sa (ó) ba(í) chóir dom dol
   a' móscailth stuic chuin féir,

mar 'sea ' bhuail sí liom 's a(í) caidhp 'na hucht
   's í ' cíora ' folt go réig,
an chúileann ghlic (ó) do(í) b'áille crot
   ná 'n eala ar shruth an éisc.   8

2.
Is mo chroí do chrith (ó) dá hiarthaí di
   cén tír (ó) gurb as an bhé:
'Nú ' tu Clíona ghlic (ó) ' chuir draíocht is bruid
   is d'fhág 'na raic an Trae,   12
nú ' tu Déirdre ' thug grá cléibh is cion
   nú Naois' do(í) cailleadh léi,
nú 'n (a) bhean do rug (i) le háilleacht crot
   an t-úll ó ioma(d) ghéir ?'   16

3.
Is do labhair sí liúm, 'Ó (n)a shéimhfhir, suig,
   go neósad duit brí mo scéil,
mar ní stuaire mi ó do ghluais anuir
   ná a mhóscail cath na Trae;   20
ach do *natives* chirt d'Uíbh Laeire mi
   do shíolraí mhaithí' Gael,
is (i) mo chôr' dein (ó) mona bpósfair mi
   go much (í) le fáinne an lae.'   24

4.
'Is a(í) bháb a' tsuilt ó ba(í) bhreátha crot
   ná 'n sneachta ar chnuc le gréin,
mar (a) d'fhágaís-se (ó) tinn breóite mi
   's ní muar é mo shos ón bpéin,   28
ach phósfainn-se gan feórlinn tu
   's ní dh'iarrfaínn (ón) leat ba ná spré,
ach (i) tá móid orùm lé óigmhnaoi dheas
   ón gcôrsanacht ruim ré'.   32

English Translation

1.
Early one morning while on my soft bed
I heard the music of the birds;
because I thought that I should go
herding my cattle to pasture;
because she met with me, her tresses flowing down her bosom,

combing her hair smoothly,
the clever fair maiden of the most beautiful shape
surpassing even the swan on the stream of fish.

2.
My heart trembled as I enquired of her
what land the beautiful woman was from;
'Are you clever Clíona who put enchantment and bonds
and left Troy in chaos,
or are you Déirdre who gave affection and the love of her heart
to Naoise who died because of her,
or the woman who won with beauty of form
the apple from stiff competition?'

3.
She spoke to me, 'oh gentleman, sit,
'til I tell you the meaning of my story:
I am not the beauty who moved from the East
nor who ignited the battle of Troy –
but I am of the rightful natives of Iveleary
descended from Gaelic nobles,
and make my coffin if you don't marry me
early with the break of day'.

4.
'Oh joyous babe of the most beautiful form
surpassing snow on the sunny hill,
because you left me sore and sick,
and I scarcely get any respite from my pain;
I would marry you without a farthing
and I would look for neither cattle nor dowry,
but I have pledged myself to a fine young woman
in the neighbourhood already'.

2(c). Maidin Mhuch ar Leabaig Bhuig [Early One Morning on a Soft Bed]

Singer: Máire Ní Ceocáin (1925–), born and reared in Cúil Aoḋa, Múrcraí, now living in Baile an Collaig, Lám le Corcaiġ.[1]

Source: Sound recording K68 from the Traditional Music Archive in University College, Cork, collected by Florence Linehan in 1975. Previously published and released in *Bláth 's Craobh na nÚdar: Amhráin Mháire Bhuí* (Ní Shíocháin 2012).

Figure A.2 Maidin Mhuch ar Leabaig Bhuig [Early One Morning on a Soft Bed]

1.
Maidin mhuch ar leabaig bhuig
do chuala guth na n-éan;
do smaoiníos-sa gur chóir dom dul
a' múscailt stuic chun féir; 4
do bhuail umam 's a ciabh 'na hucht,
's í ' cíora ' folth go réig,
an chúileann ghlic ba bhreátha cruth
ná 'n eala ar shruth an éisc. 8

2.
Mo chroí gur chrith á fhiarthaí dhi
cad é tír gurbh as don bhé:
'An tú péarla 'n tsuilth ón nGréig do rith
agus d'fhág 'na raic an Trae, 12
nú Déirdre fuair scéimh is cion
ó Naois' a cailleag léi,
nú an bhean do riug le háilleacht cruth
an t-úll ó ioma' ghéir?' 16

3.
Do labhair sí liom, 'A shéimhfhir, suig,
go n-ínsead fáth mo scéal:
ní stuaire me do ghluais thar muir
ná ' mhúscail Cath na Trae; 20
de *natives* chirt Íbh Laeire me,
is de shíolrach chlanna Gael,
is mo chôirle din mara bpósfair me
go much le fáinne 'n lae'. 24

English Translation

1.
Early one morning on my soft bed
I heard the voice of the birds;
I thought that I should go
herding my cattle to pasture;
she met with me, her tresses flowing down her bosom,
combing her hair smoothly,
the clever fair maiden of the finest shape
surpassing even the swan on the stream of fish.

2.
My heart trembled as I enquired of her
what land the beautiful woman was from;
'Are you the pearl of joy who fled Greece
and left Troy in chaos,
or Déirdre who received eagerness (or beauty) and affection
from Naoise who died because of her,
or the woman who won with beauty of form
the apple from stiff competition'.

3.
She spoke to me, 'Oh gentleman, sit,
'til I tell you the import of my stories:
I am not a beauty who moved over the sea
who ignited the battle of Troy –
I am of the rightful natives of Iveleary
and descended from Gaelic nobles,
and take my advice if you don't marry me
early with the break of day'.

3(a). A Bhúrcaig Óig ón gCéim [Oh Young Burke from Keimaneigh]

Scribe: Crothúr 'ac Coitir.

Source: LS139, Special Collections, UCC Library, University College, Cork. Previously published in *Filíocht Mháire Bhuidhe Ní Laoghaire* (Ó Donnchú 1931) and *Bláth 's Craobh na nÚdar: Amhráin Mháire Bhuí* (Ní Shíocháin 2012); previously published and translated in *Máire Bhuí Ní Laoire: A Poet of Her People* (Brennan 2000).

The first line is more commonly 'A Bhúrcaig Bhuí ón gCéim' ('Oh Yellow Burke from Keimaneigh ') in modern times. In this song, Máire Bhuí addresses her own son, imploring him not to abandon the young woman he is courting just because her dowry is small. Máire Bhuí, in advising her son on his choice of wife, lists the excellent attributes of the young lady in question, Neil ní Mhichíl Chnâig, comparing her to a noblewoman in stature, grace and beauty. She also refers, however, to the famed abilities of the young woman's family at fighting as an enticement to marriage. Ultimately, the young lady is successful in wooing the young Burke, also vindicating Máire Bhuí's poetic intervention through song.

1.
A Bhúrcaig óig ón gCéim,
mar a dtéann a' fia chun strae,
   fíll thar n-ais 'us bheir leat bean
do dhéanfaig beart dod réir.
Ná fág í siúd id dhéig
mar ghiúll ar bheagán spré;
   dá dtíodh a cleaing sa bhruín let ais
go mbuaífí leat a' *sway*.   8

2.
Mara mbeadh crosa 's fán a' tsaeil
'us bás a hathar féin,
   bheadh flúirse mhuar dá stoc ansúd
i ngaorthaíbh cûrtha ré,
marcaíocht shocair shéimh,
'us c'luith dhon tsíoda dhaor,
   leaba chlúimh féna cúm
is cruitín dúnta léi.   16

3.
'Sí Neil ní Mhichíl Chnâig
an eala mhúinte mhná,
   gaol na bhfear 's na dtíosach gceart
' thuíll clú 'gus meas riamh d'fháil,
seómraí ' brúchtaigh bháin,
'us machaí bó 'cu a' tál,
   mná dea-chlúmhail na dtithe siúd
do riarfadh flúirseach arán.   24

4.
A Bhúrcaig úd 'tá thuaig
ag ciûis na Locha Lua,
   beig ort léan má thréigeann túsa
craobhfholth na gcuach,
céile shocair shuairc
do bhé dhis ' bheadh gan ghruaim,
   go bhfuil a' *sway* 'ci féin dá réir
ó chaol a' ghlean' go cuan.   32

5.
Ar maidin Domhnaig Dé
'sí ' thaistil chúinn thar Céim
   an ainnir mhúinte chneasta chlúmhail,
ba dheas é dlúth a déid,
bhí lasa lúr' na gcaor
'na leacain úir bhuig réig,
   ba phras é a siúl ar bhárr a' drúcht'
gur sciub sí an Búrcach léi.   40

English Translation

1.
Oh young Burke from Keimaneigh
where the deer strays,
come back and bring with you a woman
that will act in your interests.
Do not leave her after you
for having a meagre dowry;
if her clan were to join the fray by your side
you would win the sway.

2.
If it weren't for the hardships of life
and the death of her own father,
she would have a generous stock of his cattle there
in fragrant smooth river-valleys,
steady gentle horse-riding,
and an outfit of expensive silk,
a feather bed under her waist,
with curtains to close.

3.
Neil ní Mhichíl Chnâig
is a refined swan of a woman,
the relative of fine men and hosts
who ever earned fame and respect,
parlours pouring forth white milk,
herds of cattle yielding milk,
the reputable women of those houses
would produce plenty bread.

4.
Oh yonder Burke to the North
on the edge of Loch Allua,
you will regret it if you abandon

the beauty of the curly tresses,
a steady cheerful spouse,
a beautiful woman without melancholy,
who has therefore won sway herself
from the narrow of the glen to the harbour.

5.
On the morning of God's Sunday
who should travel to us over the Céim
only the refined reputable kind beauty,
the form of her teeth was lovely,
she had the radiance of berries
in her soft smooth fresh cheeks,
quick was her movement over the dew
and she stole the Burke away.

3(b). A Bhúrcaig Bhuí ón gCéim [Oh Yellow Burke from Keimaneigh]

Singer: Cáit Ní Mhuimhneacháin (1918–1949), Gaorthadh na Péice, Ballingeary.

Source: National Folklore Archive, sound recording CBÉ CT0257_007a, previously published and released on compact disc in *An Joga Mór: Amhráin Cháit Ní Mhuimhneacháin* (Raidió na Gaeltachta 2001), and in *Bláth 's Craobh na nÚdar: Amhráin Mháire Bhuí* (Ní Shíocháin 2012).

Figure A.3 *A Bhúrcaig Bhuí ón gCéim [Oh Yellow Burke from Keimaneigh]*

1.
A Bhúrcaig bhuí ón gCéim
mar a dtéann an fia ar strae,
 ó fíll thar n-ais is beir leat bean
do dhéanfaig beart dod réir.
Ná fág it 'iaig an bhé
mar gheall ar bheagán spré:

dá mbeadh a *clan* sa bhruíon let ais
is leat a bhuafí an *sway*.   8

2.
Maidin Domhnaig Dé
'sea ' thaistil chúinn thar céim
    (n) an ainnir chlûil chneasta mhúinte
dob áille gnaoi 'gus scéimh;
bhí lasair dheirg na gcaor
'na leacain úrbhuig réig
    's í a' siúl an drúcht' go pras a' teacht
gur sciub sí an Búrcach léi.   16

3.
Mura mbeadh crosa 'n tsaeil
agus bás a hathar féin,
    bheadh réim is flúirse ag á stoc súd
i ngaorthaíbh cûrtha réig,
marcaíocht shocair shéimh,
is c'luith don tsíoda dhaor,
    (ó) leaba chlúimh féna cúm
's a cruitín dúnta léi.   24

4.
Ó, 's a Bhúrcaig úd aduaig
ó chiûis a' Locha Lua,
    beig léan ort má thréigeann tú
bé gheal na gcua[ch]
de chéile dheas shuairc;
do b'éigean dóibh gluais,
    is tá 'n chraobh aici ar an gCaolchuil
ón dtaobh thuir do chuan.   32

English Translation

1.
Oh young Burke from Keimaneigh
where the deer strays,
come back and bring with you a woman
that will act in your interests.
Do not leave the beautiful woman after you
for having a meagre dowry;
if her clan were to join the fray by your side
you would win the sway.

2.
The morning of God's Sunday
who should travel to us over the Céim
only the refined reputable kind beauty,
her cheek and countenance were beautiful,
she had the red radiance of berries
in her soft smooth fresh cheeks,
swiftly she moved over the dew on her way
so that she stole the Burke away.

3.
If it weren't for the hardships of life
and the death of her own father,
she would have a ranging and generous stock of his cattle there
in fragrant smooth river-valleys,
steady gentle horse-riding,
and an outfit of expensive silk,
a feather bed under her waist,
with curtains to close.

4.
Oh and yonder Burke to the North
on the edge of Loch Allua,
you will regret it if you abandon
the bright beauty of the curly tresses,
a lovely cheerful spouse;
they had to go off,
and she is the best of them all from Kealkill
to the East side of the harbour.

4(a). Maidean Mhoch 'us Me ' Feighilth mo Stuic [Early One Morning as I Herded My Cattle]

Scribe: Crothúr 'ac Coitir.

Source: LS144, Special Collections, UCC Library, University College, Cork. Previously published in *Filíocht Mháire Bhuidhe Ní Laoghaire* (Ó Donnchú 1931) and *Bláth's Craobh na nÚdar: Amhráin Mháire Bhuí* (Ní Shíocháin 2012); previously published and translated in *Máire Bhuí Ní Laoire: A Poet of Her People* (Brennan 2000).

1.
Maidean mhoch 'us me ' feighilth mo stuic
　'us dá seóla chun an fhéir

'sea bhuail umum 'sí stuaire an tsuilth,
  'us í ' duanaireacht 's ag éamh. 4
Nuair a chuala 'n guth ba shuairce liom
  le fúnn gur dhrideas léi
ba raí gach deóir lena leacain bhuig
  'us ba thrua í ' gol i gcéin. 8

2.
Ba chrothach scuabach dualach dubh
  a cuacha ' titim léi,
a cúm seang singil ba néata suite,
  's a mala dheas ba chaol, 12
a déid ba ghile 's a béal ba bhinne,
  'us a dhá cích chruinne ghéar',
'Go deimhin a bhean ba bhreá do ghean
  go moch le fáinn' an lae'. 16

3.
'An tu Céarnait ghlic an bhé cheap muilthe
  amach à t'íntinn ghéar,
nú an bhé a tugag thar bhárr na tuinne
  do mhúiscil cath na Trae, 20
nú an fíor gur tu ' thug a' t-úll so 'b fhinne
  thar mhnáibh na cruinne léi?'
Nárbh álainn deas é ' scéimh 's a gean
  go moch le fáinne an lae! 24

4.
'A sháirfhir ghlic na ráite suilth,
  ní héinne 'co san mé;
ach bé 'sea me gan chéile ar bith,
  cé gur fada mi fí léan. 28
Beir scéal anois gur daorag sinn
  ag tréadtha an uilc 's a' chlaein;
gan bhréag anois tá 'n téarma 'stig,
  beig Éire 'gainn fí réim'. 32

5.
''Á mb'aidhl leat teacht i ti'an táirne 'steach
  'us bheith páirteach seal liom féin?'
'Sé an freagra ' duairt, 'Níl cae 'gam stad,
  tá 'n fôr ar leatha im dhéig, 36
Diúc *o' York* 's a thrúp dá shlad
  ag priúnsa ceart na nGael,

'us ar a' mbliain seo chúinn beig búir go lag,
    sin cúntas ceart lem scéal'.   40

English Translation

1.
Early one morning as I herded my cattle,
steering them to the grass,
who should I meet but the joyous maiden,
singing and crying.
When I heard the voice so joyous to me
I eagerly moved towards her;
fat was every tear which flowed down her soft check
and her crying in the distance was pitiful.

2.
Wavy, sweeping, curly and black
were her flowing tresses,
her slender single waist was neatly situated,
her lovely eyebrow slender,
her teeth were the whitest, her mouth the most melodious,
and her two protruding well-formed breasts,
'Indeed, woman, your love was fine
early at the break of day'.

3.
'Are you clever Céarnait, the lady who created mills
out of her sharp mind,
or the woman who was taken over the wave
who roused the battle of Troy,
or is it true that it is you who took the fairest apple
over all the women of the world?'
Lovely were her beauty and affection
early at the break of day.

4.
'Oh fine clever man of the joyous utterances,
I am none of those;
but I am a woman without any spouse
even though I have long been in sorrow;
take this story now that we have been enslaved
by hordes of evil and bias –
without a word of a lie the term is up,
and we will rule Ireland'.

5.
'Would you like to come into the tavern
and pass the time with me?'
The answer she gave, 'I cannot tarry,
the harvest is being reaped behind me,
the Duke of York and his troop being defeated
by the rightful prince of the Gaels,
and next year boors will be weak,
that is a true account of my tale'.

4(b). Fáinnín Geal an Lae [The Dawning of the Day] by Máire Bhuí Ní Laeire

Singer: Nóra Ní Chonaill (Bean Uí Uidhir) from Ballyvourney.

Source: National Folklore Collection, CBÉ 47:66–68, collected in 1933 by Proinséas Ó Ceallaigh. Previously published in *Bláth 's Craobh na nÚdar: Amhráin Mháire Bhuí* (Ní Shíocháin 2012).

1.
Maidean mhoch ar mh'eighrí dom
   a' múscailt mo stuic chun féir,
do chuala an guth ba shuairce liom
   is le fúnn do dhruideas léi;   4
cé ' casfí orm ach a' stuaire suilth
   is í a' duanaireacht 's ag éamh;
ba raî gach deór lena leacain bhuig
   is ba thrua í ag gol i gcéin.   8

2.
Ba chíortha snaímtheach scuabach chluthar
   ' bhí a cuach' a' titim léi,
bhí a cúm caol singil 's a héadan suite
   is a mala dheas ba chaol,   12
a déid ba ghile, a béal ba bhinne
   's a dhá cín chruinne ghéar';
'Go deimhin, a bhean, nách breá do ghean
   le fáinnín gheal a' lae'.   16

3.
'Dá mb'áil leat teacht ' dtig an táirne 'steach
   is bheith páirteach seal liom féin?'
'Go deimhin a riúin, níl cae agam stad,
   tá an fôr a' lasa im dhéig: 20
tá diúic i York is a thrúp á shlad
   ag priúnsa ceart na nGael –

bliain a cúig beig búir go lag,
   sin cúntas ceart lem scéal'.   24

4.
'Is aithreach liúm an cúrsa a' meath
   ar phriúnsa ceart na nGael,
O'Connell clûil, plúr na bhflaith,
'tá a' d'iarr' ár gcirt a phlé;   28
do chua' sé 'núnn i gcúrsaí fear
   agus slán go dtigig sé
go sásta súgach is a thrúp len' ais
   le fáinnín gheal a' lae'.   32

5.
'An Céarnait tu na ráite suilth,
   nú an bhé thar lear i gcéin,
nú an bhean sa chnoc do thraoch na cuin
   lena ráinig Cath na Trae?   36
An tú an bhé nur tugag di an t-úll 's a' bile
   thar mhnáibh na cruinne go léir?
Go deimhin a bhean is breá do ghean
   le fáinnín gheal a' lae!'   40

6.
' ' sháirfhir ghlic na ráite suilth,
   ní héinne 'cu san mé,
ach bé 'sea me gan chéile ar bith
   is is fada dhom fí léan: 44
mo scéal anois gur daorag sinn
   ag tréadta an uilc 's a' chlaein;
tá an téarma istig gan breág anois
   is beig Éire againn fé réim'.   48

English Translation

1.
One early morning as I rose up,
herding my cattle to grass,
I heard the voice so joyous to me
and I eagerly moved towards her;
who should I meet but the joyous maiden
singing and crying,
fat was every tear which flowed down her soft check
and her crying in the distance was pitiful.

2.
Combed, interweaving, sweeping, and sheltering
were her flowing tresses,
her slender single waist and her face well situated,
her lovely eyebrow slender,
her teeth were the whitest, her mouth the most melodious,
and her two protruding well-formed breasts,
'Indeed, woman, your love is fine
early at the break of day'.

3.
'Would you like to come into the tavern
and pass the time with me?'
'Indeed, my love, I cannot tarry,
the harvest is lighting up behind me,
the Duke of York and his troop are being defeated
by the rightful prince of the Gaels,
in the year five [i.e. 1825] boors will be weak,
that is a true account of my tale'.

4.
'I regret that the course is declining
for the rightful prince of the Gaels,
reputable O'Connell, flower of men,
who is trying to negotiate our rights;
he went abroad for the causes of men
and may he return safely
happily merrily with his troop by his side
at the dawning of the day'.

5.
'Are you Céarnait of the happy utterances,
or the lady far away over the seas,
or the woman in the hills who tired the hounds
who started the Battle of Troy?
Are you the woman who took with her the apple and the sacred tree
over all the women of the world?
Indeed, woman, your love is fine
at the dawning of the day!'

6.
'Oh fine clever man of the joyous utterances,
I am none of those;
but I am a woman without any spouse

even though I have long been in sorrow;
take this story now that we have been enslaved
by hordes of evil and bias –
the term is up without a word of a lie,
and we will rule Ireland'.

5(a). Maidean Álainn Ghréine (An Crúiscín Lán) [One Lovely Sunny Morning (The Full Jug)]

Scribe: Crothúr 'ac Coitir.

Source: LSS141 and 144, Special Collections, UCC Library, University College, Cork. Previously published in *Filíocht Mháire Bhuidhe Ní Laoghaire* (Ó Donnchú 1931) and *Bláth 's Craobh na nÚdar: Amhráin Mháire Bhuí* (Ní Shíocháin 2012); previously published and translated in *Máire Bhuí Ní Laoire: A Poet of Her People* (Brennan 2000).

An aisling or vision poem composition attributed to Máire Bhuí Ní Laeire. Three different airs to this song exist (see 5 c–d below) (Ní Shíocháin 2012: 199–205).

1.
Maidean álainn ghréine 'us me ar thaobh chnoc na buaile
'sea ' dhearcas cúileann mhaorga 's a bréid fliuch ón luachair;
bhí gile 'us finne ' n-aonacht go gléineach 'na gruanna,
d'fhúig sí m'íntinn léanmhar 's is baolach nách buan ' bhead –
    'us gheóm arís a' crúiscín 'us bíodh sé lán.

2.
D'fhiosaras go béasach don spéirbhruinneall stuama:
'Ca bhfuilid do ghaoltha nú cá taobh as gur ghluaisís,
an bean le fán a' tsaeil thu gan chéile ar do thuairisc,
nú an fíor gur tusa Céarnait ' chuir na tréanmhuilthe ar fuaimeat?' –
    'us gheóm arís a' crúiscín 'us bíodh sé lán.

3.
"óigfhir mhúinte bhéasaig ní héinne me dhá nduaraís
ach bean do mhaithibh Ghael me 'tá léanaithe i gcruatan;
mh'ainm cheart 'sí Éire 'us mac Séarlais 'om ruagairt,
mo bhailthí puirt ag béaraibh an éirlig 's an fhuadaig' –
    'us gheóm arís a' crúiscín 'us bíodh sé lán.

4.
Do thugas crotha lámh di 'us céad fáilthe ruim a' stuaire,
cuire stad go lá dhi go sásta chun suainis,

go ndéanfainn tínte cnámh di le háthas i mbua-chnoc
d'fhúnn go mbeadh a' lá againn 'us cead ráis ar na huaisle –
    'us gheóm arís a' crúiscín 'us bíodh sé lán.

5.
Níl cae 'gam stad go lá 'gat cé gur ghá dhom a' suaineas –
caithfead triall go Clár Luirc mar thánag le tuairisc
go bhfuil Galla-phuic 's a n-áltha 's an áit seo le ruagairt
'us Clanna Gaíol 'na n-áitreamh 's is áthas liom ró-mhuar é' –
    'us gheóm arís a' crúiscín 'us bíodh sé lán.

6.
'Beig Sasanaig á thnátha 'us ní cás liom a gcruatan,
a dtithe geala bána go láidir á gcuardach,
a leathaireacha geárrtha 'na gc'ráistíochaibh uaisle
'us go siúlóig Gaeil go rábach ar a lán-chorpaibh muara' –
    'us gheóm arís a' crúiscín 'us bíodh sé lán'.

English Translation

1.
One lovely sunny morning as I was on the side of the booley hill
I saw a stately fair maid whose braid was wet from the rushes;
there was brightness and fairness combined radiantly in her cheeks,
she left my mind sorrowful and I fear I may not last long –
and let us get the jug again and let it be full.

2.
I enquired politely of the composed fair beauty:
'Who are your people or from whence have you come,
are you a woman wandering the world with no spousal protection,
or is it true that you are Céarnait who set the strong mills noisily working?' –
and let us get the jug again and let it be full.

3.
'Oh young mannerly gentleman, I am none of those you mentioned,
but I am a woman of Gaelic nobility who has been saddened by hardship;
my true name is Éire and the son of Charles is driving me out,
my port towns in the possession of bears of slaughter and plunder' –
and let us get the jug again and let it be full.

4.
I shook her by the hand and laid a hundred welcomes before the beautiful woman,
an invitation to stay until day happily in repose,

that I would make bonfires joyously in high hills
so that we would have the day and the right to send the nobles racing –
and let us get the jug again and let it be full.

5.
'I don't have time to stay until day with you even though I need the repose –
I must travel to Ireland because I have come with tidings
that foreign pucks and their families are to be driven out of this place
and Irish clans put in their stead and I am exceedingly happy about it' –
and let us get the jug again and let it be full.

6.
'Englishmen will be worn down and I care not their plight,
their bright white houses will strongly be ransacked,
the leathers in their noble carriages will be cut
and Gaels will walk with gusto over their fat fulsome corpses' –
and let us get the jug again and let it be full.

5(b). Maidin Álainn Ghréine [One Lovely Sunny Morning]

Singer: Seán de hÓra (1909–1989), Cloichear, the Dingle Peninsula, Kerry.

Source: *Seán de hÓra ó Chorca Dhuibhne* (compact disc, Cló Iar-Chonnacht, 1989). Also previously published and released in *Bláth 's Craobh na nÚdar: Amhráin Mháire Bhuí* (Ní Shíocháin 2012).

Figure A.4 Maidin Álainn Ghréine [One Lovely Sunny Morning]

1.
Maidin álainn ghréine ar thaobh chnuic na buaile
'sea ' dhearcas an chúileann mhaorga 's a bréidín fliuch ón luachair;
do bhí gile 's finne 'n aonacht go gréiníoch 'na gruannaíbh,
(í) d'fhág sí m'íntinn céasta (an), is baolach (ó) nách buan dom.   4

2.
D'fhiosaraíos-sa go béasach don spéirbhruinneal stuama,
'Ó, c(é)á bhfuil do ghaolta, cén taobh gur ghluaisís?
Nú bean lé fán a' tsaeil tu ná fuil céile ar do thuairisc?
Nú ' fíor go tusa Céarnait ' chuir na tréanmhuilte ar fuaimeant?'   8

3.
''S a (n)fhir(s) óig léannta(n), ní héinne mí dá ndúraís,
ach bean do mhaithibh Gael (ó) tá léanaíthe 'g an gcruatan,
mar m'ainm cheart-sa Éire go bhfuil mac Séarlas dá lua liúm,
go bhfuil 'ú[r] mbailte puirt ag béarthaibh an éithig 's an fhuadaig'.   12

4.
'Ligfeadsa 'nis dom dhánta - táim cráit' óna nduantaíbh,
a' bailiú cíosa 's cánach gan fáilthe ruimh a ndualgas,
mar a mbeig fitheamh leis an lá úd 'nar tháinig aon fhuascailt,
mar gur muar an galar báis liom an t-ál so do bheith fé chruasmacht'.   16

5.
'Ná lig-se 'nis dod dhánta, ná bí cráite ná buartha,
cé gur feárr mo theang' ag trácht air, tá an cháirde linn 'nis buailte,
mar gur cúileann do mhaiseach mná me do tháinig leis an dtuairisc
go raibh *Connell* ó hÍbh Ráthach is a' lá aige siúd buaite.'   20

6.
Do thugas-sa cruithe lámh di, chuireas céad fáilte ruim an stuaire,
cuire suí go lá di go sásta ar a suaineas,
mar do thógfainn tínte cnámh di le áthas ar mhuarchnuic
le súil go mbeadh an lá 'gainn – cead ráis (e) ar na huaisle.   24

English Translation

1.
One lovely sunny morning on the side of the booley hill
I saw the stately fair maid whose braid was wet from the rushes;
there was brightness and fairness combined radiantly in her cheeks,
she left my mind tormented; I fear I may not last.

2.
I enquired politely of the composed fair beauty:
'Where are your relatives, or from whence have you come?
Are you a woman wandering the world with no spousal protection,
or is it true that you are Céarnait who set the strong mills noisily working?'

3.
'Oh young learned gentleman, I am none of those you mentioned,
but I am a woman of Gaelic nobility who has been saddened by hardship;
my true name is Éire and the son of Charles is being betrothed to me,
and that your port towns are in the possession of bears of deceit and plunder'.

4.
'I will cease now from my poems – I am tormented from their compositions,
collecting rent and tax and with no welcome for their responsibilities,
where one will wait for that day in which release will come
because it is a tremendous deathly disease for me that these people should be so sorely oppressed'.

5.
'Do not abandon your poems, be neither tormented nor sad,
even though my tongue says it better, the time is now upon us,
because I am a truly beautiful woman who has come with tidings
that Connell from Iveleary has won the day'.

6.
I shook her by the hand and laid a hundred welcomes before the beautiful woman,
an invitation to stay until day happily at her ease,
that I would build bonfires joyously for her on big hills
hoping that we would have the day – the right to send nobles racing'.

5(c). Maidin Álainn Gréine [One Lovely Sunny Morning]

Singer: Áine Uí Chuíll (Ní Bhuachalla) (1956–). Was living in Bárr Duínse, Coolea, Co. Cork, at the time of this recording, but born and raised in Kilnmartyra, Co. Cork, where she now currently resides. She picked up this song from the singing of Bean Uí Shuibhne from Cúil Aodha, who used to perform in the hall in Kilnamartyra when Áine was a girl.

Source: Field recording by Tríona Ní Shíocháin in Bárr Duínse, 2011. Previously published and released in *Bláth 's Craobh na nÚdar: Amhráin Mháire Bhuí* (Ní Shíocháin 2012).

Figure A.5 Maidin Álainn Gréine [One Lovely Sunny Morning]

1.
Maidin álainn gréine is me 'r thaobh chnoc na buaile,
do casag ainnir taobh liúm 's a bréid (e) fliuch ón luachair;
bhí gile 's finne 'n aonacht go gléineach 'na gruannaibh,
is d'fhág sí m'íntinn lean(a)mhar is is (a) baolach nách buan ' bhead –
   is gheóm arís an crúiscín is bíodh sé lán.   5

2.
D'fhiosraíos go béasach don (a) spéirbhruinneal stuama:
'Cá bhfuil do ghaoltha nú cad é 'n taobh as ar ghluaisís?

An bean ar (a) fán a' tsaeil thú gan chéile ar do thuairisc?
Nú an fíor gur tusa Céarnait a chuir na tréanmhuilt' ar fuaimint?' –
    is gheóm arís an crúiscín is bíodh sé lán.   10

3.
''S a óigfhir chlûil léannta ní héinne me dá nduaraís –
is bean do mhaithibh Gael (a) mi 'tá léanaithe i gcruatain.
M'ainm ceart-sa Éire 's mac Shéarlais dhá lua liom,
mo bhailte puirt ag béaraibh an éithig 's an fhuadaig'–
    is gheóm arís an crúiscín is bíodh sé lán.   15

4.
'Stadfad feast' 'om dhántaibh, táim cráite tinn (a) buartha,
a' bailiú cíosa 's cána 's gan fáil ar aon 'ualgas,
ag feitheamh leis an lá úd 'nar tháinís chúinn dár dtuairisc,
's is muar an galar báis dúinn an t-ál so bheith fé chruatain' –
    is gheóm arís an crúiscín is bíodh sé lán.   20

5.
'Ná leog-se feasta 'od dhántaibh, ní gá dhoit bheith buartha –
gí fada dhúinn a' trácht air, tá 'n cháirde linn buailte;
is cúileann maiseach mná mé do tháinig le tuairisc
go bhfuil Ó Conaill ó Uíbh Ráthach is an lá aige siúd buaite' –
    is gheóm arís an crúiscín is bíodh sé lán.   25

7.
Do thugas-sa croithe lámh dhi is céad (a) fáilthe ruim an (a) stuaire,
cuire stada go lá dhi go sásta ar a suaineas,
do dhófainn tinte chnámh dhi le háthas i mbuaic chnuic
le súil is go mbeadh an lá againn is cead (a) ráis (e) ar na huaislibh –
    is gheóm arís an crúiscín is (a) bíodh sé lán.   30

8.
'Ní neart dom stad go lá cé gur ghá dhom an suaineas –
caithfead triall go Clár Luirc, tá na báire le buala;
beig Sasanaig 's a n-áltha gan fáltas dá ruagairt,
is clanna Gael 'na n-áitreamh 's is áthas liom ró-mhuar é' –
    is gheóm arís an crúiscín is bíodh sé lán.   35

English Translation

1.
One lovely sunny morning while I was on the side of the booley hill
I met a stately fair maid beside me whose braid was wet from the rushes;
there was brightness and fairness combined radiantly in her cheeks,

she left my mind sad and I fear I may not last long –
and let us have the jug again and let it be full.

2.
I enquired politely of the composed fair beauty:
'Where are your relatives, or from whence have you come?
Are you a woman wandering the world with no spousal protection,
or is it true that you are Céarnait who set the strong mills noisily working?' –
and let us have the jug again and let it be full.

3.
'Oh young learned reputable man, I am none of those you mentioned –
I am a woman of Gaelic nobility who has been saddened by hardship;
my true name is Éire and the son of Charles is being betrothed to me,
my port towns in the possession of bears of deceit and plunder' –
and let us have the jug again and let it be full.

4.
'I will cease now from my poems – I am tormented, sore and worried,
collecting rent and tax and with no responsibility to be had,
waiting for that day you came to see how we were,
and it is a tremendous deathly disease for me that these people should endure
    such hardship' –
and let us have the jug again and let it be full.

5.
'Do not abandon your poems, you don't need to worry –
even though we have long talked of it, the time is now upon us,
I am a truly beautiful woman who has come with tidings
that Connell from Iveleary has won the day' –
and let us have the jug again and let it be full.

6.
I shook her by the hand and laid a hundred welcomes before the beautiful woman,
an invitation to stay until day happily at her ease,
that I would burn bonfires joyously for her on the summit of hills
hoping that we would have the day and the right to send nobles racing –
and let us have the jug again and let it be full.

7.
'I can't stay until day with you even though I need the repose –
I must travel to Ireland because the match is to be played;
Englishmen and their families dispossessed and being driven out,
and Irish clans put in their stead and I am exceedingly happy about it' –
and let us get the jug again and let it be full.

5(d). Maidin Álainn Gréine [One Lovely Sunny Morning]

Singer: Cáit Ní Mhuimhneacháin (1918–1949) from Ballingeary, Co. Cork.

Source: National Folklore Archive, sound recording CBÉ CT0257, collected in 1941 by Seán Ó Súilleabháin, previously published and released in *An Joga Mór: Amhráin Cháit Ní Mhuimhneacháin* (Raidió na Gaeltachta 2001), and also in *Bláth 's Craobh na nÚdar: Amhráin Mháire Bhuí* (Ní Shíocháin 2012).

Figure A.6 *Maidin Álainn Gréine [One Lovely Sunny Morning]*

1.
Maidin álainn gréine 's me 'r thaobh chnuic na buaile
'sea ' dhearcas cúileann mhaorga 's a bréid fliuch ón luachair;
bhí gile 's finne 'n aonacht go gléineach 'na gruannaibh,
agus d'fhúig sí m'íntinn léanmhar 's is baolach nách buan a bhead -
is geóm arís an crúiscín is bíodh sé lán.   5

2.
D'fhiosraíos-sa go béasach don spéirbhruinneal stuama,
'Cá bhfuil do ghaoltha nú 'daon taobh as gur ghluaisis?
Nú an (a) bean le fán a' tsaeil thú gan céil' ar do thuairisc?
Nú an fíor gur tusa Céarnait ' chuir na tréanmuilth' ar fuaimit?'-
agus geóm arís an crúiscín is bíodh sé lán.   10

English Translation

1.
One lovely sunny morning while I was on the side of the booley hill
I met a stately fair maid beside me whose braid was wet from the rushes;
there was brightness and fairness combined radiantly in her cheeks,
she left my mind sad and I fear I may not last long –
and let us have the jug again and let it be full.

2.
I enquired politely of the composed fair beauty:
'Where are your relatives, or from whence have you come?
Are you a woman wandering the world with no spousal protection?
Or is it true that you are Céarnait who set the strong mills noisily working?' –
and let us have the jug again and let it be full.

6(a). Seo Leó, ' Thoil [Seo Leó, My Darling]

Scribe: Crothúr 'ac Coitir.

Source: LS141, Special Collections, UCC Library, University College Cork. Previously published in *Filíocht Mháire Bhuidhe Ní Laoghaire* (Ó Donnchú 1931) and *Bláth 's Craobh na nÚdar: Amhráin Mháire Bhuí* (Ní Shíocháin 2012); previously published and translated in *Máire Bhuí Ní Laoire: A Poet of Her People* (Brennan 2000).

This is a lullaby attributed to Máire Bhuí Ní Laeire in which she promises gifts and wonders to a fretting child to soothe him, and includes the sub-theme of the *Amadán Mór* (the Big Fool) from the Fiannaíocht tradition. This traditional lullaby theme is also found in the work of Eoghan Rua Ó Súilleabháin and Diarmuid na Bolgaighe (Ní Shíocháin 2013). The final verses in Máire Bhuí's lullaby, however, are of a strong millenarian character.

1.
Mo ghraidhin go brách thu, ' pháistín óig,
mar taíonn tú buartha suaite d'reóil;
má thíonn tú liomsa gheóir futhain 'us cóir,
agus gheó' tú duais nár luamh leat fós;
agus seo leó, ' thoil, agus ná goil go fóill ...

2.
Do gheóir chun bainne uaim macha breá bó,
'us gheó' tú an tarbh chun clasaithe leó,
gheóir na capaill chun branair 'us rôir,
'us gheóir fíon dearg 's a mhalairt ar bórd;
agus seo leó, ' thoil, agus ná goil go fóill ...

3.
Gheóir a' clogad 's a' sciath ón Amadán Mór,
'us gheó' tú an t-úll ón gcúilinn óig,
gheóir a' gadhar ba mheidhraí ceól
do cheangail a' laoch à héill 'na dhóid;
agus seo leó, ' thoil, agus ná goil go fóill ...

4.
Gheóir a' corn fí dheochanna sóil
do chuireadh a' draíocht ar na mílthe sló,
do gheóir a' chathair úd Dhún an Óir
a bhí 'gen nGruagach Muar chun spóirt;
agus seo leó, ' thoil, agus ná goil go fóill ...

5.
Gheóir a' lomar' do fuilceag le hór
' thug Jás 'na loíng thar toínn ar bórd,
gheóir na capaill fí bhratannaibh sróil
ó mhac Rí an Dirig cé gur fada dho id chôir;
agus seo leó, ' thoil, agus ná goil go fóill ...

6.
Gheóir Mo' Chromtha gan dabht chun bróg,
'us gheó' tú an Droichead chun *provision* lóin,
gheóir Bleá Cliath chun fiaig 'us spóirt,

'us gheóir chun stuiceanna Luimine Mhór;
agus seo leó, ' thoil, agus ná goil go fóill …

7.
Gheó' tú Béarra chun éisc ar bórd,
'us gheóir a' maraga leathan fí fheóil,
gheóir na cuanta fí bhádaibh seóil,
'us gheóir Íbh Laeire chun sméar 'us cnó;
agus seo leó, ' thoil, agus ná goil go fóill …

8.
Ar a' mbliain seo chúinn beig búir fí bhrón
'us cathair 'us dún gan smúit gan cheó,
'us gheóir gach ní nár mhaíos ort fós:
iníon a' diúic id chlúid chun spóirt;
agus seo leó, ' thoil, agus ná goil go fóill …

9.
Ná goil a thuille 'us ná ficim do dheóir,
mar beid siúd scriosta shara dtigig a' fôr,
beig a súile ' sile agus briste ar a nglór,
'us a gcóistí againne 'na ngliugaram spóirt;
agus seo leó, ' thoil, agus ná goil go fóill …

English Translation

1.
My eternal pity for you, oh little child,
for you are worried, distressed and miserable;
if you come with me you will get shelter and proper attention,
and you will get a prize that hasn't been mentioned to you yet;
and seo leó, my darling, and don't cry yet …

2.
You will get for milk a fine herd of cattle,
and you will get the bull to breed with them,
you will get the horses for ploughing and tillage,
and you will get red wine and its opposite on the table;
and seo leó, my darling, and don't cry yet …

3.
You will get the helmet and shield from the Big Fool,
and you will get the apple from the fair young lady,

you will get the dog of the merriest music
that the hero tied up with a rope in his fist;
and seo leó, my darling, and don't cry yet …

4.
You will get the cup of the sumptuous drinks
that used to enchant the thousands,
you will get that fort of Dún an Óir
that the Great Enchanter used to have for sport;
and seo leó, my darling, and don't cry yet …

5.
You will get the fleece that was bathed in gold
that Jason took over the wave on his ship,
you will get the horses under satin cloaks
from the son of Rí an Dirig even though you have long deserved it;
and seo leó, my darling, and don't cry yet …

6.
You will get Macroom of course for shoes,
and you will get the Bridge (i.e. Bandon) for lunch provision,
you will get Dublin for hunting and sport,
and you will get great Limerick for stock;
and seo leó, my darling, and don't cry yet …

7.
You will get Beara for fish for your table
and you will get the plentiful market of meat,
you will get harbours of sailing ships,
and you will get Iveleary for berries and nuts;
and seo leó, my darling, and don't cry yet …

8.
Next year coming, boors will be sorrowful
and city and fort will be without blemish without mist,
and you will get something I haven't boasted of yet:
the duke's daughter by your fireside for sport;
and seo leó, my darling, and don't cry yet …

9.
Don't cry anymore and let me not see your tears,
for they will be destroyed before harvest-time,
their eyes will be weeping and their voices will be broken,
and we will make joyous wreckage of their coaches;
and seo leó, my darling, and don't cry yet …

6(b). Seo Leó, ' Thoil [Seo Leó, my Darling]

Singer: Maighréad Uí Luínse, Ré na nDoirí, Co. Cork, initially from Ballingeary, Co. Cork.

Source: National Folklore Archive, sound recording CBÉ CT0265_0065a, collected by Seán Ó Súilleabháin in 1941. Previously published and released in *Bláth 's Craobh na nÚdar: Amhráin Mháire Bhuí* (Ní Shíocháin 2012).

Figure A.7 Seo Leó, ' Thoil [Seo Leó, My Darling]

1.
[Mo ghraidh]in go brách tú, a pháistín óig,
mar taíonn tú buartha suaite d'reóil;
má thigeann tú liomsa gheóir futhain is cóir
agus gheó' tú duais nár luag leat fós;
    agus seo leó, ' thoil, agus ná goil go fóill;
    seo leó, ' thoil, agus ná goil ná deóir.   6

2.
Seacht n-úna an domhain gan dabht do gheóir,
an Cnoc Mhaol Donn is an rann 'na threó;
' bhfuil do thalamh anis gan chíos don stór
faid a rithfig an ghrian go dian sa ló;
    agus seo leó, ' thoil, agus ná goil go fóill;
    seo leó, ' thoil, agus ná goil ná deóir.   12

3.
Gheóir Mo' Chromtha gan dabht chun bróg,
gheóir an Droichead 's a bhfuil ann do lón,
gheóir Bleá Cliath chun fiaig is spóirt,
agus gheóir chun stuice Luimineach Mór;

agus seo leó, ' thoil, agus ná goil go fóill;
    seo leó, ' thoil, agus ná goil ná deóir.   18

4.
Gheó' tú Béarra chun éisc ar bórd,
gheóir an maraga leathan fí fheóil,
gheóir na cuanta fí bhádaibh seóil,
agus gheóir Íbh Laeire chun sméar is cnó;
agus seo leó, ' thoil, agus ná goil go fóill;
    seo leó, ' thoil, agus ná goil ná deóir.   24

English Translation

1.
My eternal pity for you, oh little child,
for you are worried, distressed and miserable;
if you come with me you will get shelter and proper attention,
and you will get a prize that hasn't been mentioned to you yet;
and seo leó, my darling, and don't cry yet,
seo leó, my darling, and don't cry or weep.

2.
The seven wonders of the world of course you will receive,
the Knockmealdown mountain and its constellation of stars,
that your land now is without rent for the store
for as far as the sun will travel in the day;
and seo leó, my darling, and don't cry yet,
seo leó, my darling, and don't cry or weep.

3.
You will get Macroom of course for shoes,
and you will get the Bridge (i.e. Bandon) and all that is there for lunch,
you will get Dublin for hunting and sport,
and you will get great Limerick for stock;
and seo leó, my darling, and don't cry yet,
seo leó, my darling, and don't cry or weep.

4.
You will get Beara for fish for your table
and you will get the plentiful market of meat,
you will get harbours of sailing ships,
and you will get Iveleary for berries and nuts;
and seo leó, my darling, and don't cry yet,
seo leó, my darling, and don't cry or weep.

7(a). Cath Chéim an Fhia [The Battle of Keimaneigh]

Scribe: Crothúr 'ac Coitir.

Source: LS Í Chuív. Previously published in *Filíocht Mháire Bhuidhe Ní Laoghaire* (Ó Donnchú 1931) and *Bláth 's Craobh na nÚdar: Amhráin Mháire Bhuí* (Ní Shíocháin 2012); previously published and translated in *Máire Bhuí Ní Laoire: A Poet of Her People* (Brennan 2000).

This is the most famous of the songs attributed to Máire Bhuí Ní Laeire and is still popular among the traditional singing community in Irish-speaking Cork to this day. The song recounts the Battle of Keimaneigh, which took place in January 1822, but also articulates a millenarian political vision that orients towards the continued anticolonial struggle. It also includes reference to the famous prophecy of Pastorini, which spelled apocalypse in the 1820s, at the end of verse 4.

1.
Cois abha Ghleanna 'n Chéama i nUíbh Laeire 'sea ' bhímse
   mar a dtéann a' fia insan oíche chun síor-cholla sóil,
a' machnamh seal liom féinig a' déanamh mo smaointibh,
   ag éisteacht i gcoíllthibh le bínn-ghuth na n-eón;
     nuair a chuala 'n cath a' teacht aniar,   5
     glór na n-each a' teacht le sians,
     le fuaim an airm chrith a' sliabh
     'us níor bhínn linn a nglór.
Do thánadar go nádmhar mar a thiocfadh gárd' do chonaibh ní
   'us mo chú-sa na sáirfhir do fágamh fí bhrón.   10

2.
Níor fhan bean ná páiste i mbun áitribh ná tí 'co
   ach na gártha do bhí 'co 'gus mílth' olagón,
a' féachaint ar a' ngárda a' teacht láidir 'na dtíompall,
   a' lâch 'us a' líona 's a' scaoile 'na dtreó;
     an liú gur lean i bhfad i gcian,   15
     'sé ' duairt gach flaith nur mhaith leis triall,
     'Gluaisíg mear, tá 'n cath dhá rian'
     agus téimís 'na chôir'.
Thánadar na sáirfhir i gcoím áthais le clanna Gaíol
   agus do chumáineadar na páinthig le fánaig ar seól.   20

3.
Is gairid dhúinn go dtáinig lámh láidir 'ár dtíompall
   do sheól amach ár ndaoine go fíor-mhoch fín gceó,
an Barràch 'na bhumbáille, *Barnet* 'gus *Beecher*,
   Hedges agus Whítig, 'us na mílth' eile leó;

a Rí na bhFeart, go lagaig iad 25
gan chlú gan mheas gan rath gan séan²
i dtínte teasa i measc na bpian
gan faeiseamh go deó.
Céad mola muar le Íosa nár dhíolamair as a' dtóir
   ach ' bheith a' déanamh grínn de 'us á ínsint ar só. 30

4.
Sa bhliain seo 'nis atá 'gainn beig rás ar gach smíste,
   cuirfeam insa díg iad, draoib orthu 'us fóid;
ní iarrfam cúirt ná stáitse, beig árd-chroch 'na suí 'gainn,
   's a' chnáib go slachtmhar sníte le díolthas 'na gcóir.
     Is acu 'thá 'n tslat, is olc í ' riail, 35
     i gcóistíbh greanta is maith é ' ngléas,³
     gach sórd le caitheamh, flea 'gus féasta,
     ag béaraibh ar bórd.
Go b'é deir gach údar cruínn liom sara gcríochnaí siad deire an fhóir
   insa leabhar so Pastorína go ndíolfaid as a' bpóit. 40

5.
Do bhí Smith ar a thárr i n-áirde ar árd-leacain fhraoig dhuibh,
   ba ghránna a bhí a ghnaoi 'us gan toínte ar a thóin –
nár bheire crích is feárr iad, an t-ál so Chailbhin choîthig
   nár ghéill riamh do Chríost, ach poímp agus póit.
     Beig na sluaite fear a' teacht gan chiach, 45
     ar longa mear' is fada é a dtriall,
     's a' Franncach theas nár mheathlaig riamh
     i bhfaor agus i gcóir.
Beig catharacha á stríoca agus tínteacha á lasa leó –
   tá 'n cáirde fada díoltha 's a' líonrith 'na gcôir. 50

6.
'S a Chlanna Gaíol na n-áranm, ná staonaig 'us ná stríocaig,
   is geárr anis gan moíll go mbeig crích ar 'úr ngnó,
agus tógaig suas 'úr gc'ráiste, tá 'n t-ál so le díbirt
   go Ifreann á dtíora 'dir thínteachaibh teó:
     bíodh 'úr bpící glan' i gceart i ngléas,⁴ 55
     téig 'on chath, ná fanaig siar,
     tá 'n chabhair a' teacht le toil ó Dhia,
     agus léiríg na póirc.
Sáig isteach go dána i n-áitreamh a dtáinig rôibh,
   is mithid díbh é ' fháil 'us tá 'n cáirde maith go leór. 60

7.
Stadfad feasta 'om dhántaibh, táim lámh leis a' gcríonnacht,
    tá iomarca 'on dro-chroí 'gam i mbuín na mbolg mór,
ní gean dom a thuille ' rá leó – nára feárrde don mbuíon é
    ach ár agus scîle go dtíg ar a gcór:
        nár' díon dóibh stad ar sheal dá ngléas,   65
        nár' díon dóibh carraig, cnoc ná sliabh
        mar a mbíonn a' sineach mear dá fhiach
        'us a' ghéim aco ar seól.
Beig gach sáirfhear croíúil 's a phíce 's a shlea 'na dhóid
    gan súil le sásamh choíche ná díol as go deó.   70

English Translation

1.
By the river of the glen of Keimaneigh in Iveleary that I frequent
where the deer goes at night to sleep soundly,
thinking a while to myself and making my ideas,
listening in woods to the melodious voice of the birds;
when I heard the battle coming from the West,
the symphonic sound of the horses coming,
with the noise of the army the mountain shook
and their sound was not sweet to us.
They came treacherously as a guard of poisonous hounds
and my grief the fine men who were left sorrowful.

2.
No woman or child stayed at the homestead
but they let out cries and thousands of wails,
looking at the guard that was closing in strongly around them,
shooting and loading and firing in their direction;
the shout that resounded afar,
every warrior said he would go,
'Move quickly, the battle is being plotted,
and let us go forth'.
The good men arrived in a mountain recess of happiness for clans of the Gael
and they drove the fat men away down the hill.

3.
It was not long until the strong arm enveloped us,
our people were sent out early under mist,
Barry was the bumbailiff, Barnet and Beecher,

Hedges and Whites and thousands more;
oh God of Wonders, may you strike them down
without reputation without respect without luck or good omen
to fires of heat plunged in pains
without relief for all eternity.
One hundred praises to Jesus that we didn't pay for our pursuit
but that we can make light of it and tell the tale at our leisure.

4.
This coming year every good for nothing lump will be sent racing,
we will bury them in the ditch, covered with mud and sods;
we will seek neither court nor stage, we will have a high hanging,
with the noose neatly taut in vengeance.
It is they who hold the cane, terrible is its rule,
in ornate coaches of fine gloss,
every good thing to consume, feast and banquet,
laid out for bears.
What every accurate author [prophet] tells me before they finish the end of
    harvest time
that in this book of Pastorini that they will pay for their drunkenness.

5.
Smith was face down on a high slab of black heather,
his appearance was disgusting without a rag to cover his backside –
may they meet no better end than this, that family of foreign Calvin
who never submitted to Christ, but to pomp and intoxication.
Hordes of men will joyfully arrive,
in swift ships they travel from afar,
and the Frenchman to the South who never waned
in blades and arms (or zeal and justice).
Cities will submit and be set ablaze,
long have we been owed, and terror is in store for them.

6.
And oh beloved Gaelic clans, do not desist and do not submit,
it will not be long now before your work is done,
and raise up your courage, this crew are to be banished
to Hell to be toasted in hot fires:
let your clean pikes be at the ready,
go forth to battle, don't hold back,
help is coming with the grace of God,
and subdue the swine (or show the swine).
Boldly push in to the holdings that came before you,
it is high time for you, and their time is up.

7.
I will cease with my poems, I am nearing old age,
I have too much bad heart for the big bellied lot,
I wish not to say any more – there would be no better outcome
but for destruction and terror to descend upon that company:
may they not have the shelter of ceasing a while from their munitions,
may rock, hill or mountain provide no cover for them,
where the swift fox hunts
while game is pursued.
Every big-hearted fine man with his pike and spear in his fist
expecting never to be satisfied nor to ever pay for his deeds.

7(b). Cath Chéim an Fhia [The Battle of Keimaneigh]

Singer: Peáití Thaidhg Pheig (Pádraig Ó Tuama) (1893–1968), born and reared in an Ráth, Baile Mhic Íre, but married into na Millíní in Coolea, where he spent the rest of his life (Acadamh Fódhla 2011).

Source: Sound recording from Raidió Teilifís Éireann, collected by Ciarán Mac Mathúna and Seán Ó Riada in 1962. This rendition contains only three verses of the song; in other recordings Peáití sings additional verses (Acadamh Fódhla 2011). Previously released on compact disc *Amhráin ar an Sean-nós* (RTÉ, undated), *Bláth 's Craobh na nÚdar: Amhráin Mháire Bhuí* (Ní Shíocháin 2012), and *Peáití Thaidhg Pheig* (Acadamh Fódhla 2011).

Figure A.8 Cath Chéim an Fhia [The Battle of Keimaneigh]

1.
Cois abhainn Ghleanna 'n Chéama i nÍbh (a) Laeire 'sea ' bhímse
    mar a dtéann an fia insan oíche chon (a) síor(a)cholla sóil,
a' machnamh seal liom féinig a' déanamh mo smaointibh
    ag éisteacht i gcoíllthe le guth bínn na n-eón;
nuair a chuala an cath ag teacht aniar   5
is glór na n-each ag teacht le sians,
le fuaim na n-arm do chrith an sliabh;
        níor mhéinn linn a nglór.
Thánadar go nâdmhar mar a thiocfadh gárd' do chonaibh nî
    ach cû mo chroí na sárfhir d'fhágadar gan treóir.   10

2.
Níor fhan fear, bean, ná páiste i mbun áitribh na dtíora,
    na gártha guil do bhí acu 's na mílte olagón,
a' féachaint ar an ngárda go láidir 'nár dtíompall
    a' lâch 'us a' líona 's a' scaoile 'nár dtreó;
an liú gur leath i bhfad i gcian,   15
'sé ' duairt gach flaith nur mhaith leis triall,
'Gluaisíg go mear tá an cath dá riar
        agus téimís 'na dtreó'.
Thánadar na sárfhir; guím áthas ar chlanna Gael;
    thiomáineadar na páinthig le fánaig ar seól.   20

3.
Ba ghairid dúinn go dtáinig lámh láidir 'nár dtíompall,
    do scaipeadar ár ndaoine 's gach (a) maoilinn fén gceó,
bhí an Bùrràch 'na bhunbháille 'cu, *Barnett* agus *Beecher*,
    Hedges agus Faoiteas is na mílthe eile leó;
a Rí na bhFeart go leagaig iad   25
gan chlú gan mheas gan rath (a) gan séan,
go (d)tíonta mear' i measc na bpian,
        gan faeiseamh go deó.
Céad mola muar le Íosa nár dhíolamair as an dteóir
    ach a' bheith a' déanamh grínn de 's dá ínsint ar só.   30

English Translation

1.
By the river of the glen of Keimaneigh in Iveleary that I frequent
where the deer goes at night to sleep soundly,
thinking a while to myself and making my ideas,
listening in woods to the melodious voice of the birds;

when I heard the battle coming from the West,
the symphonic sound of the horses coming,
with the noise of the army the mountain shook
and we didn't like their sound.
They came treacherously as a guard of poisonous hounds
and my heart's sorrow the fine men who were left without direction.

2.
No man, woman or child stayed at the homesteads,
but they let out cries and thousands of wails,
looking at the guard that was closing in strongly around them,
shooting and loading and firing in their direction;
the shout that spread afar,
every warrior said he would go,
'Move quickly, the battle is being managed,
and let us go forth'.
The good men arrived; I wish happiness on Gaelic clans;
they drove the fat men away down the hill.

3.
It was not long until the strong arm enveloped us,
they scattered our people and every hillock under the mist,
Barry was the bumbailiff, Barnet and Beecher,
Hedges and Whites and thousands more;
oh God of Wonders, may you strike them down
without reputation without respect without luck or good omen
to fast fires plunged in pains
without relief for all eternity.
One hundred praises to Jesus that we didn't pay for our pursuit
but that we can make light of it and tell the tale at our leisure.

8. Tá Gaeil Bhocht' Cráite [Poor Gaels Are Tormented]

Source: Ó Donnchú papers, Ballingeary Historical Society.

Singer: Diarmuid 'ac Coitir from na Corraithe Thiar in Ballingeary. Collected by Donncha Ó Donnchú in the early twentieth century. Previously published in *Filíocht Mháire Bhuidhe Ní Laoghaire* (Ó Donnchú 1931) and *Bláth 's Craobh na nÚdar: Amhráin Mháire Bhuí* (Ní Shíocháin 2012); previously published and translated in *Máire Bhuí Ní Laoire: A Poet of Her People* (Brennan 2000).

The story goes that Máire Bhuí composed this song on her deathbed during the famine (Ó Donnchú 1931: 77), however the political discourses of the song itself, which include reference to St John's prophecy, would suggest that the song was composed much earlier, most probably in the 1820s, when the millenarian movement was at its height (Ó Gráda 1994: 86–87). This song most likely is telling of the reprisals that followed the Battle of Keimaneigh itself, and of the fate of the men involved, some of whom were hanged and some of whom were transported (O'Leary 1993: 14–15).

1.
Tá Gaeil bhocht' cráite go céasta cásmhar
    agus cúirt gach lá orthu mar dhúbailt bróin,
clanna sáirfhear dá gcrocha i n-áirde
    's dá gcur síos láithreach sa chroppy-hole,   4
tá na loingeas lán díobh dá gcur thar sáile,
    mo chú go brách sibh faoi iomad yoke,
nára fada an cáirde go bhfaighi' sibh sásamh,
    is agatsa atá 's san, a Rí na gCôcht.   8

2.
Is é ' chuala ó fháigibh go nduairt Naomh Seán linn
    go raibh deire an cháirde caite leó,
's go dtiocfadh *slaughter* ar gach piara másach
    nár ghéill don Pháis is do chaith an phóit;   12
aon chaonaí fánach ná túrfar bás do
    ag iompar mála agus é 'na dhóid,
's gan déirc sa láimh sin a thúrfadh náid do
    ach buala is cáine dá mbrú go deó.   16

3.
Is an bhliain seo atá againn 'sea ' bheig rírá againn
    tar éis búir do thnátha is do charta i ngleó;
beig tínte cnâ againn ar na mullaíbh árda
    agus adharc le háthas ag seinm ceóil;   20
mná agus páistí go mbeid dá dtnátha
    is le clochaibh an bháin 'sea do leagfaid póirc,
is le leônú an Árdmhic go dtitfid lánlag
    chô tiubh le báistig ar chnoc lá ceóig.   24

4.
Leaga is leóna agus scîle dóite
    go dtíg ar an gcóip sin 's a stór 'na measc,
an chroch 's an córda dá gcur fína scórnaig
    agus Dia nár fhóirig go mór a gceas;   28
ceangal côraic orthu ag Oscar cróga
    is é ' bheith ag gabháil go deó orthu go leóna 'n gad,

is i n-áit na n-óigfhear 'tá sínte ró-lag
    an bhuíon go brónach go deó na ngealth. 32

5.
Tá mo shúil lem Mháistir gur geárr an cáirde
    go bhfeiceam lá orthu agus tamall spóirt,
is go mbeid dá dtnátha gan chúirt gan státse
    gan fallaí bána gan fíon gan beóir; 36
go mbeig na mílthe lánphoc i n-aon pholl amháin acu
    ar a dtárr i n-áirde gan chloch gan fód,
agus Gaeil ar chlár glan ag ól mo shláinte
    is me féinig láithreach dá chnaga leó. 40

6.
Is nár théad sa bhán ghlas ná ag túirt an fhásaig
    go bhfeicead rás ar lucht bolg mór,
go mbeig rith is rás ar an ndream so ' chráig sinn,
    is d'fhúig fín mbráca gach a dtáinig rôinn; 44
nuair a gheód an lá orthu níl gnó agaibh trácht liom
    ar phiúnt, ar chárt do chur ar scór,
ach baraillí lána agus iad ar státse
    dá dtúirt do tháintibh mar dhig le n-ól. 48

English Translation

1.
Poor Gaels are tormented, troubled and in sorry plight
and court every day upon them as a double sorrow,
sons of fine men being strung up (hanged)
and being thrown immediately into the croppy-hole,
the ships are full of them being transported overseas,
my eternal sorrow that you are under the yoke,
may it not be long now 'til you get satisfaction,
only You know, oh King of Powers.

2.
What I heard from prophets is that St John has told us
that their time is up,
and that slaughter will befall every fat-arsed peer
that didn't submit to the Passion and who engaged in drunken excesses;
any poor wandering loner that isn't given death
while he carries nothing but a bag in his fist,

and with no charity in that hand that would bestow him nought
but beating and disparagement forever pressing on him.

3.
And this coming year we will have uproar
having exhausted and cleared out boors in noisy battle;
we will have bonfires on high summits
and the horn joyfully playing music;
women and children will be wearing them down
and with the rocks of the plain they will defeat swine,
and with the permission of the High Son that they will fall full-weak
as thick as rain on a hill on a misty day.

4.
Knocking and injury and burnt terror
may such befall that company and all associated with them,
the hangman's noose under their necks
and may God not help them in their plight;
brave Oscar will put them in the binds of battle
and will beat them eternally until the rope strains,
and instead of the young men that lie here dead
that crew will be eternally sorrowful.

5.
My hope is with my Master that it will not be long now
'til we shall see the day and have sport at their expense,
and that they will be ground down without court without stage
without white halls without wine without beer;
that thousands of those fat pucks will be in one hole
face down without stone nor sod,
and Gaels at a clean counter drinking my health
and I in the middle of them knocking it back.

6.
And may I not go to the green plain nor to the wilderness
until I see that the crew of big bellies are sent fleeing,
and that we will have run and race upon these people who persecuted us,
and who drove into hardship all who came before us;
when I win the day over them don't bother talking to me
about tallying a pint or a quart,
but full barrels on a platform
to be given to the masses to drink.

9(a). A Mháir' Ní Laeire [Oh Mary O'Leary] composed by Máire Bhuí Ní Laeire and Donncha Bán Ó Luínse

Scribe: Crothúr 'ac Coitir.

Source: LS Í Chuív. Previously published in *Filíocht Mháire Bhuidhe Ní Laoghaire* (Ó Donnchú 1931) and *Bláth 's Craobh na nÚdar: Amhráin Mháire Bhuí* (Ní Shíocháin 2012); previously published and translated in *Máire Bhuí Ní Laoire: A Poet of Her People* (Brennan 2000).

This song is ascribed to Máire Bhuí Ní Laeire and the song poet Donncha Bán Ó Luínse. Though this particular manuscript states that Diarmuid Ach Seámuis composed the song in conjunction with Máire Bhuí, stating that Máire Bhuí 'composed it all to the first verse', another manuscript copy (LS140, UCC) by the same scribe attributes the song to Máire Bhuí and Donncha Bán Ó Luínse, stating that 'Denis Lynch Ballyvourney composed the 1st & last verses'. Pádraig Ó Crualaoi also ascribes the song to Máire Bhuí and Donncha Bán Ó Luínse, and maintained that Donncha Bán composed verses 1, 3 and the final verse, and Máire Bhuí composed the rest (Ó Cróinín 1982: 113–16).

1.
A Mháir' Ní Laeire ó bhéal a' Chéama
   mar a mbíonn os maol dá mhúiscilt,
an amhla' ' éagais ná hairím aon phiuc
   do ghuth do bhéil á mhúiscilt,   4
nú ' bhfeacaís éinne ' gabháil moch ná déanach
   sa ghleann so taobh le Diúchuil,
do neósadh scéal duit ar chúrsaí an tsaeil seo
   'ge clanna Gael i gcúng'reacht?   8

2.
Do chualag scéal duit anis go déanach
   ó fhiodóg slé ' bhí i nDiúchuil,
go suífeadh téarma gan moíll in Éirinn
   a chuirfeadh béir ar gcúlaibh;   12
go mbeadh repéalers 's a bhfórsaí tréana,
   agus cúnamh Dé 'co á stiúra,
'gus buín a' Bhéarla gan fíon gan féasta,
   'gus stealla p'léar dhá ndúiseacht.   16

3.
Go n-eighrí an saol leis a' bhfiodóg slé 'mu
   do thug a' scéal san chút-sa

le grá 'us le méinn duit thar mhnáibh na hÉireann,
   a bhláth 's a chraobh na n-údar.   20
Ó bhís chô héasca 'gus lâch le béaraibh
   'us iad d'fhágaint tréith le púdar,
tá 'n cáirde taobh leó le grásta 'n Aon-Mhic
   do gheárr a' téarma ar dtúis dóibh.   24

4.
Beig stealla p'léar agus pící géara
   dhá gcuir 'na méadail bhrúidig,
beig cloch 'us craobh orthu ó láimh gach éinne
   'gus mùllacht Dé ar a' gcúmplacht;   28
beid siad faonlag fí spalla gréine
   gan neach sa tsaol 'na gcúram,
a gcuin 's a m*béagles* 's a gcapaill traocht[a]
   gan dúil i ngéim ná ' liú 'co.   32

5.
Tá dram an áil seo go céasta cráite
   'ge cíos 'us cáin á dtúrna,
'gus búir go táchtmhar in allaí bána
   'gus deire ' gcáirde túrtha.   36
Ní bheig féasta ar clár ach prátaí bána
   'gus salann lán do bhrúscar;
'us ní bheinn féin sásta le méid a ngátair
   go bhfaighidís bás gan bhlúire.   40

6.
Dá mbeinn ar clár glan fé thobac gheárrtha
   'us fé sholas bhán gan múcha,
go n-aireóinn rás ar a' ndram so ' chráig sinn,
   go n-eighreóinn láidir chúthu.   44
Tá mo shúil lem Mháistir ná raghad 'on bhán ghlas
   go bhficead tláth an cúmplacht,
'us go mbead á n-áireamh i bpollaibh báite
   'us le foillibh árd' á rúsca.   48

7.
Do chualag trácht ort, a mhic a' deá-'thar,
   gur mhaith do cháil id dhúthaig,
guím séan 'us áthas 'us sliocht fí bhláth ort
   a chuirfig c'ráiste 'us fúnn ort.   52

Dá gcastí lá orm thu ' dtig a' táirne,
   do thúrfainn cárt fí chúr duit
'us crotha lámh leis ag ól do shláinte,
   'gus *punch* ar clár go flúirseach.   56

8.
'S a mhic a' deá-'thar nár thuíll tu ' cháine,
   mar bhís fial fáiltheach flúirseach,
ní dhéan-sa trácht ar a thuille dánta,
   táim críonna tâch-lag brúite.   60
Bronnaim láithreach an chraobh id láimh duit,
   a bun 's a bárr 's a húlla,
'us ná caill do ch'ráiste – insa bhliain seo lámh linn
   a bheig ochalán ar bhúraibh.   64

9.
Go deimhin is dó' liom, más fíor do ghlórtha,
   gur dhinis óg arís me
chun *tally hó* ' bheith ar mhnáibh na rógairí seo
   dh'itheann feóil Dé hAoine.   68
'Sé ' deir lucht eólais go mbeid siúd brónach
   mar ghiúll ar phóit an tsaoil seo
ná leanann côirle na cléireach cóireach
   'us gabháil a' bóthar díreach.   72

English Translation

1.
Oh Mary O'Leary from the mouth of Keimaneigh
where the hornless deer stirs,
is it that you have died that I hear none
of the voice of your mouth stirring,
or did you see anyone early or late
in this glen beside Diúchuil
that would tell a tale of the happenings of this world
of Gaelic clans in difficulty?

2.
I heard a tale for you of late
from a mountain plover in Diúchuil,
that a term would reside shortly in Ireland
that would send bears retreating;

that there would be repealers and their strong forces,
and the help of God steering them,
and that English-speaking crew without wine without feast
and pelting of bullets starting them.

3.
The best of wishes for your mountain plover
who brought you that tale
and with love and affection for you over all the women of Ireland,
oh flower and branch of authors (i.e. greatest of all authors, poets or prophets).
Oh you were so adept at firing at bears
and enweakening them with gunpowder,
the time is upon them with the grace of the One Son
who created the term for them first day.

4.
There will be pelting of bullets and sharp pikes
being driven through their brutish paunches,
a stone and branch down upon them from every hand
and God's curse on the company;
they will be exhausted and weak under scorching sun
with no one in the world to care for them,
their hounds and beagles and their horses exhausted
with no desire for game or shout.

5.
Our people are tormented and troubled
by rent and tax which defeat them,
and boors (self)importantly in white halls
and their time is running out.
There will be no feast upon table but white potatoes
and salt full of dirt;
and I wouldn't be happy with the extent of their deprivation
unless they died without a scrap to eat.

6.
If I were on a white plank under cut tobacco
and under a white light unquenched,
and if I were to hear that that crew who persecuted us were sent racing,
I would rise up strongly to them.
My eye is to my Master that I won't go to the green plain
until I may see that company weak,

and until I will be counting their dead bodies drowned in bog holes
and being flung over high cliffs.

7.
I heard talk of you, oh son of the fine father,
and your reputation precedes you in the country,
I wish good luck and happiness and flowering descendants upon you
that will give you courage and vigour.
If I were to meet you one day in the tavern
I would give you a frothing quart
and shake your hand and drink to your good health,
and there would be plentiful punch to drink.

8.
Oh son of the fine father who never earned criticism,
because you were big-hearted, welcoming and generous,
I won't talk any more of poems,
I am old, weak and worn.
I give you now the branch in your hand,
its bottom, top and apples,
and don't lose courage – in this coming year
boors will be groaning.

9.
Indeed I think, if your voice is true,
that you have made me young again,
to give tally ho to the women of these rogues
who eat meat on Friday.
All those who are knowledgeable say that they will be sad
because of the drunken excesses of this life
for those who don't follow the advice of the true clergy
and stay on the straight road.

9(b). A Mháir' Ní Laeire [Oh Mary O'Leary] by Máire Bhuí Ní Laeire and Donncha Bán Ó Luínse

Singer: Cáit Ní Mhuimhneacháin (1918–1949) from Ballingeary, Co. Cork.

Source: National Folklore Archive, sound recording CBÉ CT0342_0797, collected in 1941 by Seán Ó Súilleabháin. Previously published and released in *An Joga Mór: Amhráin Cháit Ní Mhuimhneacháin* (RnaG 2001), and also in *Bláth 's Craobh na nÚdar: Amhráin Mháire Bhuí* (Ní Shíocháin 2012).

Figure A.9 A Mháir' Ní Laeire [Oh Mary O'Leary] by Máire Bhuí Ní Laeire and Donncha Bán Ó Luínse

1.
'Us a Mháir' Ní Laeir' ó bhéal a' Chéama
  mar a mbíonn an eilit mhaol dá múiscilt,
an amhl' ' éagais ná hairím aon phiuc
  de ghuth do bhéil sa dúthaig,   4
nú a' bhfeacaís éinne g'bháil much nú déanach
  sa ghleann so taobh le Diúchuil
do neósadh scéal doit ar chúrsaí an tsaeil seo
  go bhfuil Clanna Gael i gcúngracht?   8

2.
Do chuala scéilín anis le déanaí
  ó fhideóg shlé bhí nDiúchuil
go suífeadh téarma gan mhoíll in Éirinn
  (a) do chuirfeadh béir ar gcúlaibh;   12
go mbeadh *repéalers*'s a bhfórsaí tréana
  'gus cúnamh Dé dá stiúra,
agus buíon an Bhéarla gan fíon gan féasta
  'gus cáithe p'léar dá rúsca.   16

3.
Go n-eighrí an saol leis an bhfideóig shlé 'mu
  do thug an scéal san chútsa

le grá 's le méinn doit thar mhnáibh na hÉireann,
   a bhláth 's a chraobh na n-údar.   20
Ó bhís chô néata 'gus lâch le béara
   's a bhfágaint tréith le púdar,
tá an cáirde taobh leó le grásta 'n Aonmhic
   do gheárr an téarma ar dtúis dóibh.   24

English Translation

1.
Oh Mary O'Leary from the mouth of Keimaneigh
where the hornless female deer stirs,
is it that you have died that I hear none
of the voice of your mouth in the district,
or did you see anyone early or late
in this glen beside Diúchuil
that would tell you a tale of the happenings of this world
that Gaelic clans are in difficulty?

2.
I heard a little tale for you lately
from a mountain plover in Diúchuil,
that a term would reside shortly in Ireland
that would send bears retreating;
that there would be repealers and their strong forces,
and the help of God steering them,
and that English-speaking crew without wine without feast
and spraying of bullets shaking them.

3.
The best of wishes for your mountain plover out there
who brought you that tale
and with love and affection for you over all the women of Ireland,
oh flower and branch of authors (i.e. the greatest of all authors, poets or prophets).
Oh you were so neat at firing at bears
and enweakening them with gunpowder,
the time is upon them with the grace of the One Son
who created the term for them first day.

10. Máire Bhuí agus Donncha Chruíd [Máire Bhuí and Donncha Chruíd]

Storyteller: Pádraig Ó Murchadha (Peatsaí Chit) from Gort Luachra, Iveleary, born in 1871.

Source: National Folklore Archive, CBÉ 849: 438–39. Collected by Seán Ó Cróinín in 1942 for the Irish Folklore Commission. Previously published in *Bláth 's Craobh na nÚdar: Amhráin Mháire Bhuí* (Ní Shíocháin 2012).

Bhí file eile anso an uair sin agus do bhí go seóig. Is é an áit go raibh sé féin agus a mhuíntir – ar an gCloich mBarraig (barra na hÍnse Muaire, b.f. i mB. Á. Ghaorthaig). Donncha Chruíd a ghlaedís ar an bhfile. Do mhuíntir Chríodáin ab ea é. Níor réiti' sé féin agus Máire Bhuí i n-aon chor, pé cúis é. Bhídís a' déanamh véarsaí dá chéile. Conas san a duairt sé le Máire Bhuí? –

'Níor crochag riamh éinne dom mhuíntir
is níor cuireag thar loíng i gcéin
murab ionann is glamar na nÍnseach
go bhfuil na Botanies líonta 'á bpréimh!'

Crochag duine muínteara le Máire Bhuí: Cormac Ó Laeire ab ainm do. Anso thíos ar an gCíll Muair i mBéalaithe 'n Ghaorthaig a crochag é: Cormac Buí a ghlaedís air, agus do bhí gaol geairid aige le Máire Bhuí. Sin é an chúis go nduairt Donncha an chainnt sin. Bhí Máire Bhuí ar an Ínse Muair. Ansan a bhí an Búrcach. Ar Túirín na nÉan (b.f. i mB. Átha'n Gh.) a bhí a muíntir féin. Caitheag amach iad agus caitheag Donncha Chruíd agus a mhuíntir amach as an Ínse Muair. I gCorcaig a chríochnaig Donncha Chruíd. Do bhí a mhac i gCorcaig 'na dhiaig, agus do bhí an chainnt agus an fhilíocht aige sin, leis. Seán Dhonncha Chruíd a ghlaedís air.

English Translation

There was another poet here at that time and he was brilliant. The place himself and his family were living was in Cloch Bharrach (the top of Ínse Mhuar, a townland in Ballingeary). They called him Donncha Chruíd. He was one of the Creeds. Himself and Máire Bhuí didn't get on at all, whatever reason for it. They used to be composing verses for one another. How did he say it to Máire Bhuí? –

'No member of my family was ever hanged
nor sent abroad in a ship
unlike that noisy lot of the Inches
of whose roots the Botanies are full!'

A relative of Máire Bhuí was hanged: Cormac Ó Laeire was his name. Down here in Cíll Mhuar in Ballingeary was where he was hanged – in Páirc na Croise.

I don't know why he was hanged: they called him yellow Cormac and he was a close relative of Máire Bhuí. That is why Donncha said what he said. Máire Bhuí was in Ínse Mhuar; that was where Burke was. In Túirín na nÉan (a townland in Ballingeary) was where her own family was. They were evicted and Donncha Chruíd and his family were evicted from Ínse Mhuar. Donncha Chruíd ended up in Cork. His son was in Cork after and he had the talk and the poetry too. They called him Seán Dhonncha Chruíd.

11. Máire Bhuí agus an Fíodóir [Máire Bhuí and the Weaver]

Storyteller: Diarmuid 'ac Coitir, Doire na Sagart, Ballyvourney, Co. Cork.

Source: National Folklore Collection, CBÉ IML 42: 348–51, collected in 1932 by Áine Ní Chróinín. Previously published in *Bláth 's Craobh na nÚdar: Amhráin Mháire Bhuí* (Ní Shíocháin 2012).

I ndeire na hochtú haoise déag nú i dtosach an naoú haoise déag, do bhí Máire Bhuí ní Laeire i réim in iarthar Paróiste Íbh Laeire. File dob ea Máire agus lena línn féin ní raibh aon fhile eile in Éirinn chô cliste léi nú chô bínn léi. Amhrá[i]n náisiúnta is mó do cheap Máire agus is minic do cháin sí go dian na Sasanaig nó na Clanna Gall. Mar gheall ar í féin ' bheith chô maith d'fhile agus an mola muar do bhí uirthi, ní thaitnuíodh filí beaga eile léi do bhíodh ag ceapa rócán. Le línn na haimsire céanna do bhí fíodóir ina chónaí i mbaile ann go nglaotar Gort a' Phlodaig air. Do bhí smidireacht bheag filíochta ag an bhfíodóir ach ní raibh aon mheas ag Máire Bhuí air. Lá éigin do tháinig cailín óg go tig an fhíodóra le beart snáith, agus d'iarr sí ar an bhfíodóir abhar gúna do dhéanamh di don tsnáth. Ní bhíodh puínn éadaig dá cheannach insan am san insa tsiopa, éadach baile is ea is mó do chaitheadh na daoine, agus dá bhrí sin do bhíodh na fíodóirí bruidiúil. Ón nGort Luachra dob ea an cailín agus do bhí dithineas uirthi le habhar an ghúna mar do bhí sí le dul go dtí an C[h]ingcís. D'fhiarthai' sí de'n fhíodóir cathain a bheadh abhar an ghúna déanta aige, agus duairt sé ná beadh ar feag mí, mar go raibh obair mí istig aige cheana féin. Ní shásódh san an cailín. Duairt sí gur mhaith léi féin é ' fháil i gciúnn seachtaine, agus níorbh fhéidir é ' bhoga. T'réis ' bheith a' tathant is ag déircíneacht ar feag tamaill, duairt sí leis abhar an ghúna do bheith déanta i gciúnn deich lá, agus go dtúrfadh sí breab do, breab mhaith nó tabharthas éigin do i dteannta a pháig. Do bhog an méid sin an fíodóir agus duairt sé léi [teacht] dhá iarraig i gciúnn na deich lá agus go mbeadh sé déanta. Tháinig an cailín lá an choinne agus thug sí a phá chun an fhíodóra agus is dó' liom gur báisín ime a thug sí chuige mar thabharthas. Do bhí an fíodóir lán d'áthas agus do ghreann nuair a fuair sé an pá agus an tabharthas i dteannta a chéile. Shuig sé síos agus duairt sé rann beag di mar seo:

"A chailín bhig na luachra, beig gruaim ort is oighear go deó,

ag baint do bhirt gach uair mhoch go buartha agus ag aeireacht bó,
beig Sasanaig na muar-chorp go huasal a' gabháil an róid
'na gcóistí greanta ag luasca mar is dualgas é do cheapag dóibh".

Nuair a chuaig an scéal chô fada le Máire Bhuí, agus nuair a airi' sí an rann beag filíochta i ndiaig an fhíodóra do bhí sí ar deargb[h]uile. Níor mhaith le Máire B[h]uí na Sasanaig a fheiscint in uachtar i gcónaí agus seo mar ' duairt sí:

"A fhíodóir gan fuaimeint, eighrig suas anis agus caith do spól,
agus ná hairím a thuille dot dhuanta mar ní[o]r dhual duit gur bhínn do ghlór.
Níor gheallag dóibh do réir thuairimeach cead buanaíochta d'fháil go deó,
agus a chailín bhig na Luachrach, beig na sluaite fear ag rith it dheó[i]g".

Ní duairt an fíodóir a thuille.

English Translation

In the end of the eighteenth century or the beginning of the nineteenth century, Máire Bhuí ní Laeire was in her prime in the Western part of the parish of Iveleary. Máire was a poet and during her own time there was no other poet in the whole of Ireland as clever nor as melodious as her. National songs mainly is what she composed, and she strongly criticized the English or the 'Foreign Clans'. Because she herself was such a good poet and because of her being held in such high esteem, she used not like other small poets who used to be composing *rócáns* [inferior or trite compositions]. During that same period there was a weaver living in a place called Gort a' Phlodaig. He had a small smattering of poetry, but Máire Bhuí had no respect for him. One day the young girl came to the weaver's house with a bundle of yarn, and asked for the weaver to make her material for a dress out of the yarn. There used to be no clothes being bought at that time in the shop, it was mainly homemade clothes people used to wear at that time, and therefore the weavers used to be busy. The girl was from Gort Luachra and she was in a hurry to get the material for the dress because she was going to the Pentecost. She enquired of the weaver as to when he would have the dress material made, and he said it wouldn't be ready for a month, because he had a month's work in already. That didn't satisfy the girl. She said she wanted the material in a week's time, and she pressed the weaver but he wouldn't budge. After pressing and pleading for a while, she said to him to have the dress material ready within ten days and that she would give him a bribe, a good bribe or offering as well as his pay. That moved the weaver and he said to her to come and get it in ten days' time and that it would be ready. The girl came on the agreed day and I think that it was a basin of butter that she brought as an offering. The weaver was full of joy and frivolity when he received his pay and the offering at the same time. He sat down and said a verse like this for her:

'Oh little girl of the rushes, you will be forever despondent and depressed,
gathering your bunch of rushes worriedly early in the morning and herding cattle,
while big-bodied Englishmen will go nobly along the road
in their ornate carriages swaying because that is the divine duty that was their
   fate'.

When the story went as far as Máire Bhuí and when she heard the little verse of poetry from the weaver, she was fuming in anger. Máire Bhuí used not like to see the English always having the upper hand and this is how she spoke:

'Oh foolish weaver of little consequence, get up and employ your spool,
and let me not hear any more of your poems because you were not bestowed
   with sweetness of voice.
They were not, by all accounts, promised permanent rule for ever,
and oh little girl of the rushes, there will be crowds of men running after you'.

The weaver said no more.

Notes

1. Máire Ní Cheocháin (1925–), born and reared in Cúil Aodha, Múscraí, now living in Baile an Chollaigh, lámh le Corcaigh.
2. LS sian.
3. LS nglias.
4. LS nglias.

Bibliography

Manuscript Sources

LS 139	Special Collections, UCC Library, University College, Cork.
LS 140	Special Collections, UCC Library, University College, Cork.
LS 141	Special Collections, UCC Library, University College, Cork.
LS 144	Special Collections, UCC Library, University College, Cork.
LS Í Chuív	The manuscripts of Professor Brian Ó Cuív.
LS 101:10ro	The Torna Collection, Special Collections, UCC Library, University College Cork.
CBÉ 42: 348–51	National Folklore Archive, University College, Dublin.
CBÉ 45: 387–91	National Folklore Archive, University College, Dublin.
CBÉ 47:66–68, 73–75	National Folklore Archive, University College, Dublin.
CBÉ 849: 438–39	National Folklore Archive, University College, Dublin.
CBÉ 1527: 144.	National Folklore Archive, University College, Dublin.
LS 004	Ó Donnchú Papers, Ballingeary Historical Society Archives.

Sound Recordings

K68	Traditional Music Archive, University College, Cork.
CBÉ CT0257_007a	National Folklore Archive, University College, Dublin.
CBÉ CT0257_008a	National Folklore Archive, University College, Dublin.
CBÉ CT0265_0065a	National Folklore Archive, University College, Dublin.
CBÉ CT0442_0797	National Folklore Archive, University College, Dublin.
CBÉ T0649	National Folklore Archive, University College, Dublin.
Field recording 2011	Áine Uí Chuíll, Bárr Duínse, collected by Tríona Ní Shíocháin.

Discography

De hÓra, S. 1989. *Seán de hÓra ó Chorca Dhuibhne*. Indreabhán: Cló Iar-Chonnacht.
Ní Mhuimhneacháin, C. 2001. *An Joga Mór: Amhráin Cháit Ní Mhuimhneacháin*. Muskerry: Raidió na Gaeltachta.
Nic Dhonncha, M. 2003. *Bun an Bhaile: Amhráin ón mBlascaod/Songs from the Blasket Island*. Ballyferriter: Oidhreacht Chorca Dhuibhne.
Ó Tuama, P. 2011. *Peáití Thaidhg Pheig*. Muskerry: Acadamh Fódhla.
Various Artists. Undated. *Amhráin ar an Sean-nós*. Dublin: Raidió Teilifís Éireann.
Various Artists. 2012. *Bláth 's Craobh na nÚdar: Amhráin Mháire Bhuí*. Dublin: Coiscéim.

Bibliography

Acker, P. 1998. *Revising Oral Theory: Formulaic Composition in Old English and Old Icelandic Verse*. New York: Garland.
Agovi, K. 1995. 'A King is Not Above Insult: The Politics of Good Governance in Nzema Avudwene Festival Songs', in G. Furniss and L. Gunner (eds), *Power, Marginality and African Oral Literature*. Cambridge: Cambridge University Press, pp. 47–61.
Alexander, J.C. 2004. 'Cultural Pragmatics: Social Performance Between Ritual and Strategy', *Sociological Theory* 22(4): 527–73.
Anyidoho, K. 1995. 'Beyond the Communal Warmth: The Poet as Loner in Ewe Oral Tradition', in G. Furniss and L. Gunner (eds), *Power, Marginality and African Oral Literature*. Cambridge: Cambridge University Press, pp. 244–59.
Argyrou, V. 2013. *The Gift of European Thought and the Cost of Living*. New York and Oxford: Berghahn.
Atkinson, D. 2014. *The Anglo-Scottish Ballad and its Imaginary Contexts*. Cambridge: Open Book.
Barber, K. 2007. *The Anthropology of Texts, Persons and Publics: Oral and Written Culture in Africa and Beyond*. Cambridge: Cambridge University Press.
Bartlett, L. 2007. 'Literacy, Speech and Shame: The Cultural Politics of Literacy and Language in Brazil', *International Journal of Qualitative Studies in Education* 20(5): 547–63.
Béaslaí, P. 2010 [1953]. 'Coláiste na Mumhan: Laethanta Tosaigh an Choláiste', *Journal of the Ballingeary Historical Society*: 11–13.
Becker, J. 2004. *Deep Listeners: Music, Emotion and Trancing*. Bloomington, IN: Indiana University Press.
Beiner, G. 2007. *Remembering the Year of the French: Irish Folk History and Social Memory*. Madison, WI: University of Wisconsin Press.
Bergholm, A. 2012. *From Shaman to Saint: Interpretative Strategies in the Study of Buile Shuibhne*. Helsinki: FFC 302.
Bergin, O. 1970. *Irish Bardic Poetry*. Dublin: Dublin Institute for Advanced Studies.
Boland, T. 2013. 'Towards an Anthropology of Critique: The Experience of Liminality and Crisis', *Anthropological Theory* 13(3): 222–39.
———. 2014. 'Critique is a Thing of This World: Towards a Genealogy of Critique', *History of the Human Sciences* 27(1): 108–23.
Bourke, A. 1988. 'Working and Weeping: Women's Oral Poetry in Irish and Scottish Gaelic', *Women and Gender Studies Series*: 1–17. Retrieved 27 April 2017 from http://hdl.handle.net/10197/5715
———. 1991. 'Performing Not Writing', *Graph* 11: 28–31.

———. 1993. 'More in Anger than in Sorrow: Irish Women's Lament Poetry', in J.N. Radner (ed.), *Feminist Messages: Coding in Women's Folk Culture*. Chicago, IL: University of Illinois Press, pp. 160–82.

Brennan, B. 2000. *Máire Bhuí Ní Laoire: A Poet of Her People*. Cork: Collins Press.

Bromwich, R. 1945. 'The Keen for Art O'Leary, its Background and its Place in the Tradition of Gaelic Keening', Éigse 5: 236–52.

Bruner, E. and V. Turner. 1986. *The Anthropology of Experience*. Chicago, IL: University of Illinois Press.

Buchan, D. 1972. *The Ballad and the Folk*. London: Routledge and Kegan Paul.

Burridge, K. 1971. *New Heaven, New Earth: A Study of Millenarian Activities*. Oxford: Basil Blackwell.

Butler, J. 1988. 'Performative Acts and Gender Constitution: An Essay in Phenomenology and Feminist Theory', *Theatre Journal* 40 (4): 519–31.

———. 1990. *Gender Trouble: Feminism and the Subversion of Identity*. London: Routledge.

Canny, N. 1988. *Kingdom and Colony: Ireland in the Atlantic World 1560–1800*. Baltimore, MD and London: The Johns Hopkins University Press.

Cohen, A.P. 1985. *The Symbolic Construction of Community*. London: Routledge.

Cohn, N. 1970. *The Pursuit of the Millennium*. London: Paladin.

Coleman, S. 2010. 'Mobilized Sound: Memory, Inscription and Vision in Irish Traditional Music', *Irish Journal of Anthropology* 13(1): 23–29.

Cowdery, J. 1984. 'A Fresh Look at the Concept of Tune Family', *Ethnomusicology* 28(3): 495–504.

Darnton, R. 2010. *Poetry and the Police: Communication Networks in Eighteenth-Century Paris*. Cambridge, MA: Harvard University Press.

Derive, J. 1995. 'The Function of Oral Art in the Regulation of Social Power in Dyula Society', in G. Furniss and L. Gunner (eds), *Power, Marginality and African Oral Literature*. Cambridge: Cambridge University Press, pp. 122–39.

Dilthey, W. 1976. *Selected Writings*. Cambridge: Cambridge University Press.

Dlamini, S.R. 1994. 'The Messages Conveyed through Traditional Swati Female Folk Songs', in E. Sienaert, M. Cowper-Lewis and N. Bell (eds), *Oral Tradition and its Transmission: The Many Forms of Message*. Durban: The Campbell Collections and Centre for Oral Studies, University of Natal, pp. 88–97.

Donnelly, J.S. 1983. 'Pastorini and Captain Rock: Millenarianism and Sectarianism in the Rockite Movement of 1821–4', in S. Clark and J.S. Donnelly (eds), *Irish Peasants: Violence and Political Unrest*. Dublin: Gill and Macmillan, pp. 102–39.

———. 2009. *Captain Rock: The Agrarian Rebellion of 1821–1824*. Wisconsin: University of Wisconsin Press.

Dooley, A. and H. Roe. 2008. *Tales of the Elders of Ireland*. Oxford: Oxford University Press.

Draper, J.A. 2004. 'Script, Subjugation and Subversion: An Introduction', in J.A. Draper (ed.), *Orality, Literacy and Colonialism in Southern Africa*. Leiden: Society of Biblical Literature.

Dunne, T. 1998. 'Subaltern Voices? Poetry in Irish, Popular Imagery and the 1798 Rebellion', *Eighteenth Century Life* 22(3): 31–44.

———. 2001. '"Tá Gaedhil bhocht cráidhte": Memory, Tradition and the Politics of the Poor in Gaelic Poetry and Song', in L. Geary (ed.), *Rebellion and Remembrance in Modern Ireland*. Dublin: Four Courts Press, pp. 93–111.

———. 2004. *Rebellions: Memoir, Memory and 1798*. Dublin: Lilliput.

Durán, L. 1995. 'Jelimusow: The Superwomen of Malian Music', in G. Furniss and L. Gunner (eds), *Power, Marginality and African Oral Literature*. Cambridge: Cambridge University Press, pp. 197–207.

Dyubhele, F.J. 1994. '"My Song is My Weapon": Satire as a Communicative Strategy in Xhosa Folk Songs', in E. Sienaert, M. Cowper-Lewis and N. Bell (eds), *Oral Tradition and its Transmission: The Many Forms of Message*. Durban: The Campbell Collections and Centre for Oral Studies, University of Natal, pp. 142–48.

Eisenstadt, S.N. 1995. 'The Order-Maintaining and Order-Transforming Dimensions of Culture', in S.N. Eisenstadt, *Power, Trust, and Meaning: Essays in Sociological Theory and Analysis*. Chicago, IL: University of Chicago Press, pp. 306–27.

Elias, N. 1994. *The Civilizing Process*. Oxford, England: Blackwell.

Felski, R. 2015. *The Limits of Critique*. Chicago, IL: University of Chicago Press.

Finnegan, R. 1977. *Oral Poetry: Its Nature, Significance, and Social Context*. Cambridge: Cambridge University Press.

Foley, J.M. 1981. 'Tradition-Dependent and Independent Features in Oral Literature: A Comparative View of the Formula', in J.M. Foley (ed.), *Oral Traditional Literature: A Festschrift for Albert Bates Lord*. Columbus, OH: Slavica, pp. 262–81.

———. 1991. *Immanent Art: From Structure to Meaning in Traditional Oral Epic*. Bloomington, IN: Indiana University Press.

———. 1995. *The Singer of Tales in Performance*. Bloomington, IN: Indiana University Press.

———. 2002. *How to Read an Oral Poem*. Chicago, IL: University of Illinois Press.

Foucault, M. 1980. *Power/Knowledge: Selected Interviews and Other Writings*. New York: Pantheon.

———. 2011. *The Courage of Truth: Lectures at the College de France 1983–4*. Basingstoke: Palgrave Macmillan.

Freeman, A.M. 1920. 'An Irish Concert', *Journal of the Folk Song Society* 23: xxi–xxvii.

Furet, F. 1981. *Interpreting the French Revolution*. Cambridge: Cambridge University Press.

Furniss, G. and L. Gunner. 1995. *Power, Marginality and African Oral Literature*. Cambridge: Cambridge University Press.

Geertz, C. 1973. *The Interpretation of Cultures: Selected Essays*. New York: Basic.

Gilbert, S. 2007. 'Singing Against Apartheid: ANC Cultural Groups and the International Anti-Apartheid Struggle', *Journal of Southern African Studies* 33(2): 421–41.

Girard, R. 1979. *Violence and the Sacred*. Baltimore, MD: Johns Hopkins University Press.

Glassie, H. 2012. 'Historical Time and "The Swad Chapel Song"', in B. Almqvist et al. (eds), *Atlantic Currents: Essays on Lore, Literature and Language/Sruthanna an Aigéin Thiar: Aistí ar Sheanchas, ar Litríocht agus ar Theanga*. Dublin: University College Dublin Press, pp. 199–212.

Gunner, L. 1995. 'Clashes of Interest: Gender, Status and Power in Zulu Praise Poetry', in G. Furniss and L. Gunner (eds), *Power, Marginality and African Oral Literature*. Cambridge: Cambridge University Press, pp. 185–96.

———. 2009. 'Jacob Zuma, the Social Body and the Unruly Power of Song', *African Affairs* 108(430): 27–48.

Heaney, S. 1983. *Sweeney Astray: A Version from the Irish*. Derry: Field Day Theatre Company.

Hersch, I.S. 2011. 'Towards Social Progress and Post-Imperial Modernity? Colonial Politics of Literacy in the Anglo-Egyptian Sudan, 1946–1956', *History of Education* 40(3): 333–56.

Horvath, A., Thomassen, B. and H. Wydra (eds). 2015. *Breaking Boundaries: Varieties of Liminality*. New York and Oxford: Berghahn.
Howe, S. 2000. *Ireland and Empire: Colonial Legacies in Irish History and Culture*. Oxford and New York: Oxford University Press.
Huizinga, J. 1970. *Homo Ludens: A Study of the Play-Element in Culture*. London: Paladin.
Jama, Z.M. 1994. 'Silent Voices: The Role of Somali Women's Poetry in Social and Political Life', *Oral Tradition* 9(1): 185–202.
Johnson, J.W. 1995. 'Power, Marginality and Somali Oral Poetry: Case Studies in the Dynamics of Tradition', in G. Furniss and L. Gunner (eds), *Power, Marginality and African Oral Literature*. Cambridge: Cambridge University Press, pp. 111–21.
Katsuta, S. 2003. 'The Rockite Movement in County Cork in the Early 1820s', *Irish Historical Studies* 33(131): 279–98.
Knott, E. 1960. *Irish Classical Poetry: Commonly Called Bardic Poetry*. Dublin: Cultural Relations Committee of Ireland/Sign of the Three Candles.
Lord, A.B. 1960. *The Singer of Tales*. Cambridge, Massachusetts: Harvard University Press.
———. 1996. *Myth and Poetics: The Singer Resumes the Tale*. Ithaca, NY: Cornell University Press.
Mac Síthigh, T. 1984. *Paróiste an Fheirtéaraigh: Stairsheanchas an Cheantair i dTréimhse an Ghorta Mhóir*. Dublin: Coiscéim.
Mauss, M. 1966. *The Gift: Forms and Functions of Exchange in Archaic Societies*. London: Cohen and West.
McCarthy, W.B. 1990. *The Ballad Matrix: Personality, Milieu and the Oral Tradition*. Bloomington, IN: Indiana University Press.
McCulloch, M.P. 2003. 'Women, Poetry and Song in Eighteenth-Century Lowland Scotland', *Women's Writing* 10(3): 453–68.
McKibben, S. 2010. *Endangered Masculinities in Irish Poetry 1540–1780*. Dublin: University College Dublin Press.
McLane, M.N. 2011. *Balladeering, Minstrelsy, and the Making of British Romantic Poetry*. Cambridge: Cambridge University Press.
Montano, J.P. 2011. *The Roots of English Colonialism in Ireland*. Cambridge and New York: Cambridge University Press.
Morley, V. 2002. *Irish Opinion and the American Revolution 1760–1783*. Cambridge: Cambridge University Press.
———. 2011. *Ó Chéitinn go Raiftearaí: Mar a Cumadh Stair na hÉireann*. Dublin: Coiscéim.
———. 2017. *The Popular Mind in Eighteenth-Century Ireland*. Cork: Cork University Press.
Moylan, T. 2016. *The Indignant Muse: Poetry and Songs of the Irish Revolution 1887–1926*. Dublin: Lilliput Press.
Muleka, J. 2014. 'Centering the Peripheral: A Case for Poetry in Africa', *Journal of Arts and Humanities* 3(1): 150–60.
Murphy, M. 1979. 'The Ballad Singer and the Role of the Seditious Ballad in Nineteenth-Century Ireland: Dublin Castle's View', *Ulster Folklife* 25: 79–102.
Nagy, G. 1996. *Poetry as Performance: Homer and Beyond*. Cambridge: Cambridge University Press.
———. 2004. 'Transmission of Archaic Greek Sympotic Songs: From Lesbos to Alexandria', *Critical Inquiry* 31(1): 26–48.

Nagy, J.F. 1985. *The Wisdom of the Outlaw: The Boyhood Deeds of Finn in Gaelic Narrative Tradition*. Los Angeles, CA: University of California Press.
———. 1996. *A New Introduction to Buile Suibhne*. Dublin: Irish Texts Society.
Nic an Airchinnigh, M. 2010. 'Caoineadh Airt Uí Laoghaire: Scrúdú ar dhá bhéalaithris ó Nóra Ní Shindile', *Béascna: Journal of Folklore and Ethnology* 6: 69–91.
———. 2013. 'Traidisiún na Caointeoireachta in Éirinn agus sa Ghréig', in N. Ní Shiadhail, M. Ní Úrdail and R. uí Ógáin (eds), *Sealbhú an Traidisiúin*. Dublin: University College Dublin Press, pp. 25–36.
Nic an Airchinnigh, M. and L. Ó Laoire. 2015. 'Caointe agus amhráin chrúite: is le gach bó a lao agus is le gach caoineadh a cheol', *Aiste* 4(1): 155–76.
Nic Eoin, M. 1998. *B'ait Leo Bean: Gnéithe den Ídé-eolaíocht Inscne i dTraidisiún Liteartha na Gaeilge*. Dublin: An Clóchomhar.
Ní Ghairbhí, R. 2008. 'A People That Did Not Exist? Reflections on Some Sources and Contexts for Patrick Pearse's Militant Nationalism', in R. O'Donnell (ed.), *The Impact of the 1916 Rising: Among the Nations*. Dublin: Irish Academic Press, pp. 162–86.
Ní Shíocháin, T. 2009. 'Filí agus Amhránaithe, Foinn agus Focail: *Maidean Álainn Ghréine* agus Ionad an Cheoil i dTraidisiún na nAmhrán', *Béascna: Journal of Folklore and Ethnology* 5: 37–57.
———. 2012. *Bláth 's Craobh na nÚdar: Amhráin Mháire Bhuí*. Dublin: Coiscéim.
———. 2013a. 'Máire Bhuí Ní Laeire: File Béil agus Fáidh Míleannach', in S. Ó Coileáin, L.P. Ó Murchú and P. Riggs (eds), *Séimhfhear Suairc: Aistí in Ómós don Ollamh Breandán Ó Conchúir*. Dingle: An Sagart, pp. 296–311.
———. 2013b. 'Filí agus Amhránaithe, Cumadóirí agus Athchumadóirí: An Seachadadh Cruthaitheach agus an Chumadóireacht Bhéil i dTraidisiún Amhránaíochta na Gaelainne', *Béascna: Journal of Folklore and Ethnology* 8: 90–114.
———. 2014. 'Memory, Liminality and Song Performance: Understanding the History of Thought through Song', *International Political Anthropology* 7(1): 73–88.
Ní Úrdail, M. 2000. *The Scribe in Eighteenth- and Nineteenth-Century Ireland: Motivations and Milieu*. Münster: Publikationen.
———. 2002. 'Máire Bhuí Ní Laoghaire: File an "Rilleadh Cainte"', *Eighteenth-Century Ireland/ Irish an Dá Chultúr* 17: 146–56.
O'Brien O'Keefe, K. 1990. *Visible Song: Transitional Literacy in Old English Verse*. Cambridge: Cambridge University Press.
Ó Buachalla, B. 1983. 'An Mheisiasacht agus an Aisling', in P. de Brún, S. Ó Coileáin and P. Ó Riain (eds), *Folia Gadelica*. Cork: Cork University Press, pp. 72–87.
1996. *Aisling Ghéar: Na Stíobhartaigh agus an tAos Léinn 1603–1788*. Dublin: An Clóchomhar.
———. 1998. *An Caoine agus an Chaointeoireacht*. Dublin: Cois Life.
———. 2003. 'From Jacobite to Jacobin', in K. Bartlett et al. (eds), *1978: A Bicentenary Perspective*. Dublin: Four Courts Press, pp. 75–96.
———. 2007. *Aogán Ó Rathaille*. Dublin: Field Day Publications.
Ó Cathasaigh, R. 2009. *Tídil Eidil Éró: Amhránaíocht Thraidisiúnta don Aos Óg*. Ballyferriter: Oidhreacht Chorca Dhuibhne.
Ó Ciosáin, N. 1997. *Print and Popular Culture in Ireland, 1750–1850*. New York: St. Martin's Press.
Ó Coigligh, C. 1987. *Raiftearaí: Amhráin agus Dánta*. Dublin: An Clóchomhar.
Ó Coileáin, S. 1988. 'The Irish Lament: An Oral Genre', *Studia Hibernica* 24: 97–117.

Ó Conchúir, B. 1982. *Scríobhaithe Chorcaí, 1700–1850*. Dublin: An Clóchomhar.
———. 2009. *Eoghan Rua Ó Súilleabháin*. Dublin: Field Day Publications.
Ó Cróinín, D. (ed.). 2000. *The Songs of Elizabeth Cronin, Irish Traditional Singer: The Complete Song Collection*. Dublin: Four Courts Press.
Ó Cróinín, D. (ed.) 1980. *Seanachas Amhlaoibh Í Luínse*. Dublin: Comhairle Bhéaloideas Éireann.
———. 1982. *Seanachas Phádraig Í Chrualaoi*. Dublin: Comhairle Bhéaloideas Éireann.
Ó Crualaoich, G. 1983. 'The Vision of Liberation in Cúirt an Mheán Oíche', in P. de Brún, S. Ó Coileáin and P. Ó Riain (eds), *Folia Gadelica*. Cork: Cork University Press, pp. 95–104.
———. 1986. 'An Nuafhilíocht Ghaeilge: Dearcadh Dána', *Innti* 10: 63–66.
———. 1997. 'The French Are on the Say', in J.A. Murphy (ed.), *The French Are in the Bay*. Dublin: Mercier, pp. 120–37.
Ó Cuív, B. 1944. *The Irish of West Muskerry*. Dublin: Dublin Institute for Advanced Studies.
Ó Cuív, S. (ed.). 1915. 'Coirli Vaire Vy Da Mac (A Vúrcuig Ví ón Géim)', *An Claidheamh Soluis*, 6 November.
Ó Donnchú, D. 1931. *Filíocht Mháire Bhuidhe Ní Laoghaire*. Dublin: Oifig an tSoláthair.
———. 2012 [1917]. 'The Whiteboys', *Ballingeary Historical Society Journal*: 38–39.
O'Donnell, P.D. 1975. *The Irish Faction Fighters of the Nineteenth Century*. Dublin: Anvil.
Ó Foghludha, R. 1937. *Eoghan Ruadh Ó Súilleabháin*. Dublin: Comhlacht Oideachais na hÉireann.
Ó Gealbháin, C. 2015. '"Na Prátaí Dubha" agus Déantúis eile a Leagtar ar Mholly na Páirce', *An Linn Bhuí* 19: 41–62.
Ó Giolláin, D. 2000. *Locating Irish Folklore: Tradition, Modernity, Identity*. Cork: Cork University Press.
———. 2005. *An Dúchas agus an Domhan*. Cork: Cork University Press.
Ó Gráda, D. 1989. 'Na Rockites agus Cath Chéim an Fhia', *Comhar* 6: 42–45.
Ó Gráda, C. 1994. *An Drochshaol: Béaloideas agus Amhráin*. Dublin: Coiscéim.
Ó hAnnracháin, P. 1944. *Fé Bhrat an Chonnartha*. Dublin: Oifig an tSoláthair.
Ó hAo, S. 1985. *Seanachas ó Chairbre*, D. Ó Cróinín (ed.). Dublin: Comhairle Bhéaloideas Éireann.
Ó hÉalaithe, D. (ed.). 2014. *Memoirs of an Old Warrior: Jamie Moynihan's Fight for Irish Freedom 1916-1923*. Dublin: Mercier.
Ó hÓgáin, D. 1982. *An File: Staidéar ar Osnádúrthacht na Filíochta sa Traidisiún Gaelach*. Dublin: Oifig an tSoláthair.
Ó Laoire, L. 2002. *Ar Chreag i Lár na Farraige*. Galway: Cló Iar-Chonnacht.
———. 2012. 'Brolach: Ó Bhéal a' Chéama: Máire Bhuí Ní Laoghaire', in Ní Shíocháin, *Bláth's Craobh na nÚdar: Amhráin Mháire Bhuí*. Dublin: Coiscéim, pp. xx–xxiv.
O'Leary, P. 1993. 'The Battle of Keimaneigh', *Ballingeary Historical Society Journal*: 13–15.
Ó Madagáin, B. (ed.). 1978. *Gnéithe den Chaointeoireacht*. Dublin: An Clóchomhar.
Ó Madagáin, B. 1985. 'The Functions of Irish Song in the Nineteenth Century', *Béaloideas* 53: 130–216.
———. 1992a. 'Echoes of Magic in the Gaelic Song Tradition', in C.J. Byrne, M. Barry and P. Ó Siadhail (eds), *Celtic Languages and Celtic Peoples: Proceedings of the Second North American Congress of Celtic Studies*. Halifax: St. Mary's University, pp. 125–40.
———. 1992b. 'An Ceol a Ligeann an Racht', *Léachtaí Cholm Cille* 22: 164–84.

Ó Murchú. L.P. (ed.). 1982. *Cúirt an Mheon-Oíche*. Dublin: An Clóchomhar.
Ong, W.J. 1982. *Orality and Literacy: The Technologizing of the Word*. London and New York: Methuen.
Ó Riain, P. 2014 [1972]. 'A Study of the Legend of the Wild Man', in J. Carey (ed.), *Buile Suibhne: Perspectives and Reassessments*. Dublin: Irish Texts Society, pp. 172–201.
O'Riordan, M. 2007. *Irish Bardic Poetry and Rhetorical Reality*. Cork: Cork University Press.
Ó Suibhne, P. 1932. 'Seanachas ó Uíbh Laoghaire', *Béaloideas* 3: 149–69.
Ó Súilleabháin, M. 2013. *Where Mountainy Men Have Sown: War and Peace in Rebel Cork in the Turbulent Years 1916–21*. Dublin: Mercier.
Ó Súilleabháin, S. 1937. *Diarmuid na Bolgaighe agus a Chómhursain*. Dublin: Oifig an tSoláthair.
Ó Tuairisg, L. 2009. 'History, Seanchas and Memory in "Cath Chéim an Fhia"', in N. Cronin et al. (eds.), *Anáil an Bhéil Bheo: Orality and Modern Irish Culture*. Newcastle: Cambridge Scholars Publishing, pp. 27–40.
Ó Tuama, S. 1960. *An Grá in Amhráin na nDaoine*. Dublin: An Clóchomhar.
Partridge (Bourke), A. 1980. 'Wild Men and Wailing Women', *Éigse* 17: 25–37.
Perry, R. 2008. '"The Finest Ballads": Women's Oral Traditions in Eighteenth-Century Scotland', *Eighteenth-Century Life* 32(2): 81–97.
Ramey, P. 2012. 'Variation and the Poetics of Oral Performance in Caedmon's Hymn', *Neophilologus* 96: 441–56.
Rouget, G. 1985. *Music and Trance: A Theory on the Relations Between Music and Possession*. Chicago, IL: University of Chicago Press.
Scott, G. 1985. '"The Times are Fast Approaching": Bishop Charles Walmesley OSB as Prophet', *Journal of Ecclesiastical History* 36: 590–604.
Sewell, W.H. 1996. 'Historical Events as Transformations of Structures: Inventing Revolution at the Bastille', *Theory and Society* 25(6): 841–81.
Simms, J.G. 1969. *Jacobite Ireland 1685–91*. London: Routledge and Kegan Paul.
Smith, O. 2013. *Romantic Women Writers, Revolution and Prophecy*. Cambridge: Cambridge University Press.
Speer, J.H. 1985. 'Waulking o' the Web: Women's Folk Performance in the Scottish Isles', *Literature in Performance* 6(1): 24–33.
Szakolczai, A. 2000. *Reflexive Historical Sociology*. London: Routledge.
———. 2001. 'Civilisation and its Sources', *International Sociology* 16(3): 371–88.
———. 2004. 'Experiential Sociology', *Theoria* 103: 59–87.
———. 2008. 'Experiential Meanings'. Originally published in German as 'Sinn aus Erfahrung', in K. Junge, D. Suber and G. Gerber (eds), Érleben, Erleiden, Erfahren: Die Konstitution sozialen Sinns jenseits instrumenteller Vernunft. Bielefeld: Transcript-Verlag, pp. 63–99. Retrieved 27 April 2017 from https://www.academia.edu/8378113/Experiential_meanings
———. 2009. 'Liminality and Experience: Structuring Transitory Situations and Transformative Events,' *International Political Anthropology Journal* 2: 141–72.
Thomas, C.G. and E. Kent Webb. 1994. 'From Orality to Rhetoric: An Intellectual Transformation', in I. Worthington (ed.), *Persuasion: Greek Rhetoric in Action*. London and New York: Routledge, pp. 3–25.
Thomassen, B. 2009. 'The Uses and Meaning of Liminality', *International Political Anthropology* 2(1): 5–28.

———. 2012. 'From Liminal to Limivoid: Understanding contemporary Bungee Jumping in a Cross-Cultural Perspective', *Journal of Tourism Consumption and Practice* 4(1): 59–93.

———. 2013. 'Anthropology and Social Theory: Renewing Dialogue', *European Journal of Social Theory* 16(2): 188–207.

———. 2014. *Liminality and the Modern: Living Through the In-Between*. London: Ashgate.

Tóibín, N. 1978. *Duanaire Déiseach*. Dublin: Sáirséal agus Dill.

Turner, V. 1969. *The Ritual Process – Structure and Anti-structure*. London: Routledge and Kegan Paul.

———. 1982. *From Ritual to Theatre: On the Human Seriousness of Play*. New York: PAJ.

———. 1986. 'Dewey, Dilthey and Drama: An Essay in the Anthropology of Experience', in V. Turner and E. Bruner (eds), *The Anthropology of Experience*. Urbana, IL: Illinois University Press, pp. 33–44.

———. 1987. *The Anthropology of Performance*. New York: PAJ.

———. 1990. 'Are There Universals of Performance in Myth, Ritual, and Drama?', in R. Schechner and W. Appel (eds), *By Means of Performance*. Cambridge: Cambridge University Press, pp. 8–18.

Ua Súilleabháin, S. 1994. 'Gaeilge na Mumhan', in K. McKone et al. (eds), *Stair na Gaeilge: in Ómós do Phádraig Ó Fiannachta*. Maynooth: Maynooth University, pp. 479–538.

Uí Ógáin, R. 1981. 'Máire Ní Dhuibh', *Sinsear*: 101–7.

———. 1985. *An Rí gan Choróin*. Dublin: An Clóchomhar.

———. 1988. 'Ceol ón mBlascaod', *Béaloideas* 56: 179–219.

———. 1995. *Immortal Dan: Daniel O'Connell in Irish Folk Tradition*. Dublin: Geography Publications.

Uí Ógáin, R. and T. Sherlock. 2012. *The Otherworld: Music and Song from Irish Tradition*. Dublin: Comhairle Bhéaloideas Éireann.

Van Gennep, A. 1960. *The Rites of Passage*. London: Routledge and Kegan Paul.

Van Krieken, R. 2011. 'Three Faces of Civilization: "In the Beginning All the World Was Ireland"', *Sociological Review* 59(1): 24–47.

Vansina, J. 1985. *Oral Tradition as History*. Wisconsin: University of Wisconsin Press.

Voegelin, E. 1975. *From Enlightenment to Revolution*. Durham: Duke University Press.

Weber, M. 1948. 'The Social Psychology of the World Religions', in H.H. Gerth and C.W. Mills (eds), *From Max Weber: Essays in Sociology*. London: Routledge, pp. 267–301.

———. 1978. *Economy and Society*. Los Angeles: University of California Press.

Whelan, K. 1996. *The Tree of Liberty: Radicalism, Catholicism and the Construction of Irish Identity, 1760–1830*. Cork: Cork University Press.

Wydra, H. 2009. 'The Liminal Origins of Democracy', *International Political Anthropology Journal* 2(1): 89–108.

Zimmermann, G.D. 2002. *Songs of Irish Rebellion*. Dublin: Four Courts Press.

Index

A
'A Bhúrcaig Bhuí ón gCéim', 83–84, 144–48
'A Mháir' Ní Laeire', 59, 64, 66, 75, 87–90, 102–3, 120–28, 179–185
'ac Coitir, Crothúr, 64, 73–74, 77, 116, 121, 132, 136, 143, 148, 154, 163, 169, 179
'ac Coitir, Diarmuid, 60, 98, 118, 134, 175, 187
aisling, the, 29–31, 54, 58, 70, 73, 78, 90, 94, 96, 105–108, 134, 136, 154
Akan oral tradition, 13
Allah-Amin, 13–14, 17
anarchy, 5, 82, 89, 96, 106
apocalypse, 89, 98, 124n3, 128, 169
'Ar Leacain na Gréine', 78, 134–36
Argyrou, Vassos, 7
authority, 2, 5–8, 11, 14, 18, 21, 31, 41, 43, 49, 56–7, 60, 63, 90–93, 97, 101–3, 109–12, 116–18, 120–21, 125, 128
Avudwene, 41–2, 49

B
Barry, James, 85, 93, 98, 99, 169, 172, 174, 175
Battle of Keimaneigh, the, 63, 78, 81, 84, 85, 93–99, 109, 113, 115, 120–22, 176. *See also* 'The Battle of Keimaneigh'
Becker, Judith, 35, 54–55, 110
Bourke, Angela, 17, 19, 27–28, 31–32, 50, 65
Bromwich, Rachel, 65
Butler, Judith, 6–9

C
caoineadh. *See* lament

Captain Rock, 80, 81, 94
'Cath Chéim an Fhia', 11, 30, 39, 85, 87–89, 93–99, 102, 112, 114, 122, 169–175
chanson de jeune fille, 46
chanson de la mal-mariée, 40
charisma, 2, 51, 57, 79, 86–93, 112, 116–17
Cohn, Norman, 86, 90, 91, 94, 130
Coleman, Steve, 114–16
colonial subject, creation of, 5, 130
colonial subjection, 4–5, 116, 125, 129–30
composition in performance, 65–69
contestation, 7–8, 10–16, 23, 33, 112
creative transmission, 9, 37, 40, 83, 116
crisis, 5, 48, 52, 57, 82, 85–93, 98, 99, 117, 129
Cumann na mBan, 120–23

D
de hÓra, Seán, 38–39, 139–141, 156–58
Diarmuid na Bolgaighe, 65–66, 70–72, 124n2, 164
Dilthey, Wilhelm, 129, 130
dissolution of order, 57, 79, 82, 92, 111, 125
disqualified knowledge, 6–8, 10
Donncha Chruíd, 83, 186–87
Donnelly, James S., Jr., 80–82, 94, 99, 124n3
Dyula oral tradition, 15, 17

E
'Early Before Phoebus Shone'. *See* 'Go Moch Ruimh Lúra Phoébus'

'Early One Morning as I Herded my Cattle'. See 'Maidean Mhoch 'us Me ' Feighilth mo Stuic'
'Early One Morning on a Soft Bed'. See 'Maidean Mhoch ar Leabaig Bhuig'
ecstasy, 2–4, 21, 25, 32, 34–6, 39–40, 51, 54, 86–88, 90, 104, 113–120, 126, 130
Eisenstadt, Shmuel N., 5, 17
Ekpe, Komi, 50
ekstasis. See ecstasy
Ewe oral tradition, 42–43, 50
experience, 1–5, 12–26, 32–41, 48, 51–56, 82, 85, 88, 90, 94, 99, 103, 109–20, 125–30
experiential ideas, 4, 17, 111, 114, 127–28

F
famine, 2, 48–50, 57, 59, 82, 117, 119, 175
fios, 29, 86
Finnegan, Ruth, 42
Foley, John Miles, 2, 12, 36, 69, 104, 113
formulas, 104–6, 110, 113, 124n2, 126
    formulaic phrases, 65, 69, 72–3, 76, 113
    formula system, 69, 70–73
Foucault, Michel, 2, 7, 8, 10, 88, 92–93,
Freeman, A.M., 39–40, 120
French Revolution, the, 53, 78, 91, 104, 111, 125, 135

G
gender trouble, 9. See also oral trouble
Ghana, South West, oral tradition, 13
Glassie, Henry, 10, 12, 115, 116, 126
'Go Moch Ruimh Lúra Phoébus', 106

H
heat, 4, 32–34, 55, 119
Horvath, Agnes, 52
Huizinga, Johann, 13, 15, 21, 46

I
Irish Volunteers, 114, 120, 121
Irish War of Independence, 116, 120, 121, 123
izibongo, 16

J
Jacobinism, 4, 53, 78, 95–96, 99, 102, 119, 126, 134
Jacobitism, 57–59, 96, 103, 106–8, 119, 126
Jelimusow, 34

K
Katsuta, Shunsuka, 94, 99
keen. See lament
kúrubi songs, 15–17

L
lament, 16–19, 27–29, 31–32, 41, 50, 53, 62–66, 75, 124n1
liminality, 4–5, 23–26, 30–5, 40, 50–55, 94, 110–15, 125–130
    antistructure, 3, 5, 23–26, 33–34, 36, 36–42, 46, 50, 53, 54, 110, 114, 128, 130
    communitas, 3, 25, 26, 33, 34, 44, 51, 53, 57, 110, 111–13, 130
    democracy and liminality, 128
    elders, 41
    passing through, 3, 4, 24, 31, 35, 125, 127–29, 140
    poetry as liminal, 26–31
    post-liminal forms, 24–25, 130
    potentiality, 3, 13, 24, 26, 36–41, 43–51, 53, 79, 108, 110, 111, 117, 120
    powers of the weak, 44, 50
    revolution as liminal, 111–12
    ritual powers of liminality, 41–44
    satire, 41, 42, 46, 54, 58
    seer of communitas, 51–55, 57, 110
    shaman, 29–31, 34, 56
    social death and re-birth, 24–26, 112, 130
    statuslessness, 24–25, 27–30, 53
    wilderness, 24, 27–31, 43, 89, 94
literacy, 5–13, 17, 19–20, 54, 65, 79, 130
Lord, Albert B., 2, 10, 16, 18, 36, 40, 65, 69, 72–75, 77, 102–5, 110
lullaby, 31, 66, 70, 89, 109, 163–68

M
'Maidean Álainn Ghréine', 37–38, 88, 105, 131, 154–163

'Maidean Mhoch ar Leabaig Bhuig', 74–75, 107, 131, 136–143
'Maidean Mhoch 's me' Feighilth mo Stuic', 73–74, 76–77, 89, 148–154
Mali oral tradition, 34–35
millenarianism, 2, 4, 19, 54, 56, 85–86, 89–91, 94, 97–103, 109, 112, 124n3, 130, 164, 169
mimesis, 115–16, 130
Molly na Páirce. *See* Ní Dhroma, Máire
Moynihan, Jamie, 120–21, 123
mouvance, 40
Muleka, Joseph, 7, 8, 19

N

Nagy, Gregory, 2, 18, 36, 40–41, 115–16, 130
Nagy, Joseph Falaky, 28–29, 86
ngaara, 34–35
Ní Chadhlaigh, Mairéad, 62
Ní Cheocháin, Máire, 117, 131, 141–43
Ní Chonaill, Eibhlín Dubh, 63
Ní Chonaill, Nóra, 73–74, 77, 106, 131, 151–54
Ní Chruadhlaoich, Máire, 62
Ní Dhonnagáin, Máire, 62
Ní Dhroma, Máire, 48–50, 62
Ní Dhuibh, Máire, 62–63
Ní Mhuimhneacháin, Cáit, 37–38, 113–14, 121, 131–32, 146–48, 162–63, 183–85
Ní Riain, Máire, 62
Ní Shúilleabháin, Nóra, 62
Nic Dhonncha, Máiréad, 40, 45
Nic Eoin, Máirín, 62–63, 124n1

O

Ó Coileáin, Seán, 36, 65, 75
Ó Crualaoi, Pádraig, 59, 66–68, 83, 179
Ó hAo, Seán (Hamit), 67
Ó hÓgáin, Dáithí, 29, 42, 66–67, 86
Ó Giolláin, Diarmuid, 10, 99
Ó Laeire, Cormac Buí, 186
Ó Laeire, Crothúr Buí, 84–85
Ó Laoire, Lillis, 32–34, 41, 51–53, 108, 110, 114, 124n1
Ó Longáin, Mícheál Óg, 65, 79
Ó Luínse, Amhlaoibh, 45
Ó Madagáin, Breandán, 31–32, 40–41, 52, 69, 110, 114–15
Ó Muiríosa, Seán, 73, 75, 77
Ó Murchadha, Pádraig, 83, 186–87
Ó Sé, Diarmuid na Bolgaí. *See* Diarmuid na Bolgaighe
Ó Súilleabháin, Eoghan Rua, 30, 62, 65–66, 69–70, 72–73, 76, 96, 105, 124n2, 164
Ó Súilleabháin, Mícheál, 121–22
Ó Súilleabháin, Tomás Rua, 42, 65, 66, 85
Ó Tuama, Pádraig, 39, 114, 120, 132, 173–75
O'Connell, Daniel, 4, 19, 22n2, 79, 85–86, 106–7, 152–53
'Oh Mary O'Leary'. *See* 'A Mháir' Ní Laeire'
'Oh Yellow Burke from Céim'. *See* 'A Bhúrcaig Bhuí ón gCéim'
'On the Sunny Side of the Hill'. *See* 'Ar Leacain na Gréine'
'One Lovely Sunny Morning'. *See* 'Maidean Álainn Ghréine'
oral aesthetics, 9, 41, 65–78, 104, 109, 126
oral composition, 2, 9, 13, 16, 18, 19, 62–78, 87, 102, 110, 113
oral transmission, 9, 12, 18, 37, 40, 67–78, 114, 116
oral trouble, 9, 11, 12. *See also* gender trouble
orality, 3, 6–20, 30, 41, 58, 65–79, 85, 104–10, 130
orthography, 132–33

P

Palmer McCulloch, Margery, 20
parrhesia, 2, 4, 47–48, 56, 85, 91–93, 119, 123
Parry, Milman, 18, 67
Partridge, Angela. *See* Bourke, Angela
Pastorini, 85–87, 95–97, 101, 124n3, 169
Peáití Thaidhg Pheig. *See* Ó Tuama, Pádraig
Peatsaí Chit. *See* Ó Murchadha, Pádraig.
performance, 1–6, 9, 11–21, 23–24, 32–42, 50–56, 58, 65–78, 87–88, 92, 104, 110–17, 123–24, 127, 129, 130, 132, 134

performativity, 2, 3, 5–9, 12, 14, 24, 29, 33, 39, 50, 57, 130
play, 3–4, 13, 15, 21, 23–26, 32–34, 36, 39, 41, 43, 45–46, 53–55, 105, 113, 119, 130
'Poor Gaels are Tormented'. *See* 'Tá Gaeil Bhocht' Cráite'
power, 2–19, 23–24, 32–35, 41–43, 44, 46, 48, 49, 50–51, 54–56, 87, 89, 96, 99, 101, 105, 110–18, 121, 125–30
precompositional period, 67
print, 4, 20–21, 54–55, 58, 88, 91–92, 97, 100–1, 121
Proclamation of the Irish Republic, the, 118–19
prophecy, 11, 29, 85, 86–104, 106, 124–29, 169, 175

R
Raftery, 64–65, 85
re-composition, 37, 40–41, 76–77
re-creativity, 2, 4, 9, 12–16, 19, 23–24, 36, 38–39, 41, 51, 54, 56, 70, 72–73, 77–79, 82, 95–97, 101–8, 110, 113, 116, 119, 127, 129
revolution, 4, 22n2, 43, 78–79, 82, 89, 91, 95, 96, 100–104, 110–125, 127–28, 134.
ritual, 4–5, 17–19, 21, 24–35, 41–44, 51–54, 62, 88, 111, 115, 129, 130
Rockites, 54, 78–82, 84–87, 93–95, 97–100, 112, 123, 129

S
Saint John, 88, 100–1, 124n3, 175, 186–7
satire. *See under* liminality
savoir des gens, 10
scribal culture, 79, 123–4
seer, 86. *See also* liminality: seer of communitas
'Seo Leó, ' Thoil', 70–71, 89, 109, 131, 163–68
'Seo Leó, My Darling'. *See* 'Seo Leó, ' Thoil'
shaman. *See under* liminality: shaman
societal transition, 9, 52–53, 110–13
Somali oral tradition, 9, 13–17, 50
South African oral tradition, 15–17
Suibne Geilt, 26–29, 53

supernatural knowledge. *See* fios
Szakolczai, Arpad, 4, 52, 88, 127–128, 130

T
'Tá Gaeil Bhocht' Cráite', 82, 87–89, 99, 132, 175–79
'The Battle of Keimaneigh'. *See* 'Cath Chéim an Fhia'
theme, 13, 16, 29–31, 36–41 43–37, 52, 54, 56, 65, 69–78, 89–90, 94, 96, 103–109, 113, 126, 163–164.
Thomassen, Bjorn, 5, 24, 26, 52, 111–12, 125, 127
Turner, Victor, 3, 5, 21, 24–26, 29, 32–34, 39, 41, 43–44, 51, 53, 56–57, 110–11, 113, 126–27, 129–30

U
United Irishmen, the, 4, 21–22, 78–79, 97, 99
United Irish Rebellion, the, 22n2, 78, 97, 100, 114
Uí Chuíll, Áine, 37–38, 117, 131, 158–61
Uí Luínse, Maighréad, 131, 167–68

V
van Gennep, Arnold, 3, 23–27, 29–31, 34–35, 43–44, 50–52
Vansina, Jan, 11–12
Voegelin, Eric, 8

W
Walmesley, Charles. *See* Pastorini
waulking songs, 16–19, 31–32
Weber, Max, 2, 4, 6, 87–88, 92, 112, 114, 116–19
Whelan, Kevin, 4, 79, 81–82, 99
Wild Sweeney. *See* Suibne Geilt
Wolfe Tone, Theobald, 4, 19, 22n2, 54, 78–79, 125
Wydra, Harald, 52, 111–12, 128

X
Xhosa folk songs, 13

Z
Zulu oral tradition, 16

CPSIA information can be obtained
at www.ICGtesting.com
Printed in the USA
JSHW040253150721
16930JS00008B/291